Ellyn and Caroline Found

"It is difficult to comprehend how heartbreaking the story of the Found family is—a loving mother, Ellyn, diagnosed with a terminal cancer, a beautiful teen-age daughter, Caroline, killed in a freakish moped accident—both buried within a fortnight. That the father, Ernie, somehow managed to courageously rise above this devastating calamity, to carry on with grace, and that the town and Caroline's school and volleyball team came together to cherish the memory of the two women, is the story of unbounded love. That there is a victory in sports, as well, is but a glorious bonus. Nothing can cure the sadness, nothing can undo the horror, but what Bill Hoeft's book tells us is that even the worst tragedy can uplift us if we care enough and are unafraid to bare our hearts."

—Frank Deford, Senior Contributing Writer *Sports Illustrated*, NPR commentator, correspondent on HBO's *Real Sports With Bryant Gumbel*, & award-winning author, including *Alex: The Life Of A Child*

"Not all have the good fortune to know a Caroline—a rare and great spirit who instinctively knows how to feed the pulse and soul of everyone she encounters. Bill Hoeft shares this rare story of grit through grief which transforms a family, a team, and a town to embrace a new legacy, to LIVE LIKE LINE."

—Geoffrey Lauer, Executive Director, Brain Injury Alliance of Iowa

"A powerful, heartbreaking, triumphant story, told with honesty and conviction. A stirring testament to the strength and courage of a Family, to the enduring bonds of Community, and to the eternal, transcendent, healing power of Love."

—Dan Knight, Steinway Artist, Pianist, Composer

"Bill Hoeft not only captures the depths of the tragedies, but also the elation of the highs in both Caroline and Ellyn's life stories. Live Like Line provides a truly inspirational account of the Found family that proves touching for readers of all ages."

—Ally Disterhoft, University of Iowa Women's Basketball, Iowa City West High alum ('13)

""A wonderful tribute to a beautiful family and their own extraordinary love. The ability to share and receive the love of family and community in the wake of such heartbreak is remarkable. We are all lucky to share a special community made richer by the Found family.""

—Margaret & Fran McCaffery, Head Coach, University of Iowa Men's Basketball

LIVE LIKE LINE
Love Like Ellyn

BILL HOEFT

ICE CUBE PRESS, LLC
NORTH LIBERTY, IOWA

Live Like Line, Love Like Ellyn:
A Community's Journey from Tragedy to Triumph

Copyright © 2015 Patrick William Hoeft
Isbn 9781888160987 (trade paper edition)
Library of Congress Cataloging Number: 2014958931

Ice Cube Press, LLC (Eſt. 1993)
North Liberty, Iowa 52317
ſteve@icecubepress.com
www.icecubepress.com

Manufactured in United States of America.

All rights reserved.

No portion of this book may be reproduced in any way without permission, except for brief quotations for review, or educational work, in
which case the publisher shall be provided copies. The views expressed
in *Live Like Line, Love Like Ellyn* are solely those of the author not the
Ice Cube Press, LLC.

The paper used in this publication meets the minimum requirements
of the American National Standard for Information Sciences—
Permanence of Paper for Printed Library Materials, ANSI Z39.48-
1992.

Disclaimer: Both author and publisher have made every effort to
ensure that the information in this book was correct at press time. The
author and publisher do not assume and hereby disclaim any liability
to any party for any loss, damage, or disruption caused by errors or
omissions, whether such errors or omissions result from negligence,
accident, or any other cause. Some names and identifying details have
been changed to protect the privacy of those individuals.

Assiſting Project Editor: Jennifer Moy

Cover photo provided courtesy of Tom Ward www.twardphoto.com
Photo shows Caroline and Ellyn in color.

A portion of the sales from this book will be donated to the Found Family
Memorial Foundation.

Dedicated to
Ernie, Ellyn,
Gregg, Catharine,
and Caroline Found

Contents

Preface
by Ernie Found

I remember the day as if it were yesterday.... A Sunday morning in the late fall of 2011, in between church services. A vertically challenged, stocky, well built, dark haired gentleman (clearly a former wrestler... the nose and ears gave it away) approached me and introduced himself: "Hi, Mr. Found. My name's Bill Hoeft, and I'm a writer and I'd like to write the moving and amazing story of all that has happened to you and your family and friends, to West High School, and to the Iowa City community." I formed a bolus of dry spit in my mouth and tried to swallow it whole, thinking about how to respond. Tears formed in the corners of my eyes, making it hard to visually and mentally focus. A zillion thoughts ran through my mind. I pondered the value of attempting to put such strong emotions of so many people into words. "Let's think and talk about it," was the best that I could come up with.

We started with a short conversation at my house. After we spoke the first time I kept inviting him back. During my conversations with him, I discovered a reliable and trusted friend. His heart began to beat in rhythm with all of ours. His sensitivity and intuition became almost comforting. He became someone I know has my whole family's best interest in his heart.

No father is ever prepared for the sudden death of one of his children. No husband at ease with the loss of a dear and loving wife. The writing of this book is bittersweet for me. In fact, I have not read the whole thing and I may never read it all. I am forever grateful for Bill entering our lives and for recounting the most challenging of experiences of so many folks. Bill has been another example of how many good things have come from something so bad.

I tip my hat to him.

Chapter One
A Tragic Night

As for man, his days are like grass;
   he flourishes like a flower of the field;
for the wind passes over it, and it is gone.
—Psalm 103:15

Death always comes like a thief.
—Christopher Pike, *The Last Vampire*

On a nearly deserted city street, a moped sliced through the humid and heavy Midwest summer air. The engine whined loudly at night without daytime noise dampening the small vehicle's song. The rider, Caroline Slocum Found, was a seventeen-year-old natural beauty with golden hair and twinkling eyes the color of the sun-soaked Pacific. When she smiled, her eyes provided a hint of mischief which usually meant something fun was about to happen.

August 11th, 2011, was an otherwise typical Thursday night in Iowa City, Iowa. Caroline, or "Line" as she was called by those who knew her best, slowed down, letting the car in the next lane draw even with her. The incoming senior at Iowa City West High School turned and flashed a brilliant smile to one of her best friends and classmate, Leah Murray. Leah returned the smile as she passed Caroline.

The girls were headed home following a church youth group meeting at a friend's house. Caroline was already late for curfew after an extra stop at a frozen yogurt shop. Line's insatiable sweet tooth drew her like a magnet to the relatively new establishment for daily doses of the tasty treat. At around six-dollars per container the yogurt was an expensive addiction for the elite volleyball player, but one she allowed herself.

They negotiated a single file turn from Highway 6 onto 1st Avenue, which seamlessly becomes Mormon Trek Boulevard at the invisible line that divides Coralville and Iowa City. Mormon Trek is a well-lit, four-lane divided street which the pair had traveled countless times before. Caroline took the left lane closest to the median, accelerated, and pulled alongside her friend. The side-by-side vehicles then hastened to the posted speed limit of 35 mph.

Mormon Trek has a large island separating the north and southbound lanes of traffic. For aesthetics, the city planted prairie grass in the divider surrounding a single row of young trees spaced evenly down the middle. A large curb bounded the plantings, so the median served the dual purpose of traffic divider and large planter. It was a nice addition to the street that bears the name of the Mormons who, in 1846, passed through Iowa City on their way to a better life out West.

The majority of Mormon Trek Boulevard is straight as a runway, save the S-curve section the girls approached. Over the years, more than one distracted southbound driver had failed to negotiate the abrupt right bend and wound up on the prairie grass median. Other than some banged up cars, nothing serious resulted from the sharp bends in the road.

Caroline smiled at Leah, who was bouncing her head to the beat of a song on the radio. Leah glanced at Caroline, and together they laughed. Leah was thrilled to see her lifelong friend enjoying herself.

It had been a stressful year for the Found family. Caroline's mother, Ellyn Found, was in the hospital under twenty-four hour care, nearing the end of her courageous four-month battle with pancreatic cancer.

"Turn it up," Caroline yelled.

Their interaction took no more than a couple of seconds. Caroline failed to veer right with the road. The moped's front tire struck the median full force, popping the front end off the ground and then dropping the tire on top of the curb. The back tire followed the path of the front causing the moped to wobble precariously on top of the curb for a brief moment.

A panicked Caroline cranked the handle bars hard right in an attempt to get the moped off the curb and back onto the road, but her oversteer put the front tire into a bouncing skid along the top of the curb. When the tire gripped the cement it acted as a brake. The vehicle's momentum sent it barrel-rolling to the left, which flung Caroline violently to the right, off the moped, head first onto the ground.

Caroline's body moved another thirty-feet, sliding through the waist-high prairie grass. She came to rest feet-first at the base of the third small tree in the middle of the median.

Two witnesses, in separate vehicles, were right behind the girls. A physician walking on a well-traveled sidewalk beside the road also saw the accident. All witnesses stopped immediately and rendered aid.

It was less than thirty seconds from the time Caroline went down to when the physician was by her side. Due to the massive head injury she sustained, it was too late—Caroline was already gone. That didn't stop the Good Samaritan doctor, and soon thereafter the paramedics, from trying to resuscitate her.

When Caroline crashed, an extremely shaken Leah still had the wherewithal to stop her car and turn on her emergency flashers. Her friend's accident was by far the most traumatic thing she had seen in her young life. In spite of the trauma, Leah maintained the presence of mind to call her mother, Lisa, who told her she was on her way and to dial 9-1-1, which she did.

Lisa and Leah's older sister, Grace, were by her side quickly. Grace helped a distraught Leah out of the car when she said she might be sick. Lisa made sure Leah was doing okay and then went to check on Caroline.

Because Caroline was under eighteen, the police were initially tight-lipped about her condition, pending parental notification. They were no match, however, for a motivated mother acting on her terminally-ill best friend Ellyn's behalf. Lisa's persistence paid off when veteran Iowa City police sergeant and mother, Vicki Lalla, pulled Lisa aside and calmed the situation. "She knew the right words and made us feel like everything would be okay, no matter the outcome," Lisa said.

Boyd Murray, Leah's father, was next on the scene. After finding out what happened to Caroline, he had concerns about his daughter's physical and mental condition. The former paramedic was no stranger to trauma and its effects on people. "Leah was in shock; she was struggling." Once the police said it was okay for her to leave the scene, Boyd took Leah directly to the University of Iowa Hospitals and Clinics' emergency room to be checked out.

In the days following the accident, a police report filed by the accident investigator specified the single-vehicle accident was caused by inattentive driving. The officer indicated that due to the lack of skid marks on the roadway before the vehicle struck the curb and the straight line tumble path of the moped, Caroline didn't know the curb was coming and had no chance of saving herself. He speculated that the massive trauma she sustained on the back of her head was caused by striking the cement, probably the curb.

Chapter Two
The Aftermath

Death is a grim reality.
Death is relentless and cannot be satisfied.
Death is a significant enemy, the ultimate evil power.
—Author unknown

The death of a beloved is an amputation.
—C.S. Lewis, *A Grief Observed*

Ernest "Ernie" Found Jr., waited impatiently for his daughter to get home. She was late, and he hadn't heard from her. He was annoyed and worried about her tardiness.

Ernie was annoyed because, for weeks, the man with both a bad back and hip folded his 6'6" frame into a bed designed for someone a foot shorter to be by his wife's side at the hospital. The plan that night was for Caroline to be home at 9 sharp. He would drive her to the hospital to stay with her mother while he went home and stretched out on his own bed for a few hours of much needed sleep. Ernie would return at 2 AM and relieve Line.

Ernie was worried because he knew the type of person Caroline was. She liked to push boundaries. If something was fun to do, she would do it, consequences be damned. "She was rarely a rule offender but certainly a rule bender," Ernie said. Compounding his worry was that Line hadn't been in contact with him. She may have been late from time-to-time but always managed to text him her location and when he could expect her home.

Ernie and Ellyn were always concerned about Caroline when she was behind the wheel of a car. Because she was such an aggressive driver, they had enrolled her in a University of Iowa study on teenage driving habits. A camera was permanently mounted on the dashboard of her car and captured images while she drove.

Although Caroline's study results were not good, they were rather typical of drivers her age. She was easily distracted when passengers were with her. She took corners way too fast and sometimes exceeded the speed limit. And the volume knob on her stereo was always on one of two settings: eardrum rattling or teeth shattering.

Ernie's anxiety would have increased dramatically—and he certainly wouldn't have approved—had he known Caroline was on a borrowed two-wheeler that night. He and Ellyn didn't mind Line riding the moped, owned by family friends, but only as long as she stayed in the immediate neighborhood. She adhered to her parents' rule for several weeks, but the allure of riding the moped around town eventually won out.

The August evening was perfect for a ride, at least that was how Caroline justified taking the moped that night. Besides, the owners kids were grown, so the two-wheeler sat idle in their garage collecting dust. Line saw it as a crime to have something as fun as a moped go unused.

Because she loved the wind in her hair and the bugs in her teeth, Caroline wouldn't wear a helmet when she borrowed the moped. This was a dangerous endeavor no doubt, but not an illegal one. Iowa is one of three states, along with Illinois and Colorado, without a helmet law of any kind for motorcyclists and moped riders.

At 10 PM, a distraught and bone-weary Ernie called and texted Caroline every few minutes. When he didn't get a response by 10:30, he knew something had to be wrong and called her friends. Unable to reach Leah, he called Line's close friend and volleyball teammate, Kelley Fliehler. Caroline had been staying at the Fliehler's home all week. Kelley told Ernie she hadn't heard from Line, but she would make some calls to see if anyone had seen her.

The week-long sleepover at the Fliehlers' was a good distraction for Line. It helped divert her attention from Ellyn's rapidly deteriorating health. Staying with Kelley also meant that, while Ernie spent most of his nights at the hospital, Caroline wouldn't have to feel so alone at night in their hundred-year-old farmhouse with all its creaks and groans.

The first number Kelley dialed was Caroline's cell phone. The call didn't go through, and she immediately remembered why. Ellyn and Ernie placed a block on Caroline's phone so she could neither make nor receive non-emergency calls or text messages after 11 PM on weeknights. This was to prevent Caroline from staying up all night texting with friends. Whether seeking advice or a shoulder to cry on, Line was the go-to contact for kids struggling with one of 10,000 issues teenagers struggle with.

Kelley called Shelly Stumpff, another teammate and close friend, to enlist her help finding Caroline. The trio had spent much of the summer together talking about Line's mother, their upcoming senior year, and the volleyball season. Shelly worked the phones from the opposite end of their contact list. The girls figured, between the two of them, they would find Caroline.

When Ernie's worry became too great to keep him at home any longer, he left to look for his missing daughter. Since Caroline was supposed to be with Leah, his first stop was the Murray's. No one answered the door. Before he left for the Murray's, he asked Ellyn's sister, K.C., who was staying at the Found's house, to stick around in case Caroline came home or checked in while he was gone.

Because of Ellyn's fragile condition her brothers and sisters came to Iowa City, one or two at a time, from the east coast and stayed at the Found's farmhouse. Ernie's sisters, Marilyn and Grace, also came in shifts to help Ernie and Caroline with their daily lives. Ernie and Ellyn's two older children, Gregg and Catharine, were each living away from home.

Ernie combed the city for Caroline, going to her friends' homes and her favorite hangouts. He repeatedly called the Murrays' cell phones, but they had been asked by the officers at the accident to neither accept nor make any calls until the investigation was complete and proper notification made to Line's parents.

While Ernie was away, a Johnson County Sheriff's Deputy turned from the country road onto the Founds' long rock driveway. He let the vehicle coast down the dark lane, not looking forward to passing along the dreaded news. Giving parents their child's death notification is, and always will be, the worst job a law enforcement officer has to perform.

K.C. heard the familiar grind of rocks under a vehicle's tires and initially thought Ernie had found Caroline until there was a knock at the door. She saw the deputy's uniform and asked what bad news the official was there to deliver. The deputy was reluctant to tell her anything because she wasn't Caroline's parent, but he relented at her insistence. He immediately regretted his decision when Caroline's aunt gasped and broke down in tears. K.C. pulled herself together enough to invite the deputy inside to wait, but he declined. He waited in his squad car more than an hour for Ernie to come home.

Anxiety filled Ernie's stomach as soon as he saw the squad car parked in his drive. He knew the news that awaited him could only be bad. His sister-in-law's silhouette, standing at the storm door with a hand over her mouth, confirmed it. His intuition knew right away whatever the deputy had to tell him was about Caroline and not Ellyn. He braced himself as his pickup truck rolled to a stop behind the deputy's vehicle.

K.C. watched from behind the glass door as the two men climbed out of their cars. Ernie towered over the deputy. K.C. couldn't hear them through the storm door, but she knew the minute the message was delivered. Ernie's knees buckled and his whole frame nearly went down on the rocky drive. He stumbled to the wooden fence surrounding the family swimming pool and used it to steady himself. He stood under a canopy of stars and sobbed.

Mike and Barb Recker had been to a late movie and were just getting home when Ernie called with the news about Caroline. "Ernie broke over the phone. We left for the farm immediately." Mike recalled.

The Recker's arrived at the farm to see Ernie weeping near the pool. "He was hanging on to the fence to keep himself upright, so we stayed by his side and comforted him."

After twenty minutes in the dark, Ernie forced himself to go into the house. He stood in the kitchen and tried to get a handle on the news that no parent ever wants to accept—he had outlived one of his children. His thoughts shifted from abject grief to wretched horror at the realization he would have to tell his dying wife she had outlived her youngest daughter. Before going to the hospital to inform Ellyn, he called Gregg and Catharine and broke the news.

K.C. worked the phones to get her brothers and sisters mobilized and headed to Iowa. After contacting her husband, Barry, the second call she made was to her eldest brother, Mark Slocum. Mark had recently retired as chief financial officer for the IBM Corporation-Europe Division. He was a man accustomed to making things happen and making them happen quickly.

Mark and his wife, Trish, had already planned a trip to Iowa a week later to take their turn helping Ernie and Caroline. When the call came from a hysterical K.C., Mark's first thought was their sister had passed. "I girded myself for that news and said, 'Look K.C., I know you are calling to tell me that Ellyn is gone.'"

"It's not Ellyn, it's Caroline." K.C. shot the words out between sobs. "She's been killed, and I can't handle it. You have to come out here right away."

Soon after news of Caroline's accident spread, Lisa Murray arrived at the Founds' place to join Mike and Barb. Together, they all accompanied Ernie to the hospital so he could pass the awful news to Ellyn. The Founds were members of St. Andrew Presbyterian Church, and at Ernie's request, Head Pastor Matt Paul was there when the group arrived.

Meanwhile, doctors in the emergency room had given Leah a light sedative to calm her down. She and Boyd had been there about two hours. During that time, Boyd called Leah's youth minister, Randy Hausler, who was able to rally the congregation at St. Andrew.

It wasn't long until Randy and Associate Pastor Kyle Otterbein sat with Boyd and Leah in the Emergency Room. Ernie, Lisa, and Pastor Matt went into Ellyn's room. Ernie asked Lisa to tell Ellyn the news. He didn't think he could. Ellyn had experienced unbearable abdominal pain for quite some time, and the doctors had her on very strong pain medication. The meds made her spacey, so comprehending information was difficult. "Because of all the pain medication, Ellyn wasn't Ellyn anymore," Lisa said.

Lisa told Ellyn that Caroline had been in a moped accident and didn't survive. Her words took some time to find their way through the drug-induced haze that clouded her brain. One look at the sheer grief on her husband's face though and the awful news took hold. Ellyn's eyes filled with tears as she repeated a simple question to him, "Are you sure? Ernie, are you sure?"

Pastor Matt asked if they could pray together. Standing in the darkened room, Matt prayed a simple but fitting prayer, "Jesus is the light that shines in the darkness. God, don't let the darkness overcome the light."

In a moment of clarity, Ellyn demanded to see her daughter one last time to say goodbye. Ernie knew it was too risky to Ellyn's health for her to leave, so Caroline's body would have to be brought to the hospital, which was no easy task. University of Iowa Hospitals and Clinics has a hard and fast policy that forbids bringing a dead body into the facility for any reason but an autopsy.

Amid concerns that this would be the only opportunity for Ellyn to see Caroline, a plan was set in motion to bring Caroline's body into the basement of the hospital so Ernie and Ellyn, together, could say, "goodbye." The conspirators knew a successful plan required favors cashed in, and browbeating if necessary.

There's some mystery as to who gave the final clearance to bring Line's body into the hospital morgue. Any action circumventing hospital policy certainly put jobs on the line. If there was ever a time when compassion superseded the rules, the night's tragic circumstances certainly qualified.

Back in the emergency room, Boyd was informed of Ellyn's request and the subsequent plan. Caroline's body would need to be wheeled through the emergency room to get to the basement. While Boyd was glad Ellyn would get to see Caroline, he was concerned what might happen if Leah, who was now calm, saw Caroline's lifeless body on a gurney. He requested the emergency room personnel hold off bringing Caroline's body through the emergency room until Leah was gone. The ER staff, knowing the hospital policy assured Boyd that would never happen. Once the ER staff was made aware of the temporary change in protocol, they made sure Leah and her father were out in plenty of time.

When word came that Caroline's body had been delivered to the morgue, a team of nurses and physicians went to work transferring the medicines and monitors attached to Ellyn from stationary to mobile. With a nurse on each side of her, they gently pulled her arms to a seated position, right on through to standing, and then finally seated her in a wheelchair. Despite the strong pain meds, pain shot through her abdomen causing her to groan.

Repositioning Ellyn took no more than a few seconds, but the cancer had been destroying her body for months, so even with assistance, moving from the bed to the wheelchair took every ounce of her energy. They covered her delicate frame with blankets to keep her warm for the ride through the air conditioned hospital.

Ellyn was wheeled through the empty hallways by the hospital entourage, pushing and carrying all of the machinery and medicines attached to her. A security guard navigated the processional toward the elevators which led to the basement where Caroline's body had been placed. The trip through halls normally bustling with activity was eerie.

The group was too big for one elevator so they divided up and rode down in two groups. The medical staff, security guard, and Matt rode with Ellyn. Meanwhile, Pastor Kyle, family and friends rode with Ernie, who also requested a wheel chair because of his bad hip and back.

Riding in silence, Ellyn noticed the security guard had a cast on his hand. A former occupational therapist, she gently grabbed the stranger's casted hand and asked him what happened. She identified which corrective measures the physician had performed and recommended local therapists to help with his recovery. Considering her grief and pain level, the act astonished Pastor Matt. "It was surreal. Here we are in this terrible moment and she was caring about a stranger's problems," he remembered. Had it been anyone else, the interaction on the elevator might have been attributed to the pain medication, or maybe trying to avoid the reality of the situation. But this was Ellyn, for whom caring and compassion came as naturally as breathing.

The group negotiated the narrow passageways until they arrived at the morgue. Caroline's body was in a small room. Pastor Kyle and Matt Paul accompanied Ellyn and Ernie in and gave them some time. Ellyn touched her daughter's cheek. "That's my Caroline without the smile." Kyle approached and asked them to take their hands and make a sign of the cross on Line's forehead. Ernie grabbed Ellyn's hand and together they gently made the sign of the cross with their index fingers, just below her hairline. Pastor Kyle stepped forward and did the same while giving a blessing: "The Lord bless you and keep you; the Lord make his face shine on you and be gracious to you; the Lord turn his face toward you and give you peace."

The grieving parents stayed a bit longer with their Line. They were quiet and touched their daughter's arm, and caressed her face. There wasn't much left to do except say, "Goodbye."

Chapter 3
Bad News Travels Fast

Nothing travels faster than the speed of light with the possible
exception of bad news, which obeys its own special laws.
—Douglas Adams

The friend who can be silent with us in a moment of
despair or confusion, who can stay with us in an hour of
grief and bereavement, who can tolerate not knowing...
not healing, not curing...that is a friend who cares.
—Henri Nouwen

By midnight, Kelley Fliehler had dialed the last number on her contact
list. She scrolled to the top and started back through again—hoping
someone would report a Caroline sighting since the last time she had
asked. By 12:30 AM, she went into panic mode. The people she had
called a short time ago were no longer answering their phones.

As Kelley started down her list a third time, Shelly called her back.
She was in hysterics. Shelly needed a minute to calm down enough
for Kelley to understand her. Once Kelley got the message that Line
hadn't survived a moped accident, she went numb and initially refused
to accept what Shelly told her.

Once Kelley accepted the news as real, she woke her parents and told them what happened. Unsure of what to do, but feeling the need to do something, she grabbed her cell phone and called her volleyball coach, Kathy Bresnahan.

Coach Bresnahan, or "Brez" as all her students and players call her, was in a deep sleep when the phone rang. Startled, the twenty-year veteran teacher and coach immediately sat straight up in bed.

She shook the echoes of a dream out of her head, and then her mind scrolled through the list of possible reasons for the call. Brez's parents were still living but getting up there in age. It could have been about Ellyn. She grabbed the receiver and answered the call that would change her life forever.

Coach Bresnahan was convinced that when Kelley told her Line was dead, she actually meant Ellyn. She questioned her a few times. Once Brez was persuaded there was no mistake, she went outside and paced on her back porch.

Losing Caroline was devastating from a team perspective. Line was the team's setter, the equivalent of a quarterback on a football team. Coaches rely on setters to be their extension on the court. The setter is a very demanding, high stress, and high profile position, and by its very nature thrusts the player occupying it into a leadership position. A setter picks the team up when they are down and loosens them up when they are tight.

Setters usually receive the heat when things go wrong yet very few of the accolades when things go as planned. Great ones embrace the pressure and are as rare and valuable as flawless diamonds. Caroline was the best all-around setter Brez had ever coached. She was the team's beating heart. Brez explained, "Caroline Found *was* West High volleyball."

Alone on her back porch, the coach reflected on how far she and Caroline had come together and how close they had grown. Fleeting snapshots of moments they shared whirled through her mind. Suddenly it was three-years ago…

Coach Bresnahan stood in the middle of the gym floor while sophomore volleyball coach, Kelli Nance, made a case for why Caroline should be her future setter. She ticked off Line's attributes: determination, natural athletic ability, quick and critical decision making, …. Brez heard very little of her pitch because of the activity behind her.

Brez watched as her "future setter" bear crawled across the gym floor commando-style, barking orders at another participant in the faux military mission, "You better get your butt down or you're going to get it shot off some day, soldier!" Then Line rolled on the floor as she laughed herself silly. The coach thought to herself, "Not a chance in hell."

Her thoughts skipped ahead to the 2010 season. Although a junior, Caroline led the way during practices as well as games. She pushed and encouraged her teammates, even the seniors. When they advanced to the state championship game, Caroline, the confident floor general, led the team to both the school and Bresnahan's first state title.

Coach and Line built a trust. Line confided in her coach and sought her advice "Whenever she had free time she was in my classroom," Brez explained. Line normally was very up-beat, telling stories about this kid or that, or what she had going on in her life. One morning she came in and was subdued, so Brez asked what was going on. "My mom has been diagnosed with Stage 4 pancreatic cancer. Please tell me she is going to live," Caroline pleaded.

The coach and health teacher, never one to beat around the bush, has a New Yorker's directness occasionally misinterpreted by some as rudeness or even meanness. Brez's no-nonsense communication style was the hard truth Caroline had come to depend on. "Caroline, Stage 4 is tough stuff. The life expectancy is not good, but if anybody can do it, your mom can."

After that, Brez was one of the people Caroline leaned on for guidance and hope in coping with her mother's illness. As the months progressed, her coach pulled double duty as teacher and counselor. She made herself available for Caroline day or night with words of encouragement and moral support.

Still pacing back and forth across the porch, Brez thought about the practice scheduled for later that morning. Her players would be looking to her for answers and guidance in the face of the sudden and tragic loss of their leader and friend. Brez, the farm girl from Wisconsin who'd grown up fishing, hunting, and barrel racing at rodeos around the country had no frame of reference with the issues she would soon be forced to deal with. She called trusted confidant and principal at Xavier High School in Cedar Rapids, Tom Keating.

Before taking an administration position, Tom Keating was psychology teacher, activities director, and volleyball coach at Dubuque Wahlert high school. Brez and Tom started coaching around the same time. The seven-time state coach of the year with eleven state titles to his credit was, at first, her biggest rival. Over the years he became a mentor to Brez and eventually one of her best friends.

Coach Bresnahan called and told Tom what happened. "He cried when he heard who it was. He thought the world of Caroline, and she thought he was a god," she said. As principal at Xavier, he had lost two students in his nine years there. He knew the pain of losing students, especially those as special as Caroline and the trauma her death would bring to the student body, teachers, administrators, parents, and the community as a whole.

Once Tom gathered himself, he told Brez how sorry he was. He said he was sorry for her and the team, but he was most sorry for what was coming. He knew from experience the hurt she was feeling was only going to get worse. "As coaches and teachers, we all get drawn into these kids' lives, and I knew how her heart was just going to ache," Keating explained.

Brez confessed to Tom that she had no idea what to do next. She questioned if she should postpone the first game or even the first few games of the upcoming volleyball season. She went so far as to consider whether or not they should cancel the whole season. Keating told her the worst thing she could do was postpone anything. She needed to help guide the girls back to living their lives as soon as possible and not let their teammate's death consume them.

This was only one of several difficult obstacles he pointed out she would have to deal with in the upcoming days and months. He told her she had to get the kids through the death, the wake, and the funeral. The next hard part would be to get them back on the court when all they wanted to do was avoid anything that would remind them Caroline was gone, especially playing volleyball.

The Xavier principal's advice was the last thing she wanted to hear and only added to her list of concerns. She had doubts about being able to pull off such monumental tasks. She also worried how she would handle coaching without Caroline on the floor and in her life.

A list of questions raced through her head. How hard could she push them? Could she push them at all without them cracking under the emotional strain? How would she hold up? After all, she was feeling the same heartache as her players.

After much consideration and pacing Brez called her assistant coach and right hand, Scott Sanders. There was no answer. He finally was rattled awake by his vibrating phone at 1:30 AM. He answered and promptly received an earful from the head coach. "Brez was cussing me out for not having my ringer on," Scott said.

Scott and Brez had already talked about contingency plans for the setter position should Ellyn pass away before or during the season and if Caroline wasn't mentally prepared to play. "In the end we decided against it because if anyone could fight through the loss of her mother it would be Caroline. This would be her release, and she would probably have her best season ever," Brez believed.

At around 2 AM, Coach Bresnahan's phone rang for the first of what became a constant barrage of incoming calls and text messages until she left for the practice, scheduled at 8 AM. Friends, family, and coaches from all across the state contacted her to see if what they had heard was true, express condolences, and offer assistance.

At 7 AM, Coach Sanders walked into the dark, empty gym at West High. He went to Brez's small office and plopped down on the well-used couch. He hadn't slept since getting the call and rubbed his throbbing temples. A few minutes later Brez walked in. There were no words, none could be found, just tears and an extended hug.

Shelly Stumpff and Kelley Fliehler were the first players to show up at around 7:30. When they saw Brez their already red and puffy eyes once again filled with tears. They collapsed into their coach's arms and wailed. Brez figured none of her players had slept, and so, in her mind, changed the scheduled practice to a team meeting.

Brez checked her watch which read 8 AM. The two coaches stood and left her office. She planned the team meeting as they walked the short distance to the gym. She had decided to have the girls sit as a team on the ten-foot-line, which was Caroline's position on the court. Brez figured she would let the girls lead the team meeting if they wanted to. If not, they would talk about how they were feeling. She would allow them all the time they wanted, but wouldn't keep them long.

All plans went out the window when the coaches entered the gym. Instead of just finding the volleyball players, there were about three hundred teenagers, many crying hysterically. Brez's initial reaction to the interlopers was resentment. She felt like they were intruding on the team's grief. But she instantly felt ashamed of herself for such a selfish thought. Then she wondered how the students had found out and assembled so quickly.

The coach had no way of knowing, but members of the grief-stricken West High student body had been communicating. By midnight, news of Caroline's death was moving at lightning speed across social media channels and did so all night long. Once word spread, the Fliehlers' back porch was full of people who would stay a while and then when they would leave, replaced by more. Some were West High students, and others were West graduates who were only familiar with Caroline through their association with Gregg and Catharine.

These visits continued until first light. "On one hand it was nice that people were there to try and comfort us. They knew how close we were with Line. On the other hand, I just wanted people to get out of my face, but I couldn't tell them that," Kelley said.

All the additional students wanted to be there to grieve and show support for the volleyball team. The group grew, including the entire volleyball team from cross-town rival Iowa City High and players from the West football team. Many didn't want to interfere or intrude on the team meeting so they hung back in the shadows. Brez knew they were there to honor the kid who would have been the first one to invite every one of them to join such a meeting, so the coach invited them to sit on the court with the team.

Brez looked across the gym floor at all of the devastated kids— rudderless and searching for something, anything, in the way of guidance. Sleep deprived and heartbroken, Brez couldn't say with any certainty where the inspiration for what she did next came from, but it didn't matter. "I had someone find us boxes of tissues and just talked about Caroline the person. I led them in a moment of silence and then started joking with them a bit, 'Wouldn't Line love this? All these people here and she's the center of attention.'"

Brez asked one of her assistant coaches to find pencils and paper for everyone in the gym. She asked each of them to write a letter to Caroline and a letter to the Found family. The only instruction was to write from the heart. Sniffles and sobs echoed off of the stacked bleachers while hundreds of kids, some of whom may not have even known the Founds, poured out their hearts.

By 10 AM, Brez wanted to get the kids out of the stuffy gym and into the fresh air. She told them to go get flowers, cards, and mementos then meet her down by the accident site. When the police caught wind of the plan, they redirected vehicle traffic so the group could walk safely and unimpeded.

Word spread about the impromptu vigil. By the time Brez arrived, there were between 400-500 people crowded around the small, but now symbolic, tree. People spilled out into the street on both sides of the divider and onto the grassy areas on both sides of Mormon Trek.

Caroline's green No. 9 volleyball jersey was suspended from the tree. People hung keepsakes on the limbs as if it were a Christmas tree. Other items too big for the limbs like flowers, pictures, stuffed animals, a Spiderman or two (Line's favorite superhero), and countless other symbolic items were stacked at the base of the trunk.

Brez stepped back and scanned the crowd. Students from West and City stood side by side, and many, including burly West High football players, were in tears. The coach was especially touched by the tribute from City High students.

Standing amongst the crowd, the players and coach were exhausted and wrung out. Brez looked on while her players sobbed and embraced one another. She had no idea how they were going to make it through the upcoming season, or if they even would. They would just have to take it one day at a time. Standing together, around a tree, filled with remembrances of their fallen teammate, leader, and friend was Day One.

Chapter 4
By The Thousands

Come back to me, little dancing feet that roam the wide world o'er,
I long for the lilt of your flying steps in
my silent rooms once more;
Come back to me, little voice gay with laughter and with song,
Come back, little heart beating high with hopes, I
have missed and mourned you long.
—Lucy Maud Montgomery, *The Old Home Calls*

And we wept that one so lovely should have a life so brief.
—William Cullen Bryant, "The Death of Flowers"

By 10 AM Friday, about the time of the impromptu memorial at the crash site, Ellyn's oldest brother, Mark, pulled into Iowa City having traveled through the night. His long journey from the East Coast had started about 1 AM that morning in the sleepy state of Vermont.

After Mark first heard the news, he hung up the phone, sat on the edge of his bed, and contemplated his options. He was accustomed to making important decisions for one of the largest companies in the world—but only after weighing every shred of information afforded him. The only definitive information he had at his disposal in this situation was that his niece was dead.

He decided additional information was useless bec[a] would be the same: his family was hurting and needed h while his wife stuffed suitcases with their clothes, Ma computer and organized transportation to Iowa.

At 2 AM they were in the car and racing the two-and-a-half hours to the Manchester, NH, airport for a 5:45 AM flight. "I could not have repeated that in a million years. But hearing the desperation in my sister's voice, I kept imagining how much my sister Ellyn and Ernie would need help dealing with this. I knew we had to get there no matter what," Mark said.

Unsure when other family would be coming, Mark prearranged a block of rooms at the Marriott in Coralville. Although exhausted, they spent Friday at the hospital in an attempt to comfort Ellyn and Ernie and ensuring Gregg and Catharine made it home safely.

Of the two siblings, family members were more concerned about Catharine than Gregg. She had been at home all summer and spent much of it worrying about her family. She worried about her mother's failing physical condition, the stress her father was under, and how Caroline would cope if her mother passed while she was away at school.

Gregg also worried about his mother and family and would have gladly been there had the requirements of his job at ESPN not mandated he stay in Connecticut. His work served as a distraction until he needed to be home. He was relieved with all the familial support in his absence.

As the start of her final year in college rapidly approached, Catharine was focused on none of the things her classmates were. She wasn't thinking about her final volleyball season, graduation, or future. Instead, the 21-year-old concentrated on figuring out her role without her mother. After much deliberation, she decided to delay her return school so she could be Line and her father's foundation when Ellyn died.

Catharine told her mother she needed more time at home and wanted to push back returning to school. Ellyn wouldn't hear of this, and she made her daughter promise she would go back to San Antonio on August 9th. Due to Ellyn's drug-induced forgetfulness, every time Catharine walked into the hospital room her mother would ask if she had made arrangements to head back to school. It didn't matter if she was out of the room for two minutes or two days. The minute Ellyn saw her she asked Catharine the same question. Each time she gently reminded her mother that aunt Aileen was taking her back on August 9th.

The night before she was scheduled to leave, Catharine assured Caroline she wouldn't be gone long. Her timeline did nothing to calm Line's uneasiness about her sister leaving town. "It was hard leaving her, but I had to go. I made a promise to Mom," Catharine explained.

Catharine hadn't even had enough time to settle in when she got a call from Ernie, on the night of the 11th, wondering if she had heard from Caroline. Something in her dad's tone gave her an uneasy feeling and so she started making inquiries of her own. Finally, early in the morning, Ernie called with the devastating news about Caroline. Catharine dropped to the ground and sobbed. Her roommates quickly came to comfort her, help her pack, and get her to the airport safely before she could even inform anyone on the volleyball team. She was distressed and numb as she boarded the airplane.

Catharine took her seat on the plane and images of her sister laughing, dancing, and singing overwhelmed her brain. She never noticed the plane taking off.

Sometime between lifting off and landing she wondered, how could the same joyful mental pictures of Line that sustained her while away the past three years now crush her heart like it was being squeezed in a vice?

The trip home reminded Catharine she would never go for another summer ride with Line in her car. They would never again ride with the windows down, singing along to music blasting on the radio, while they smiled and waved to curious onlookers. She and Gregg would never again race their little sister up Mt. Monadnock during their annual trip to New Hampshire. Catharine would never again share a new experience with Caroline. The realization landed heavy on her heart, leaving it empty.

As K.C. and Catharine wheeled the car onto the Founds' driveway, Catharine remembered an expression from Helen Keller: "The best and most beautiful things in the world cannot be seen or even touched. They must be felt with the heart." The saying made her smile as she suspected her sister was behind the otherwise random thought. Caroline, like her mother, was a big fan of inspirational sayings, and she could recite one to suit any situation—just what Catharine needed to help ease her pain.

With Catharine and Gregg home, the entire family spent the remainder of the night grieving together. They cried and laughed. Recalled their fondest memories of Caroline, and cried some more. "It's when we felt like we could really let loose of our emotions," Mark said. They needed the time to be vulnerable. The following day they would be strong.

Planning for Caroline's visitation and funeral began Saturday morning at the Founds' farmhouse. The same place where countless social and commemorative occasions had been planned over the years—graduation parties, weddings, family gatherings, or simply a spontaneous Ernie bonfire so big the flames flared ten-feet high.

Most of the planning was done by Ernie, Gregg, Catharine, and the funeral director, Dan Ciha. The family decided to wait until Monday, August 15, to have the visitation with funeral services the following day. The delay was more for logistical reasons than anything else. In the meantime, the medical examiner wanted to do an autopsy, and Caroline had donated her vital organs, eyes, and ligaments to people in need of them. The Founds also wanted to give both sides of the family time to get to Iowa City over the weekend.

While the Founds worked on the content of the services, Dan worked on the logistics of the events. His biggest concern was the visitation and where it should be held. With media reports and the outpouring of support from friends and neighbors, he knew there was no way the visitation could be held at the funeral home. An alternative site with more space would be needed, and soon.

Dan called West High Principal, Dr. Jerry Arganbright, to see about the possibility of holding the visitation at the high school. Dr. Arganbright was understandably reluctant. West High was a place for education, and the last thing they needed was to set a precedent for funerals.

There was also the dilemma of finding a space within the school large enough to accommodate the numbers they were anticipating. Despite the expansive size of the school, the cafeteria and the gymnasium were the only two rooms large enough. With the number of extra-curricular activities West High offers, both were typically used from sun up to sun down, seven days a week.

The principal was conflicted with the funeral director's request. He thought about his longstanding personal relationship with the Founds and how active they had been at West. Ellyn was the consummate parent volunteer, only refusing his repeated requests for help if she had a prior commitment. He also considered the Founds' willingness to open their doors and entertain sports teams and a multitude of kids at their home.

He thought about Caroline and how her very essence stood out among the nearly two-thousand students. She was a positive role model who befriended the friendless. She greeted people enthusiastically in any number of ways. "I never saw her have a bad day. She was an indiscriminate hugger," Principal Arganbright said with a smile.

The principal had first-hand knowledge of Line's hugging prowess. One day as he walked down a hallway, he noticed Caroline at the other end. When she saw him, she beamed and charged him at full speed. Sprinting down the hall she screamed, "Dr. Arganbright!" Not slowing a bit, she launched herself into his arms nearly knocking the unsuspecting, suit-laden, middle-aged head-of-the-school to the ground. She wrapped her arms around him and squeezed as if he were a long lost sibling, not the principal of the school.

Dr. Arganbright saw her hug people many times after his own experience. When Caroline wanted to give a hug, which was often, there was no prior verbal request, text, email, or carrier pigeon asking for permission. The beneficiary was given a hug they wouldn't soon forget. The reasons for the displays of affection were as varied as the recipients—sometimes it was preceded by a monumental event, good or bad, other times it was because the person happened to be in her line of sight. After much reflection, the principal's choice was clear. He would allow Caroline's visitation to be held in the gymnasium.

By Sunday, the plans were in place, and most of the family were in town. The Marriott became the command and staging center for this improvised family crisis team. They met each morning at the hotel restaurant for breakfast, and assigned daily tasks.

Ernie and Ellyn's siblings scurried around town preparing programs, putting various photo collages together, and scouring the Founds' home for other meaningful reminders to display at the visitation and funeral. A job Mark assigned himself was to take Gregg to the local men's clothier and buy him a suit for the visitation and funeral. The Slocum sisters did the same for Catharine. "Gregg and Catharine just found out that their little sister had died. Under those circumstances, no one thinks about what tie to pack," Mark said.

While the rest of the family dashed about completing ancillary tasks, one particular family member was planning Caroline's funeral. Ellyn sent Pastor Matt Paul a text message from her hospital bed. "She was emphatic that I lead not only Caroline's, but her funeral when the time came. It certainly made it easier on Kyle (the associate pastor) and me because it eliminated the need for that discussion later on," Matt explained.

Ellyn had leaned heavily on Matt Paul since his arrival as the new head pastor of St. Andrew just three months earlier. Their relationship started before he was ever offered the job. Ellyn was on the Pastor Nominating Committee tasked with finding a new pastor after the former pastor of twenty-six years retired. It wasn't that Ellyn didn't have a strong relationship with Associate Pastor Kyle Otterbein; she did. Her decision was a result of another church team Ellyn belonged to which, in part, prompted her decision.

The church had developed a Reconciliation Team in response to a fracture in the congregation whether to relocate and construct a new church building or to renovate the existing facility. The issue, which had been festering for years, became so contentious the church had lost dozens of long-standing members.

Many of the initial pastoral candidates pulled their name from consideration when they were informed of the daunting issue they would face as a new pastor. Matt Paul didn't pull his name from consideration; on the contrary, it was the very issue that sold him on the job. That impressed Ellyn, and she advocated strongly for Matt.

Ellyn knew the right pastor could bridge the divide between the relocate and renovate sides of the congregation, but only if the members accepted him as the new head of the church. Convinced that Matt was the right man for the job, Ellyn did everything in her power to convince the Paul family to pull up their stakes in the Pacific Northwest and relocate to Iowa City. When the Pauls' came to visit, it was Ellyn who showed them around town.

Pastor Matt and Ellyn's relationship blossomed after he accepted the position and moved to Iowa. They relied on one another. She knew the pulse of the church and its members and could advise him on quirky Iowa ways such as when he should initiate a handshake or when he should let others offer their hand first. Ellyn, in turn, relied on the new pastor for spiritual guidance during the monumental physical, mental, and emotional difficulties associated with cancer.

Ellyn sought Pastor Matt's counsel when she had trouble sleeping because of her treatment, medication, or any number of reasons that a person with cancer can't sleep. The pastor gave her Psalm 46:10 "Be still and know that I am God."—and suggested that, as a meditation exercise, she repeat the passage, dropping the last word or phrase each time through:

"Be still and know that I am God."
"Be still and know that I am."
"Be still and know."
"Be still."
"Be."

This became Ellyn's mantra while she faced some pretty rocky months. She didn't keep the mantra to herself though, she passed it to many friends and family, some of whom use it to this day.

On Monday the farmhouse was bustling with activity, with one no-ticeable absence—Ellyn was simply too weak and in too much pain to consider attending even a fraction of the visitation. The Slocums and Founds, carrying heavy hearts and dressed in their Sunday best, piled into vehicles and made their way to West High.

Ernie asked that family and close personal friends gather in the gym at least forty-five minutes to an hour before the start time of 1 PM. He wanted to allow for any last minute adjustments and provide family members just arriving in town a chance to chat with others and pay their respects. The first indication of how long their day might be came when the family processional reached the school a full hour before the scheduled start time and had to negotiate a queue of cars already lined up in the parking lot.

Family intermingled with Caroline's closest friends in the gym. They milled about and exchanged hugs, pleasantries, and tears. They told stories of the golden-haired girl who touched all of their lives. They looked at picture collages and watched a slide show on a flat-screen TV that ran on a loop.

Ernie insisted that another group be there early—the West High volleyball team. The team showed up together in their green and white jerseys. The sobbing girls surrounded Ernie and hugged him harder than they had hugged anyone before. The coaches hung back. Brez looked away and bit hard on her lower lip, fighting back tears. Ernie spoke to the team huddled around him. His words made them both laugh, and sometimes cry. He walked them up to the casket so they could say goodbye to Caroline.

To lay out the most efficient receiving line possible, Dan Chia had to pull from his decades of experience organizing funeral visitations. They were expecting large numbers of people who would be standing in lines stretched well beyond the air conditioned interior of the school.

The outside temperature on that muggy August day was 90 degrees and climbing when they opened the doors to the public. The bleachers in the gym were extended to provide seating for people who needed a cool place to sit after waiting for hours in the oppressive weather.

People parked up to a half-mile away from the school. Some stood outside in the sweltering heat up to three hours before entering the building. For seven solid hours, from the time the sun blazed high overhead until it started to drop, people arrived.

The Found and Slocum families from out east were amazed at the outpouring of support from the community and wanted to do whatever they could to show their appreciation. "I took water out to people standing in line. They had to be miserable, but nobody was complaining or criticizing," Mark said.

Inside the gym, the line of people horseshoed around the outer edge of the basketball floor to the other side where Ernie, Gregg, and Catharine received them. The slow-moving queue allowed people plenty of time to stop at the corners of the room where the picture collages of Caroline and flower arrangements were on display.

Brez's colleague and friend, Tom Keating, waited in the heat with many others who had come to pay respects. Tom nodded politely to some of Caroline's classmates on either side of him and couldn't help but take in their endearing conversations. Once in the gym, he chatted with the volleyball team. The team shared fond memories of her. He talked with the family, and they had stories of their own.

There was a recurring theme with each conversation Keating overheard or took part in, and none were about Caroline's prowess on the volleyball court. Instead, every story was about how Line touched people's lives with her spirit, love, compassion, and understanding. The tales he heard were as varied as the people telling them.

Keating used his time sweltering in the August heat to advantage. Hearing about Line became the theme of a prayer he put together and would share during a school-wide assembly the first day of classes. He spoke of Line's inclusiveness and how everyone and anyone was her friend. He talked about her kindness and how she never spoke ill of anyone. He told of her compassion and willingness to listen and be there for support. He articulated her zest for life and love of the little things others ignored or took for granted.

Ernie, with bad back and hip, stood on the unforgiving gym floor and greeted every one of the estimated three thousand people who came. He warmly thanked friends and strangers for coming. Many shared anecdotes and pleasant experiences about Caroline, asked how Ellyn was doing, or simply wondered what they could do to help.

As the never-ending line of sympathizers continued throughout the day, Ernie took breaks from time to time. He needed just a few seconds to get a drink and reset before greeting the next wave of well-wishers. Each time Ernie moved to the bleachers, he saw a frail-looking young man shifting his weight nervously back and forth. Whenever Ernie looked at him, the young man diverted his eyes, but it was clear that the kid had something he wanted to say. Ernie finally asked him if he was looking for someone, and the boy burst into tears and managed to choke out between sniffles, "I'm Jimmy Peterson. Caroline was my best friend."

As it turned out, Caroline was one of Jimmy's only friends. They met through a mentoring program at West when she was paired with the undersized freshman with special needs. Try as he might to make friends at school, his personality was off-putting at best.

Caroline embraced Jimmy as a friend and spent countless hours with him at school. She asked for his cell phone number, and they exchanged text messages. Line encouraged her more popular friends to say, "Hi" to him in the halls.

Jimmy was on the football team, but he generally was shunned by the other players. Caroline pressed some of the star players to include him and make him feel like part of the team. Jimmy struggled mightily when Caroline died, but because of her efforts, his new buddies were there to help soften the blow.

The day wore on, and Mark marveled at the steady stream of people coming to pay their respects. He couldn't help but feel more than a little embarrassed as he reflected on his initial reaction when Ellyn told him that they were moving to the Midwest. "I was appalled that they were moving to Iowa. I didn't think there was anything worthwhile west of Chicago until you got to California," Mark confessed.

All totaled, Mark spent twenty-one days in Iowa. In that time his perception of the Midwest and particularly Iowa dramatically shifted. "Everyone was just so friendly and accommodating. Whether it was staff at the Marriott in Coralville or strangers we met in Iowa City, they welcomed us with open arms. We felt like part of the family," Mark admitted.

As Mark marveled at the outpouring of love and reverence heaped on the family, he couldn't help but acknowledge the irony that the one person who would have reveled in it most wasn't there. "Caroline would have thought this was cool, that all of these people were here for her. She would have been dancing and clicking her heels together," Mark said.

Caroline, rejoicing at a gathering of people on her behalf, wouldn't have been selfishness or egotism. Caroline not only loved spending time with special people in her life but connecting them with one another. Thousands of people congregating in the same place and forging new relationships with her as the singular common denominator would have been Line's nirvana.

Mark blurred his vision, and he could envision Line on the gym floor, moving from group to group and exchanging hugs, telling jokes, and laughing at punch lines with everything she had. For a brief moment he felt she was the life of the party. As quickly as she appeared, she was gone. Mark smiled, thankful for the short-lived vision.

Chapter 5
Sweet Caroline

I arise in the morning torn between a desire to improve the world
and a desire to enjoy the world. This makes it hard to plan the day.
—E. B. White

Children have neither past nor future, they enjoy the
present, which few of us do. So stop and smell the roses,
sing to yourself, and enjoy what we have while it lasts.
—Caroline Found

The Iowa City community is not unfamiliar with losing high school
students to tragic circumstances. So why did Line's death draw such
a massive outpouring of love, respect, and admiration from family,
friends, and strangers?

Caroline Found was an enigma: a teenage riddle wrapped in a puz-
zle. Ask twenty people to describe her, and twenty distinct answers
would be given. While descriptions would vary dramatically (fun, crazy, silly, gregarious, insightful, loving, understanding, bold, loyal, leader,
and friend), one theme would be constant—she cared.

Caroline blossomed into a beautiful, affectionate, giving young
woman, which was hard to imagine for those who knew her as a little
girl. Baby Line came kicking and screaming into the world on a sun-

soaked Sunday, June 19, 1994. Ernie couldn't possibly think of a better Fathers' Day present.

Ernie and Ellyn decided well before the blessed event that three children was a good number and Caroline would be the last. Most parents with two or more children can attest the youngest is treated differently. Baby Caroline was no different. She soaked up the added attention, and whenever possible, used it to her advantage.

Line clung to her parents, particularly Ellyn, during many of her formative years. She always wanted to be held or near her mommy and daddy, especially at night. "She slept in my parents' room way longer than most kids do," Catharine recalled. During her first few years of school Caroline, more than once, faked being sick so she could stay home with her mother.

She was much more regimented with her activities as a child than when she was older. She had routines like watching the same movies over and over or eating the same foods. Caroline was a thumb sucker, so much so it may have impacted her appearance later on. Her two front baby teeth were replaced with prominent incisors with a sizable gap between them.

Young Caroline had the innate ability to change moods as quickly as changing temperatures on a water faucet. "She'd go from hot to cold, and once she'd get her way, back to hot again," Gregg said. When things didn't go her way, Caroline would flash her puppy dog eyes and a sad little face that melted hearts.

After seeing the routine one too many times, her family gave the face a nickname, "Poor Pitiful Pearl," after the melancholy-faced doll popular in the 1950s. With the combination of sucking her thumb and curling up on the couch to pout, the fitting moniker stuck. It was later shortened to "PPP" and became commonplace among her aunts when mentioning her antics.

Of the three siblings, Catharine and Caroline had a more natural connection because they were closer in age, both girls, and volleyball players. Growing up the oldest and eight years Caroline's senior, Gregg saw himself less as friend and more the protector of his younger sisters. Life, age, and wisdom have allowed him to see what great friends he had in his sisters, a friendship which continues today with Catharine.

Caroline tried to ingratiate herself to both Gregg and Catharine's friends, but not for the same reasons. Each required her to play different roles within each group. She tried to be a peer on level-footing in Catharine's group. With Gregg and his pals, she was happy playing the little sibling, allowing herself to be picked on a bit, even playing the role of the annoying little sister.

Line had the ability to always achieve something out of any relationship she started with someone. She learned the benefits and pitfalls of being a junior high and high school girl from Catharine and her friends, giving careful consideration to choosing friend groups. She gained information which gave her a leg up on girls her age who didn't have the benefit of an older sister's brain to pick.

What she acquired from her brother and his friends was more valuable than anything from the girls—an insider's perspective on the male species. She heard crude noises, embraced the joy of slapstick comedy, and learned how to trash talk as well as how to give and take a joke.

But the best thing Caroline received from Gregg and his friends was a fiery competitiveness and a strong distaste for losing, which was forged in the fire of countless athletic competitions. Gregg's cluster was no different than most groups of guys; everything they did turned into a competition: "I bet I can throw farther, run faster, or chug more soda and belch louder."

Caroline and Gregg connected through competition, and Line expected to win every game she played against him. What didn't occur to her, or wouldn't have mattered if it had, was her opponent was an older, taller, stronger brother who felt an obligation to show his younger sister the proper pecking order of the Found family. When Caroline found a home in organized team sports against her peers, her motivation came from every loss to her brother and his friends. The losses drove her to outwork her opponents in a dogged pursuit of victory.

Caroline emulated Gregg and his friends in manner, dress, and even hair style. She went through a tomboy phase when she was younger, embracing activities generally considered disgusting by girls her age. She didn't mind having dirt under her fingernails or picking up slimy fish and frogs. But she had quirks too. What disgusted her above all else, for instance, was vomit—she couldn't stand the sight, the smell, or the act. If Line saw someone retching she would cover her ears, close her eyes, and run away screaming. Once the action and associated noise was over, curiosity would get the better of her and she would ask the sick person, from a safe distance, to describe the color, texture, and what was in the vomit.

By the time she hit junior high school though, a sensitive side emerged with a child-like sensibility that endeared her to all she met. Line wasn't typical even when it came to her choice of movie genre. While her peers flocked to horror, action, or sappy love story movies, Line preferred make-believe and fantasy Disney films. *Peter Pan* was one of her favorites. The idea of never having to grow up was something she connected with.

She saw nearly every movie Disney made and had the unique ability to watch a movie like *Air Bud: Golden Receiver* eight times in a row without tiring of the story line. If it wasn't Disney, it was super hero stories, particularly Spiderman. The redeeming and inspirational themes of one individual going out of their way to help those in need really appealed to her.

Caroline's relationship choices were as divergent from her junior high friends' as their movie selections. Most teenagers conclude that adults, especially their parents, are the dumbest people on the planet. Caroline, however, found value and wisdom in the words of adults and sought out their counsel when she could.

The first adult she connected with outside her family was her seventh-grade math teacher, Mike Recker and then his wife, Barb, or "Mo" and "Bo" after Caroline hung the nicknames on them. Neither Mike nor Barb can articulate why she chose to attach herself to them, but they were thankful she did because she changed their lives forever.

It was normal for Mike to have at least one annoying kid who got under his skin in class each year. Five minutes into the 2007 school year, the veteran teacher pegged Caroline as that kid. During the very first class, he had to constantly remind the chatty girl to pay attention. She wasn't disrespectful—she was polite and had a bubbly and infectious personality. Mike had been wrong before, but any hope that Line might not be a pain in his neck disappeared with her antics at the end of their first class together.

Caroline was the last to leave the room when class dismissed. Without a word, she walked by Mike's desk and inexplicably rearranged everything. Satisfied with what she had done, she rushed toward the door and turned off the lights on her way out. The stunned teacher was left sitting alone in the dark at a desk that looked like it had been hit by a tornado. He heard her laughing hysterically as she ran down the noisy hallway. All he could do was shake his head and smile while putting things back in order.

A teacher for thirty years, Mike was not easily rattled or surprised by what students did, so he was mystified as to why he pulled out his cell phone and texted his wife about this new girl he had in class. Barb picked up her buzzing phone and read the text message from him:

"New girl in class reminds me of our Caleb. I think she's going to be a lot of fun." Caroline intended on being a lot more to Mike and his family than just another of his students—Line knew it, they didn't.

Adding Line into their fold was an easy transition for the Reckers. As Mike noted in his text, their youngest son, Caleb, was also a free spirit with a big heart, and like Caroline, could be a bit annoying. "My son drove teachers crazy sometimes, but the ones that gave him a chance were usually happy that they did," Mike said.

Caroline was the kind of kid who begged the teachers she really liked to come and watch her play sports—and she played nearly every sport offered. "That's really how our relationship got started, by us watching her play sports," Mike said. Little did Mike know that he and Barb were already in the second phase of their relationship with Line.

Mike and Barb agreed to attend Caroline's athletic events since they had become empty nesters, plus they were already attending the sporting events of Charlie Rogers, a student they were mentoring through their church. Most of their off time was spent bouncing between Caroline and Charlie's events, cheering loudly at each.

Despite their common denominators of sports and an association to the Reckers, Charlie and Line didn't become close friends until high school when they made the Recker connection. After that, they spent quite a bit of time together at Mike and Barb's house. Occasionally they would do homework, but usually they just hung out and raided the refrigerator, which was perpetually stocked by Barb with their favorite snacks.

For Caroline, Mike and Barb were a supplemental set of adults she could turn to for advice, hang out with, or receive occasional tutoring. They were one of the first people she went to for consolation when her parents informed her of Ellyn's diagnosis.

The Reckers' biological kids, older than Caroline and Charlie, adopted them into the family as though little brother and sister. Ernie and Ellyn didn't mind at all that Caroline spent time at the Reckers. Ellyn's only concern was if Caroline would overstay her welcome and become a pest. Mike and Barb's connection with Line, at her insistence, eventually expanded to them being family friends.

Mike and Barb supported Caroline in whatever she did and let her know why when they didn't. They were adamant, however, that they would never lie to her parents to cover for her. Line tested that rule one day before she had four tests and had done little studying for any of them.

The morning started with Caroline telling her parents she was scheduled to work at Charlotte's Deli that day and then to Mike and Barb's for a late study session.

Barb's phone rang around 6 PM. It was Caroline asking Barb to cover for her if Ellyn called. Barb cut her off mid-sentence and reminded her that she wasn't going to lie to her parents. "Caroline said, 'Fine, I'll figure that part out, but I'm not going to be there until about 7, and I'll explain everything then.'"

When she finally got to the Reckers', Barb asked her where she had been all day. Caroline said she had picked up Charlie and his friend Anthony Brown. They had lifted weights and then decided to stop at a park to play football.

Line told Barb the three of them had been having a great time until Line's cell phone rang. Ellyn was calling to say she and Ernie were headed to Charlotte's to have a bite to eat for a late lunch. Caroline went into full panic mode. She hustled everyone into the car and dropped them at Charlie's house. She drove like the wind to Charlotte's, put on an apron, and smeared some food on it just before her parents walked into the restaurant. "That was Caroline," Barb said. "She pushed things to the limit causing her and Ellyn to butt heads quite a bit."

Caroline thought she had dodged a real bullet. Not only was she supposed to be studying for her tests, but she had been restricted from weight training or any physical exertion for two weeks because she was recovering from a back injury. That timeline didn't fit with Line's workout warrior weight training schedule, however.

Her prowess in the weight room and physical stamina was the stuff of legend, even with football players like Charlie and Anthony. After the guys exhausted themselves with three sets of regular squats, the winded pair watched in amazement as Caroline did squats on one leg with the other leg extended straight out in front of her body. Called "Pistol Squats," the guys could only do a couple before crumpling on the floor. Caroline did them in rapid fire succession. "Caroline was crazy with those things," Charlie stated.

The next day, which happened to be April Fools' Day, Barb devised a plan to teach Caroline a little lesson about deceiving her parents. She sent Line a text message informing her that Ellyn found out she wasn't where she was supposed to be and was extremely upset. Before she could send the "April Fools'" payoff message, Line called her mother and chewed her up one side and down the other for calling Barb and meddling in her business.

Ellyn calmly informed her daughter she had no idea what she was talking about. She assured Caroline there would certainly be consequences coming her way for using such bad judgment. Line fumed that she had told on herself and put Barb directly in her crosshairs. "Caroline called yelling at me, 'I can't believe you told me that. I'm grounded again. I hope that you're happy.'"

While Caroline spent a lot of time at the Recker's home, they could never take the place of her own parents and primary mentors. Line's essence, in fact, was a perfect mix of Ellyn and Ernie. It was as if she understood what made them such special people and adopted those traits from each. She always told people that she had the best role models a kid could have.

Caroline was a philanthropist at heart, just like her mother. She gave her time, friendship, and money to those in need. She befriended special need kids at school, not for school credit, or social standing, but because they didn't have a friend. She didn't just spend one-on-one time with the friendless; she would pull them into her world, forcing the sometimes reluctant athletes or "cool" kids to accept them as well.

When Caroline befriended someone it was always with a feet-taped-to-the-pedal commitment. She actually got into a spot of trouble at school for sneaking a mentally challenged student off campus during the school day to hang out with her "in-crowd" friends. To the marginalized and uncool, the popular kids in high school were unattainable. Caroline provided them a conduit to that world, which was as special to them as a thousand Christmases. To Caroline, the bit of trouble was worth it. She knew everyone needed a friend.

Line learned the valuable lessons of true friendship the hard way— by experience. When she was a sophomore Coach Bresnahan pulled her from the sophomore volleyball team up to varsity. Any coach can recognize raw talent, but Brez saw in Line leadership skills and a tenacious work ethic. These rare qualities can't be coached and are infectious to a team.

Caroline incorrectly assumed that being on the varsity team also meant automatic inclusion into the friendship circle of the older girls. The juniors and seniors on the team included her during the season by default. Once the season was over, Line was generally excluded which crushed the girl with the heart the size of a mountain. Caroline vowed never to exclude anyone based on something as trivial as age, intelligence, looks, social status, economic standing, or sexual orientation.

If someone was in need, she wanted to help, even if it meant doing something that her parents may not approve of; or might run afoul of school policy. When Charlie and Anthony came to her with a sob story about how they hadn't studied for an American Literature test and would be ineligible for football if they failed it, she didn't lecture them. She asked what she could to do help.

They devised a plan so Caroline could help them cheat. Because both of Charlie's parents were deaf, he was fluent in sign language. He showed Caroline and Anthony how to sign the first four letters of the alphabet so she could give them the answers.

All three were caught. Each tried to fall on the sword and take blame away from the others. Charlie and Anthony felt horrible, and not because they were caught or for the consequences they faced, but because they had betrayed the people who truly cared about them and the trust of Caroline's friendship.

The boys were devastated when Ellyn, Ernie, Mike, and Barb told them how disappointed they were in them. From the guys' perspective, letting down the positive role models in their lives was worse than any punishment from their football coach. Which was really saying something considering what the football coach put them through on the practice field—heaps of wind-sprints, push-ups, and up-downs.

Caroline received an in-school suspension for the incident and was required to serve detention as well. She went to the detention room after school and immediately recognized some of the kids. A few of them had extremely rough home lives. She knew the only meals they could count on were the breakfasts and lunches the school provided.

Always the giver, Caroline made sure that no one was hungry if she could help it. Using her cell phone, she ordered a large pizza for all in detention to share. The teacher proctoring the punishment was initially upset when the pizza delivery person showed up, but when Caroline explained her rationale for ordering the food, he was so moved by the gesture he overlooked the violation and even had a slice with the group.

Her charity wasn't confined to inside the school walls. She was well aware of her blessed circumstances and wanted to share them with those less fortunate. When she learned how much it cost to feed the local homeless population in Iowa City, she and close friend Adrienne Jensen sold cookies to football fans walking to and from the stadium at the Iowa Hawkeye games. Every bit of the money went to help feed the homeless.

In addition to helping others, Caroline loved real-life adventures and was always on the lookout for opportunities to create them. Her sense of adventure and humor came directly from Ernie. People fed off her boundless energy and no group more so than her volleyball teammates. If they were uptight before a big game, Line would give them a laugh by dancing and singing along to a song during warm-ups. As with any Line activity, there were no casual observers allowed—everyone had to participate, so she had everyone dancing with her.

Caroline created adventures for friends when they hung out together. They were generally activities intended to entertain her and push others outside their comfort zone. If you were a girly-girl, she may have you at a pond catching frogs. A car ride with Line might be designed to get an introverted friend out of her shell by honking and waving at every pedestrian they passed. Sometimes the adventures were born purely out of inspiration and opportunity. Kelley found this out during a sleepover.

The girls were in the middle of a scary movie marathon when the doorbell sent them into hysterics. The fear caused by the pizza delivery gave Caroline an idea. She left the room and returned with a ski mask on her face and a butcher knife raised menacingly above her head. She growled and chased her terrified and screaming friends all over the house, yelling in a deep voice, "I'm gonna kill you!"

Kelley's mother was not amused to be roused out of a sound sleep at midnight by what sounded like an axe murder taking place in her house. She was even less amused when Caroline shook a two-liter bottle of Mountain Dew and gave it to an unsuspecting Kelley to open in her room.

The adults in Line's life weren't immune from her adventures either. Mike and Barb learned this when Caroline stayed with them one weekend while Ernie and Ellyn went out of town. Line came to the house with a "bucket list" of activities. One of which was teaching the rhythm-challenged Mike how to dance to hip hop music.

Neighbor after neighbor drove by honking and laughing at the sight of the red-faced Mike dancing awkwardly in his shorts and white tube socks to a bass-thumping hip hop song blasting from Line's car in the drive. Why the tube socks? For some reason, Caroline couldn't stand the sight of bare feet and made the Recker's wear socks whenever she came over.

Caroline lived by her own set of rules, which sometimes ran counter to the norm. Despite being less than a year from voting or serving in the military, Caroline viewed life through the lens of a child. Her enthusiasm made it acceptable to do activities which were considered silly or childish. She got great joy seeing a smile on someone's face as he/she swung on the family's barn swing, hunted for frogs, played in a pile of leaves, or let out a satisfying belch after a long pull from an ice-cold soda and laughed themselves silly.

Line had a larger than life personality and appeared impervious to normal teenage angst. Her confidence, carefree attitude, and compassion for people caused people to forget she was still a teenager with a teenager's insecurities. Ironically, the girl who worked so hard to get others to try new things outside of their comfort zones had several self-doubts of her own, but only her inner-circle of friends ever saw them.

One of her insecurities was wearing attractive clothing. She wanted to but felt self-conscious because she had worn sweats and jeans to school nearly all of her freshman and sophomore years. She worried such a drastic change to her wardrobe would draw negative attention and ridicule. Caroline, to her credit, faced her fashion insecurity head on and changed things up. She turned to Kelley who always dressed well and was the closest person to a fashion consultant she knew.

When Caroline did decide to wear something nice, she was always nervous because she thought everyone would judge her. When Kelley's phone rang on a school night, she knew who it would be even before checking the caller ID. Caroline would be double checking if an outfit she put together for the following school day looked good.

The self-aware high school junior accepted there were those who saw her views on life and corresponding actions as foolish and sometimes immature. Line never denied or offered an apology to those who were critical or dismissive of her carefree lifestyle. If the criticism ever bothered her, it never showed.

To those who misunderstood her, she offered an explanation and some sage advice in an article she penned for the school's newspaper, *West Side Story*: "I am often thought of as childish. I prefer to interpret that as childlike. I still get wildly enthusiastic about little things, tend to exaggerate, fantasize and think big. I still watch cartoons, play with leaves, skip down the street, sing to myself and can't go outside without getting dirty. I still believe in Santa Clause [sic]. And that is something I will never, EVER let go of...Children have neither past nor future, they enjoy the present, which few of us do. So stop and smell the roses, sing to yourself, and enjoy what we have while it lasts."

It was with these thoughts that people came, some from thousands of miles, to stand in the sweltering heat to pay their respects. For the same reasons, people packed a church the following day to say, "goodbye" to the girl who gave so much of her goodness to so many.

Chapter 6
There Is No Finish Line

"But now 'tis not thy hand that buries me, but I, on
whom is come old age with loss of home and children,
am burying thee, a tender child untimely slain. Ah
me! Those kisses numberless, the nurture that I gave
to thee, those sleepless nights—they all are lost!"
—Hecuba in Euripides' *The Trojan Women*

She kept at true good humor's mark,
the social flow of pleasure's tide:
She never made a brow look dark,
nor caused a tear, but when she died.
—Thomas Love Peacock

On Tuesday morning, the day of Caroline's funeral, a lengthy discussion was happening amongst the Hospice workers assigned to care for Ellyn, the staff of the church, and family members. Hospice had created a list of non-negotiable demands to be followed if, by some miracle, Ellyn were able to attend the funeral service. Because of her dire physical condition, confidence she would be attending was not high.

While the head of the church listened intently, Pastor Matt Paul was mentally rolling his eyes at the list of Hospice expectations. They wanted an area left cleared in the parking lot for an ambulance. The lot was sure to be packed with cars—along with the lawn, sidewalks, and every other space a car might squeeze on to the property. They wanted to pick where to wheel her in and out quickly. And if she felt ill, there needed to be a contingency plan. "I was fine with it because it was Ellyn and I'd do anything for her, but it did seem fairly theatrical. Knowing Ellyn, it also seemed like this was the Hospice folks' wishes, not hers," said Matt Paul.

Even with less than an hour before the funeral, Ellyn's oncologist, Don McFarland, was skeptical she had the strength to attend. Ellyn's condition had advanced past any benefit from treatment. The doctors had shifted their focus on keeping her alive long enough to attend Caroline's funeral.

Dr. McFarland was described by some colleagues as a Scottish hard-ass. Oncologists need to have a certain amount of gristle on them because despite their best efforts, a high percentage of their patients' prognosis is death. Overwhelmed, Ernie asked best friend and colleague, Dr. Larry Marsh, to consult with Dr. McFarland on managing Ellyn's condition so he could focus on Caroline's visitation and funeral. It certainly wasn't something Larry looked forward to, but he readily agreed.

The tragedy of keeping a dying woman alive long enough to be present at her daughter's funeral was ironic to the otherwise unflappable doctor. "Don said to me one day after Ellyn passed, 'Larry, I'm an oncologist. I deal with death and dying on a weekly basis; that's what I do. I've never seen anything like this,'" Dr. Marsh said.

People arrived at St. Andrew with a variety of questions still unanswered. Primarily they wanted to know, "Why did this happen to such an amazing person who had so much life yet to live, and so much love left to give?" Another question that consumed the roughly one thousand grief-stricken funeral attendees was, "Why would God let this happen to such a good family?" Such questions are common and even necessary when confronted with the sudden and tragic loss of a teenager.

People work hard to assign meaning to their lives. They want to feel they are at least partly in control of what happens to them. When a tragedy occurs, or something they can't assign meaning to, it's scary and makes them feel vulnerable. They are left with an unanswerable question, "Why?"

"'Why' is not something that can be answered because the premise of the question is that there was some purpose to it," Pastor Matt explained. "I don't think it's a 'why' as much as it's a trying to affirm, 'Where is God? What is God doing now?' If it's a 'why,' God has some checklist and pen, 'okay, got that one done.' My sense is that God is weeping too."

People squeezed into the pews until it was impossible for anyone else to fit. The box normally reserved for the choir was opened to the public and overflowed with people as well. Once the pews were full, people were allowed to stand along the walls. The doors to the sanctuary were left open and rows of chairs were placed in the Narthex. Video feeds were located in Fellowship Hall and two Sunday school classrooms for those unable to view in person. Just prior to the start of the funeral, the only empty seats were the two front pews, reserved for immediate family.

Family members were in the choir room at the opposite end of the church. It was their space to gather, reflect, and have some alone time away from all the people in attendance. They were saddled with a question of their own, "Would Ellyn be well enough to attend?"

Determined, the family waited for Ellyn to arrive as long as they could. Finally, the funeral was ready to start, and all felt her absence. Disappointed, they started down the hall toward the sanctuary when, suddenly, an ambulance eased to a stop in front of the glass doors at the east wing of the church. They rushed to the double doors and erupted into cheers and applause when Ellyn emerged from the vehicle's back doors. Guests seated in the Narthex turned to see what might cause the unexpected sound of cheers at a funeral.

The church doors were opened for Ellyn, who was pushed in a wheelchair by a hospice worker. There wasn't a dry eye among the family as an overwhelmed Ernie bent and lovingly kissed his wife. Her face was gaunt and cheeks sunken, yet she looked magnificent with her makeup and shoulder length brown hair done perfectly. She wore an elegant blue and black dress.

Her smile and made-over face masked the devastating toll the cancer had exacted on her body. Her muscle mass was gone, making her weak and unsteady to walk. She was on so many pain killers to counteract the excruciating abdominal discomfort that her eyes were glassy and distant.

None of this mattered at the time. The family was thankful she had the strength to attend and for the intimate moment they shared, separate from the hordes of friends and community members. It was a chance for them to acknowledge her presence, and the happiness it gave them in the midst of everything that had happened, and was about to happen, just a hallway's walk away.

The hospice-approved plan was that Ellyn would ride into the sanctuary and helped into her seat. Immediately after the service, she was to be wheeled out of the church, into the waiting ambulance, and driven back to the hospital. The hospice workers insisted there be no deviations from the plan. "I remember that she wanted to walk down the aisle of the church. Everyone thought it was a bad idea because no one thought she'd have the strength to do it," Ernie said.

The black-robed pastors led the procession into the sanctuary with Ernie pushing Ellyn in the wheelchair behind them, the rest of the family filed in behind. The murmur of the guests stopped, and all eyes moved to Ellyn.

About halfway down the aisle, Pastor Matt turned to make sure he wasn't getting too far ahead of Ernie and Ellyn. He stared in astonishment as Ellyn gripped both wheels of the chair bringing it to a dead stop. She motioned for Ernie, who quickly stepped around the chair by her side and bent down.

"Help me up, I'm walking," Ellyn said.

After he lifted the footrests out of her way, she stood up, took her husband's arm, and together the couple walked down the remainder of the aisle.

Matt Paul is not one to use the word "miracle" broadly. In any other circumstance and setting, he would have dismissed describing what happened in that light as hyperbole, but he knew how sick she was. "The strength she had to do that was miraculous; it was a Rocky-type moment that could be felt throughout the church by everyone. I still don't know how she did that," he marveled.

After Pastor Matt walked to the pulpit, he took a moment to scan the crowd. He looked at the grief-stricken volleyball team and their coaches seated together—some sobbing, others consoling. The pastor regarded Line's friends and classmates comforting each other as they dabbed their eyes with tear-soaked tissues. He watched as Ernie and Ellyn's friends squeezed their kids tighter than ever before. If he could have reached his own sons and daughter at that moment, he would have done the same.

The pastor's eyes drifted to the family. He glanced at Gregg with his arm around Catharine's shoulder, both of them stunned and expressionless. Finally, he fixed his gaze on Ellyn and Ernie. He saw a look he had seen countless times, and as a parent himself, never found easy to accept. The couple wore similar dazed faces, twisted into painful and grief-filled inquiry. With furrowed brows they desperately searched for answers. There would be no "ah-ha" moment for the devastated couple on a quest for a meaning to their nightmarish reality. There never is.

Pastor Matt, who had presided over many funeral services, knew this one presented a unique set of circumstances. This day was to celebrate Caroline's life, but glancing at Ellyn, he knew that there was no way to completely separate Caroline from her mother considering the circumstances surrounding Ellyn's situation.

"You couldn't do either service without thinking about the other person," Matt said. "Yet when Caroline died, it wasn't Ellyn's service because she was still with us." In the days leading to Caroline's service, he had struggled with how he would negotiate the fine line between acknowledging each person individually for who they were and ensuring this day was ultimately about Caroline.

Another challenge the pastor faced was the magnitude of the communal event. So many people wanted to be involved. This was a wonderful problem to have in that it spoke volumes about Caroline and the number of people she impacted during her short time on earth. While Matt wanted to give a voice to as many as he could, he realized the importance of not having a five-hour funeral service.

Mindful of all these things, Matt Paul took a sip of water, and soon his amplified voice filled the sanctuary: "The questions come flooding into our minds: How could this happen? Why do tragedies happen to good people? It's natural to ask these questions. It's our way of trying to make sense of this tragedy. We ask these questions because of the suddenness of it all. We ask these questions because seventeen-year-olds are expected to become eighteen-year-olds."

The pastor went on to try to answer, "How could this happen?" The question that loomed so large on everyone's mind. He spoke of the mysteries of life and that a relationship with Jesus didn't make us immune to tragedy. "So while the 'why' questions of suffering still mystify us, the question of God's presence is one that we can answer. God is with us. I know this because while the world is full of suffering, it is also full of recovering from it. Where has God been these last few days? Right here, helping us overcome the pain of loss."

The remainder of the service was devoted to honoring Caroline and celebrating her life. Caroline's aunt and former opera singer, Marilyn Found, sang a beautiful rendition of "Smile." Once Marilyn finished, Pastor Kyle Otterbein took the podium and pulled a copy of a prepared statement by Ernie and Ellyn. The original was in the breast pocket of Ernie's jacket. Pastor Kyle had been provided a copy in case Ernie found himself unable to read.

As Kyle unfolded the words and faced the congregation, he looked at Ellyn with her head on Ernie's shoulder and knew the real reason he was reading the statement instead of Ernie. This was the first time in a long while, and potentially the last time, Ernie would sit with his wife when she wasn't in a hospital bed with IVs and monitors attached to her. The couple listened to their testament to Caroline read back to them.

"The company Nike, through the years, came up with several marketing slogans to help with their success, 'Go For It' and 'Just Do It.' But one they had that never became quite so commonplace was, 'There Is No Finish Line.' How true that is in life. You are going to celebrate your accomplishments and reflect on a job well done and prepare for the next event. Caroline's spirit and love are not finished. They will live on forever in us. Caroline is not finished. Her eternal life lives on in us all. 'There is no finish line,'" Pastor Kyle paused and let the Founds' words find the hearts of those gathered.

Person after person told of the amazing Caroline and how she positively impacted them and those around her. Coach Brez spoke about Caroline the teammate and unconventional leader who sometimes drove her crazy—but it was exactly that free-wheeling, care-free attitude that endeared her to the coach. She spoke of Line's tremendous love and admiration for her family. Mostly she talked about Caroline's huge heart—"At school all we as educators had to do was pick out that child that didn't have any friends or was struggling and Caroline would walk right up to them, stick out her hand and say, 'Hi, I'm Caroline Found. I'll be your friend.' Her sense of humor, zest for life, and compassion for others will be her legacy," Brez said.

The coach's succinct closing statement, while spoken to everyone, was intended to put Caroline's teammates on notice—they would play this season and give it their all no matter the outcome. "Line, we'll do you proud this season, thank you," Brez's voice trailed off, choked with emotion, as she left the pulpit and rejoined the team.

Next, Scott Jespersen positioned himself behind the podium. Line's junior high school social studies teacher spoke of Caroline the person and how lucky he felt to have had a personal relationship with her. She started his class as an annoying kid who had a happy knack for disruption. Before he knew it, she changed into a person he was willing to break his self-imposed rule—no personal friendships with students. It was an exception that changed his life.

The day of her funeral, Scott freely admitted an error in his thinking. He believed he had witnessed her transformation from a teen-aged-goofball into an amazing young woman. After some personal reflection, he realized she hadn't changed a bit; her daily positive attitude transformed him into a better person. "Caroline was who we all strive to become, no matter what our age or our station. She was sincere and strong, true to herself and to those around her. Her ability to put her faith in others was a trait that made her a great friend and teammate. She was fueled with a fierce desire to make us all happy, to make us all better," Scott said.

Gregg and Catharine were next and spoke of their little sister with the colossal heart. Gregg told of her pleasure in little things: "a comfortable sweatshirt, a cheesy movie, a wet tongued-dog, and two-bowls of ice cream." He spoke of her excitement at the prospect of who she might get to meet each and every day. Her brother touched on how lucky he felt to be her friend.

Catharine told of their cherished experiences together as sisters. She smiled warmly as she regaled of the time the two of them came upon a dead deer in the ditch. They went home, quickly donned any perceived hunting attire, and grabbed the dogs and a camera. They returned to the carcass of the animal and laughed heartily while snapping pictures giving the impression that they, avid animal lovers, hunted the deer themselves.

Pastor Matt closed the service by leading the congregation in the Lord's Prayer and providing a benediction. He moved to Ernie and the two men exchanged an extended hug. Together they helped Ellyn to her feet. The pastor she was so instrumental in bringing to the church gave her a hug as well, his eyes wet with tears.

After the embrace she immediately sat down to conserve her energy. Ellyn had a plan and, as usual, was thinking three steps ahead of everyone else. As the pallbearers positioned the casket and started down the aisle, the familiar deep crescendo of Neil Diamond's "Sweet Caroline" was piped through the sanctuary speakers.

Once the pallbearers cleared the front aisle, a hospice worker scurried over with the wheelchair and a look of expectancy that Ellyn stick to the plan. Ellyn's smile said it all, "Silly boy, you don't know me very well." While Neil Diamond's song filled the sanctuary, Ellyn grabbed Ernie's arm and they walked up the aisle.

They moved arm-in-arm the entire length of the sanctuary. Ellyn reached out, touched shoulders, and grabbed the hands of the people still struggling under the weight of the unanswered questions surrounding Caroline's death.

In typical Ellyn fashion, she was there more for their comfort than the other way around. Simultaneously, and as if on cue, the song's lyrics belted out, "Hands, touching hands, reaching out, touching me, touching you."

As the couple made their way out of the sanctuary, Ernie pumped a fist into the air as they sang along with, "Sweet Caroline, good times never seemed so good." The song would become the grieving community's anthem, a constant reminder of their very own sweet Caroline. Even today, fans at West High sporting events continue to sing the song with gusto, often drowning out Neil, "Sweet Caroline, bumm, bumm, bumm, good times never seemed so good!"

The celebration of Caroline's life continued at a reception immediately following the service, where uplifting stories were exchanged of the marvelous impact she had on people from all walks of life. Caroline lived a short but purposeful life, doing more in seventeen years to enrich peoples' lives than many do in seventy. She gave those fortunate enough to know her unconditional love, laughter, and friendship until the day she died. Hers was a life well spent.

After the official reception, a more intimate gathering of friends and family took place at the farm. Ellyn insisted on being there, contrary to doctors' orders. She wanted to be surrounded by friends and family during her time of grief, in the place she felt most comfortable. She sat on her favorite chair in the living room, a flurry of activity going on around her. Many people showed up to the intimate affair. They exchanged pleasantries with Ernie and the kids, but mostly they stopped to visit briefly with Ellyn. Most hadn't seen her in a long time, and it was their chance to both say, "Hello," and "Goodbye."

Ellyn lasted about two hours—longer than most thought she would. She simply could no longer ignore the abdominal pain. At the hospice workers' insistence, she agreed to leave the place that meant more to her than any place on earth. Family assisted her onto a hospital gurney and stood by her side as she was wheeled outside.

When Ellyn was loaded into the ambulance, parked just outside the back door, she drew the outside air into her lungs as deeply as the pain in her stomach would allow. The familiar smells of the farm brought on a rush of comforting memories, like vivid snapshots seen in a View-Master projector. Each smell was like pressing the lever of the toy, showing another memory collected on the farm. She smelled chlorine and *click* a still-shot of the kids in the pool with Ernie, using him as a diving platform. The whiff of burned wood, and *click* thirty of their friends perched on logs by a roaring bonfire that Ernie tended while holding court with a magic trick. On it went, *click* birthdays, *click* Christmases.

The family stood and waved to Ellyn as the ambulance rolled slowly down the drive. Her heart filled with longing as she watched her family and house shrink through the emergency vehicle's narrow back door window. When she lost sight of the property, a dreadful thought conquered her mind and despair invaded her heart. There was a very real possibility she had seen her home for the last time. The paradise where she had created a blessed life with lasting friends and an exceptional family more than likely a memory.

Chapter 7
A Tough Start

Your present circumstances don't determine where you
can go; they merely determine where you start.
—Nido Qubein

There are things that we don't want to happen but have
to accept, things we don't want to know but have to learn,
and people we can't live without but have to let go.
—Author Unknown

The first day of school at West High started, on the surface, as normally as any other school year. There was an 8 AM traffic jam in the
student parking lot, and most everyone was generally excited to be
back after the summer break. The two-hundred faculty and staff went
about their morning making last minute preparations for the 2011-12
school year.

Although things seemed normal, there were noticeable differences.
The decibel level wasn't nearly as high in the halls as kids prepared for
their first day of classes. Laughter and excitement were dulled by tears
and sobs. The happy embraces between friends reconnecting after a
summer apart were supplanted by consoling hugs for the grieving. The
walls seemed dull despite a fresh coat of paint. Something was amiss.

Everyone knew it wasn't something, but someone, and her funeral service had been less than two days earlier. No one needed to say it. People could just feel it. Sadness hung in the air.

West High has become one of the largest schools in the state and a true educational success story, but only after going through significant growing pains. The school opened its doors in 1968 to much head scratching and laughter because of its proximity to nothing at the time but adjacent farm ground. The school board and local governments understood that significant growth was happening on the west side of Iowa City and there was a need for schools at every level, including a new high school.

West High was built not only to serve Iowa City but also the neighboring communities of Hills, University Heights, Coralville, and North Liberty. Like most new high schools, West was considered by some a lesser version of its well established and larger eastside sister school, Iowa City High. "City" had long been a shining example of public education excellence—a perennial powerhouse in and out of the classroom.

As development filled in around West High, the school's enrollment grew. The five towns the school served now had a high school to call their own, and West began to inspire a communal feel, a real identity.

After establishing West High as an excellent school, Principal Ed Barker, retired. He was followed by DuWayne W. Carnes and Ed Hauth (interim) when a young high school principal from Lincoln, Nebraska, Dr. Jerry Arganbright, answered an advertisement for the West High principal position. "We had no connection to Iowa. I saw the job, applied, and for some weird reason they hired me," Jerry explained.

Principal Arganbright quickly put his philosophy for educational excellence in place. His three keys to achieving quality education haven't changed during his tenure—quality teachers, quality facilities, and creating a team atmosphere among staff. On the surface, Arganbright's keys for success seem embarrassingly simplistic, but therein lies the genius. "Everyone has a job to do and one is not more important than another," Dr. Arganbright pointed out.

His ideas seem to have worked. Academically, West High has a ninety-three percent graduation rate, with eighty-eight percent of 2012 graduates attending two- or four-year universities. The school's ACT average is four points above the national average. In 2012, West High boasted twenty-seven National Merit Scholarship semifinalists and twenty-five finalists. West was ranked the No. 1 high school in the state of Iowa for the 2011 school year and ranked 290th best public high school in the nation by *Newsweek* magazine.

Exceptional or not, no school is safe from grief. On that first day of school the administration put the school's five guidance counselors on high alert. As the students went about learning new locker combinations or the best routes to take between classes, the counselors were ready to reach out to anyone who showed signs of struggling with the loss of one of their own.

The students were encouraged to visit their counselor any time they felt compelled. Some did, and for days on end there were wet spots on the carpeting in the counselors' offices from all of the tears shed. Most of the tears came from the kids, but the counselors weren't immune, especially on the heels of losing a kid like Caroline.

Because of the magnitude of the loss for West High, and because it was so close to the start of school, the Area Education Association sent its Crisis Intervention Team (CIT) to assist. CIT is a group of grief counselors used when a school's own counselors could be overwhelmed with the sheer number of students needing to talk things through.

CIT also kept a very close eye on one of their own. Amy Kanellis, a counselor at West with twenty-eight years of experience, was extremely close with the Found family. She was one of Ellyn's best friends and known Line from the time she was born. She had worked with Caroline on coping skills since Ellyn's cancer diagnosis the prior Easter.

When Caroline died she had to put her own concerns and personal feelings on hold though. Amy refocused her efforts and shifted from caring for Caroline to caring for the people who cared for Caroline. She understood the volleyball team and all of the kids who Line personally touched would need help. Most of these kids had never experienced this level of loss, and without the necessary coping skills, their emotional needs would take precedence over her own.

Meanwhile, the crisis team hovered over Amy like overprotective mothers. She finally had to assure the assistant principal she would be okay and, while she appreciated the concern, she didn't need to process with the crisis team.

Amy knew counseling high school kids after one of their own dies was a balancing act. Many teenagers are still in the "everything matters and nothing matters" phase of development, the "time marches on" approach can be too cavalier for young people who tend to personalize everything in their lives. "It's all about them, and you need to make it all about them, at the same time giving them the skills to know they are going to be okay. That became the mantra, 'You're going to be okay,'" Amy explained.

Amy and the other counselors received help spreading the "you're going to be okay," message in an unexpected way. Maddie Vernon, a classmate and friend of Caroline's, was looking for a way to honor Line. She had repeatedly seen the phrase "Live Like Line" (LLL) on social media. It was catchy and simple yet spoke volumes to those who knew the type of person Caroline was. She thought the saying would make a great t-shirt.

Maddie approached her father with the idea. Mark Vernon owned a local embroidery and print shop in Iowa City, and was a loyal supporter of West High. He told her if she put a design together and brought him the orders, he would only charge for the cost of the shirts. He agreed to eat the cost of the design screen and labor costs in order to maximize the girls' profits. They planned to donate sales to the Found Family Memorial Foundation created after Caroline died.

Maddie's friend, Kaitlyn Robinson, came up with a design as simple as the saying itself. A basic blue t-shirt with "LIVE LIKE LINE" stacked on the front in large, white block lettering and an orange border. "FOUND" would be printed in white on the back of the shirt along with a "9" underneath, which was Line's jersey number.

Maddie and Kaitlyn decided the initial order of shirts would be on a pre-order basis because they had no idea if anyone would even want one. They advertised the shirts on Facebook and almost instantly 200 shirts were requested, with additional orders flooding in. Once word spread, demand from hundreds more West students poured in.

Mark rushed the initial printing. When they were ready, the girls planned to pass the shirts out over lunch periods. They were soon so overwhelmed that friends were recruited from each lunch period to help. Some kids expecting a shirt were so excited to get them they were unwilling to wait, and so Maddie left some at the school's main office as well.

As more and more LIVE LIKE LINE shirts were seen outside of the school walls, orders exploded. Parents and siblings of West students, friends of West students from other schools, and volleyball teams from around the state asked how to get them.

Even students from cross-town City High wanted shirts in mass quantities. "We had City High kids coming to West every day on their lunch break to pick up t-shirts," Maddie said.

Mark initially printed up a case of shirts. Each subsequent order grew until he was forced to put up an exclusive page on his business website designated solely for the t-shirts.

It seemed around each corner of the Iowa City area someone was sporting a LIVE LIKE LINE t-shirt. The positive impact on the grieving community was immeasurable. LIVE LIKE LINE quickly went from an expression to a way of life. The three small words were a constant reminder to busy people to be nicer to one another, maybe reach out to someone they'd had a problem with and mend fences. It was a testament to the girl who never met a stranger, never excluded a soul, and was excited each sunrise at the prospect of who she would get to meet that day.

From a psychological standpoint, the phrase LIVE LIKE LINE had a deeper meaning for the student body at West. It meant even though they were mourning the loss of a friend and fellow student, they weren't going to shut down and stop living. "Instead we were going to embrace life, smell the roses, look around, and appreciate the people that were walking the halls with us. We were going to live life in a more positive way," Amy declared.

Soon after the start of the school year, most everyone had transitioned into their routines. Freshmen were less lost. The upperclassman settled into their classes. The varsity football team had their first game under the lights on Friday night. The marching band, cheer and pom teams put on a great halftime show, and behind the support of a rowdy student section, the game ended with a lopsided West victory.

There was still a group at West struggling to adequately adjust to the new school year. The volleyball team was adrift in a sea of sadness over the loss of their leader and friend. Each day was sadder than the last. They were easy to spot at school amongst the rest of the students. They walked through the school hallways with glazed expressions, stared into oblivion during classes, and usually had no appetite at lunch.

After-school practice did nothing to buoy the girls' feelings. In fact, it had the opposite effect. Their grief intensified ten-fold when they stepped onto the gym floor. Last year if a player had a bad day at school, they knew they could count on the fun-loving Line to boost their spirits.

The team had been practicing less than a week before school started. The game many of them were devoted to and usually couldn't wait to play now was unthinkable. Volleyball became nothing more than another in a long list of reminders of Line's absence and the emptiness they felt. "I didn't think we'd be on the court for a while, but Brez knew that we needed it. She knew that's what Caroline would have wanted," Kelley Fliehler recalled.

When Coach Brez and Scott walked into the gym after the first day of school, the players sat along the wall, grudgingly putting on their shoes. The practice was scheduled for the main gym, but Coach Brez moved it to the small gym across the hall. The main gym was Caroline's house and now considered sacred ground.

The coach decided to start them out with a warm-up run around the gym. A few of the girls managed only a couple of steps before they fell on the floor crying. One-by-one the other girls lost control and dropped to the floor, wailing. The sight of the players scattered around the gym floor sobbing caused the coaches to bite their own lower lips in a futile attempt to keep from crying themselves.

Brez tried to have the team do some rudimentary drills, which amounted to the girls going through the motions with barely any effort at all. "I was on the court just standing there with tears streaming down my face. I couldn't even see the ball. So when it came to me, I just kind of stuck my arms out," Hannah Infelt recollected.

After forty minutes of going through the motions with zero energy or competitiveness, coupled with uncontrollable fits of sobs, Brez had no choice but to change practice into a team meeting. The coach instituted a new "rule"—any player could step out of practice at any time if she needed to. This was a rule every player needed to use at one time or another throughout the season.

It wasn't fair to call what they did the first week "practice." Adjusting to a gym without Caroline was no easy task because a gym without Caroline was deafeningly quiet. Line loved practice, and each day she could be up to any number of things, usually loudly, to get the team pumped up—she might sing along, at full volume, to country music piped over loud speakers, or just laugh, which was often, and always from the belly and infectious.

The prior season the Women of Troy had claimed the school and coach's first volleyball state title. Brez had just about every starter back from last year's team, and they were now seniors. Brez had been game planning lineup combinations before the 2010 school year even ended. The 2011 team would arguably be the strongest squad of her career, and conventional wisdom had every other team in the state finishing a distant second, but everything had been centered around Caroline.

Brez now found herself in uncharted territory. She had lost key players in the preseason to injury before, but she was always able to fill the vacated spots with suitable substitutes. But never had she faced anything like the devastation created by the loss of a player like Caroline. She was one of a kind.

Brez immediately shifted her focus away from wins and losses and repeating as state champions. Instead she concentrated on the girls' mental, physical, and emotional well-being as her goal for the season.

Brez's shift in coaching philosophy would not have been possible without her spending time away from the game, during a brief retirement from 2000-2004. Before her exit from competitive sports, Brez was an old school, in-your-face type coach. She embraced the mantra of the Green Bay Packer's legendary coach, Vince Lombardi: "Winnings isn't everything; it's the only thing." She didn't take losing well. "I'd go bonkers," she said.

She spent the four-year hiatus on a newly purchased house boat fishing off of the back. She was able to quiet her mind, breathe in the air, and appreciate every day as a gift. Being away from the game provided her the serenity to realize there was more to life than wins and losses. It was this perspective that prepared her to handle the loss of Line.

Her current situation, however, was not what she signed up for when she came back to teaching and coaching. She had no way of knowing if she would have enough strength to get herself through what would surely be an emotionally turbulent season. If she broke down how could she expect to lead a group of distraught teenagers?

Despite Coach Bresnahan's own doubts and reservations Tom Keating had no question she could handle it. "I wouldn't wish this on anybody, but if my daughter was on a team that was going through something like this, I'd want Kathy leading."

While Brez certainly appreciated and factored in the vote of confidence from her friend, what she really needed was assurance from someone else. One day, the coach found herself standing alone in the locker room by Line's locker, crying. She needed to know Caroline was okay, so she looked skyward and asked for a sign from her former setter. It didn't need to be a thunderbolt. Something small would suffice. Nothing happened.

Dejected, Brez looked down at the ground where she found two pennies in close proximity, both heads-up. Remembering that finding three heads-up pennies was considered a sign that someone was watching over the recipient, she hunted the locker room for a third.

A couple of students walked in and saw their P.E. teacher combing the locker room for something.

"Quick, we need to find another penny," Brez exclaimed. They searched in vain for a third penny. The discouraged coach headed towards the door with the two pennies in her hand. In desperation, she took a cursory glance back where she had just come from, and there was a heads-up penny in all its shiny bronze glory. "Pennies from heaven," Brez said, and snatched the penny from the ground, relieved.

Coach Bresnahan thought about the upcoming season she and the team faced and how much they needed something positive in their lives to counterbalance all the anguish they were feeling. She also thought about the student body and how they desperately needed something good to cling to. Brez thought about Ernie and everything he had been through. With so many people hurting, volleyball might just be the conduit for healing.

She understood all they could do was put their best foot forward and lean on each other when times got tough. The team's philosophy for the season would be, "fake it 'til you make it."

Chapter 8
Alone into the Alone

… When fond expressions on dull ears fall,
when the hands clasp calmly without one thrill,
when we cannot muster by force of will
the old emotions that came at call.
… But no tears soften this dull, pale woe;
we must sit and face it with dry, sad eyes.
If we seek to hold it, the swifter joy flies—
we can only be passive, and let it go.
—Ella Wheeler Wilcox, "Desolation"

Ellyn's health deteriorated rapidly after Caroline's death. From then on, it was a matter of keeping her "medically comfortable," which is doctor-speak for the disbursement of significant pain medications. Ellyn and Ernie's siblings continued to help with the day-to-day routines at the farm, and to visit Ellyn, whose time on earth was now being measured in hours and days.

Family stayed in the hospital room with Ellyn on a rotating basis. It wasn't a typically small hospital room. There were a few chairs and a couch. There was an additional room just outside for people to gather. The family's hope had long disappeared that Ellyn would ever see the farm again, so they did what they could to make this her new home by bringing special mementos and furnishings from the farm house.

One of Ellyn's greatest joys was hosting people at the farm—no matter if they were friends, the kids' friends, or friends of friends—the important thing to her was that everyone felt like a member of the family. Visitors were treated with delicious snacks, with extras to take home.

Ellyn enjoyed hearing about people's lives. Nothing was just polite conversation with her. She remembered specific details—no matter how mundane they may have seemed to others. Thus, rest assured, on the next visit, she would ask how great Aunt Millie was getting along after her hip replacement or if Uncle Fred had learned to separate the wash into like colors yet.

When Ellyn became extremely ill, the list of visitors was restricted to her closest friends and family. The consummate host with an elephant's memory now spent much of her time in a semi-conscious state, fighting the effects of the strong drugs.

Ellyn's failing health eventually rendered her speechless. Her electrolytes were so far out of balance that a simple task like talking became insurmountable. She had slipped into a place only someone battling to stay alive would know. It was best described by the famed writer C.S. Lewis in *A Grief Observed*. Lewis' cancer stricken wife told him, in her last days, that it felt like she was going, "alone into the alone." An isolated place reserved only for those nearing the end of their life. The rest of Ellyn's time on earth moved along that desolate path, rendering family and friends helpless onlookers.

Ernie spent most waking moments at her bedside praying, though he didn't pray for an eleventh-hour miracle. Ernie wasn't a foxhole Christian either—making last second ultimatums with God. He prayed for Ellyn, his children, and the family to be at peace. He prayed for strength. He hoped she would be well enough to talk to him one last time. Unfortunately that day never happened.

The couple didn't share any long orations or romantic sonnets. There was no need, because they had lived it. The hopelessly romantic couple had expressed their love for one another through words and deeds over twenty-five years of marriage. "There were lots of 'I love you' from me and a lot of hand squeezes from her. At that point it was just being in each other's heart," Ernie explained.

Ellyn slipped into unconsciousness on Saturday, August 20. A fighter until the end, there were times her eyes rolled under her lids. Occasionally she moaned and moved, but she never regained awareness.

After the first twenty-four hours of her downgraded condition, it was inescapable that she had very little time left. "The hospital was really great about letting us sleep there as opposed to going to another facility," Ernie said. "I thank the hospital administration for that."

On August 23, at around 5 PM, K.C. relieved her brother-in-law at the hospital so he could get something to eat, which the family had to demand of him by now. Ernie hosted an emotionally and physically exhausted family that night for dinner. He planned to eat, pack an overnight bag, and head right back to the hospital.

At around 7 PM, the ringing phone startled Ernie. Hearing K.C. was on the line, he stopped packing his bag. He reluctantly grabbed the phone and confirmed what he suspected—Ellyn's monumental battle with cancer had ended. She died peacefully.

Notifications went out to families who had returned home after Caroline's funeral. Planning for Ellyn's visitation and service amounted to nothing more than tying up loose ends and picking dates. Most of the planning was handled by Ernie and Ellyn prior to her passing.

It was a familiar scene, with many of the same people sitting in the Founds' home dealing with a death just twelve days after the first. A devastated Ernie left much of the finalizing to family and the funeral director. One thing he insisted on was speaking at Ellyn's service. He shrugged off family and friends' skepticism whether he would be able to hold it together. "I wanted to do it. I had to do it," Ernie stated. "I wanted to make sure that it came off well and with love."

What skeptics didn't know was that as Ellyn's disease progressed, Ernie had thought a lot about what he would say at her funeral. He hoped harder than anyone she would be one of the rare two-percent who beat pancreatic cancer, but Ernie was a physician and a realist. He knew very well this type of disease was typically a death sentence. In the eventuality the disease took her, it was important to him that he was prepared to honor her memory with dignity, courage, and strength.

Word of Ellyn's passing spread quickly. Newspapers across the region were peppered with stories of the Iowa City daughter and mother dying a dozen days apart. Because there wasn't adequate time for people to process their grief after Caroline passed, when Ellyn died, grief piled atop existing grief.

Chapter 9
Fake It 'Til You Make It

The only courage that matters is the kind that
gets you from one moment to the next.
—Mignon McLaughlin

Character cannot be developed in ease and quiet. Only
through experience of trial and suffering can the soul be
strengthened, ambition inspired, and success achieved.
—Helen Keller

Ellyn's death had a profound impact on the already distraught West
High volleyball squad. If losing their leader and friend wasn't bad
enough, the girls lost their unofficial team mom twelve days later. Her
importance to the team went way beyond post-game snacks. "Whenever I would see her, she would always ask how I was doing and ask me
about my future plans. Whenever you needed help with anything you
could call Ellyn," Hannah Infelt said.

Other mothers were supportive and involved with the team, but if
one of the girls was having a bad day, more times than not, Ellyn could
sense it and would fix it with a homemade chocolate chip cookie, an
encouraging word, a hug, or any combination of the three. Hannah Infelt remembered Ellyn's compassion the prior season after she played

poorly in a particular game and was down on herself. "Ellyn told me that I did my best, but I felt like my best just wasn't good enough. She gave me this huge hug, which was exactly what I needed. She knew exactly what to do, and she would do it every day."

From a team perspective, losing Ellyn couldn't have come at a worse time. Prior to her death, the girls had finally inched closer and closer to an actual practice. Their practices lacked the intensity and competitiveness of the prior season, but at least they were doing meaningful drills. Ellyn's passing caused a second crushing loss—and just two days before the season opening tournament.

After Ellyn died, Brez couldn't hold the players' focus during practice more than twenty minutes at a time. Anything longer and they seemed to experience any range of unexplained and immediate emotional outbursts from weeping to laughing—sometimes separately, other times simultaneous.

Even the rule of twenty minutes didn't always hold the players' attention. In the middle of a drill, one of the girls might erupt into a fit of uncontrollable laughter, which then became contagious. During conditioning, Shelly would kick Kelley in the butt, which led to retaliation and then an outbreak of horseplay. Brez knew her team needed the release and generally let the interruptions go, but it wasn't easy for a coach known for running some of the most competitive and intense practices of any volleyball program in the state.

The one time Brez's empathetic constraint couldn't outlast the girls' erratic behaviors was when her all-state senior leader, Shelly Stumpff, inexplicably picked up a volleyball and kicked it across the gym. At over six-feet tall with long powerful legs, Shelly probably could have taken the punter's job on the varsity football team if she wanted to. Brez ignored the disruption hoping it was an isolated incident. The coach's hopes were dashed when Shelly grabbed another ball, took a long stride, and launched it off her foot.

"Knock it off, Shelly," Brez said without raising her voice.

Shelly ignored her coach and continued to pull balls from the bag and, one after another, punted them across the gym. Brez's annoyance level elevated with each ball her star player let fly. As she pulled yet another ball from the bag, the now fuming coach told her, "If you kick another ball, everyone runs."

Without hesitation, Shelly booted the ball in her hands. The outraged coached watched as it rocketed through the air towards a bell-shaped air vent attached to the ceiling. The ball slammed into a thin metal fixture causing it to rattle violently and left a sizable dent.

Brez said, "Everyone except Shelly, ladders!" The players toed the out of bounds line at one end of the gym floor and waited for the whistle. Brez made Shelly stand on the sideline next to her and watch as her teammates were punished for her actions.

Shelly stared in agony as her friends sprinted to the first line on the floor, touched it, pivoted 180-degrees, and dashed back to the starting point. Back and forth they ran, puffing and panting, one line at a time they advanced the length of the floor.

A groundswell of sadness grew amongst the girls with each stride they took. It was just a matter of time before the rush of emotion overwhelmed the first player and she dropped to the floor in a wailing heap. Eventually they were all reduced to an inconsolable, sobbing group scattered about the gym floor. They were emotional casualties of the moment, one of many moments they experienced during the season.

Brez knew it wasn't just Caroline's death that made this year's practices a stark contrast from the past two seasons. Line's absence left a leadership void on the floor. Line was one of the most vocal players on the team, and even as a sophomore everyone tended to followed her lead. "She charged the girls up when they were flat and calmed them down when they were tight," Brez said.

Practice after practice, the team was reminded how rare a player Caroline had been. She had enjoyed every aspect of volleyball—even loved conditioning and challenged her less-than-enthusiastic teammates to keep up with her, reminding them that practice was nearly over. Repeating the same fundamental drills can become monotonous. When the drudgery of practice raised its ugly head, Caroline made it fun with her crude sense of humor. Line was big into bodily functions. She wasn't just into them, she saw them as an art form. Caroline considered gastric noises and their release to be the brush and paint, an unsuspecting friend or teammate, the canvas.

She would wait until the team was gasping from a marathon conditioning session and then walk past and belch in a teammate's face. She didn't accidentally burp, give off, or hiccup, then cover her mouth with her hand and giggle in embarrassment. She let loose—a mouth-opened, prolonged roar of gas conjured from deep inside her stomach. If you were in her direct line of fire you might end up looking like a dog with its head stuck out the window of a fast moving car. Even her friends on the football team were in awe of her belching prowess.

Without Caroline every aspect of the early part of the season was exacerbated. Even the normally even-keeled Hannah struggled with emotional outbursts adjusting to team changes. A 4.0-student and a National Merit Scholar finalist, Hannah wasn't accustomed to doing anything without a detailed plan. She was the rare breed of high school student with a future career path already mapped out, having decided to be an engineer like her parents.

Hannah wasn't just fraught with sorrow over Caroline's absence, she, like Kelley, was dealing with a position change. Out of necessity, and because it was the right move, Brez moved her from outside hitter position to the middle, pairing her with Olivia Fairfield on the front row. It was the first time Hannah ever played a new position and the new spot came with its own intricacies she needed to quickly learn.

Inside hitter drills that were second nature to Olivia took Hannah twice as long to figure out. Understandably, she made mistakes, making the normally stoic Hannah uncharacteristically irritable and prone to yelling at teammates during practice. Brez recounted, "Hannah lost her confidence. She'd snap at people; she was mean. That's not Hannah, she's kind and intelligent."

Everyone hoped Hannah would settle into her new spot and return to her normal sweet self. After a couple days of her verbal tirades towards teammates with no immediate sign of them subsiding, the coach had enough. Brez pulled her aside and asked what was going on. This was the perfect open-ended question and allowed Hannah to vent her frustrations, and she took full advantage, "I'm in a new position that I suck at, and I just don't have any confidence! Caroline gave me confidence, and now she's gone."

While the last part of Hannah's statement resonated with the whole team, her teammate, Kelley, was able to appreciate the full weight of her sentiment. "Being a player that had to switch positions, I totally got that," Kelley admitted.

On the eve of the season-opening tournament, the team still didn't have a definitive setter. Not from a lack of discussion though. In fact, Brez and Scott were constantly wondering who should fill Caroline's spot.

Caroline's backup was Erin Weathers. The junior had the potential to be a good setter, but she was still a season away from playing the position at the level expected by her demanding coach. Brez's plan had been for Erin to study under the tutelage of Caroline and be ready the following season. Laynie Whitehead, a freshman, was heavy on ability and showing promise, but she was light on experience and still a project.

The night the girls stepped into the Cedar Rapids Prairie High School gym for the Mississippi Athletic Conference-Mississippi Valley Conference (MAC-MVC) tournament, there was something amiss. It felt to them as if they had forgotten a piece of equipment back at West. Unlike a pair of knee pads or a bag of volleyballs, the thing they missed couldn't be retrieved or replaced and caused anxiety amongst the team.

As well, the state volleyball circles weren't completely convinced the Women of Troy would bounce back from such sorrow. When the pre-season volleyball rankings were released, West was ranked fourth in the state.

The first match of the year always caused a certain amount of nerves, but the feelings the team had went way beyond nerves. Every last player was on the verge of crying. They were about to play a game without Caroline and were guilt-ridden about it. They felt they were doing something wrong, and the apprehension showed on their faces.

Brez made an executive decision at the eleventh-hour to try her first idea, to have Erin Weathers and Laynie Whitehead act as duel setters in an experimental 6-2 offense.

Coach Bresnahan gathered the girls by the line of folding metal chairs serving as the team's bench. She opened a duffel and pulled out a pair of shoes. The girls immediately recognized the well-used black volleyball shoes as Caroline's by the hand-written words in white marker. Caroline had put messages on her shoes after her mother's diagnosis: "ELLYN FOUND" on the left shoe and "FIGHT 4 MOMMA" on the right.

"I'm not going to allow any of you to play for Caroline. It's unnecessary pressure to put on yourselves, and it would be too easy to feel like

81

you let her down if you make a mistake or lose a game. Instead, we'll play with Caroline, who is in all of our hearts. We'll have these with us for each game and keep them right here," Brez said. She placed the shoes under the first chair in the row, and the team agreed that the chair would remain empty during games.

An already emotionally charged night became even more so when Ernie, Gregg, and Catharine walked through the gym doors. All eyes fell on the Founds as they made their way to the bleachers. The normally noisy pregame gym was reduced to nudges and whispers by the heartfelt crowd, shocked to see the trio on the eve of Ellyn's wake. The family, who had lost so much, was a walking, talking reminder of the frailty of human life.

Brez's eyes welled up at the sight of the Founds. Their support was overwhelming to her in light of their circumstances. "I told the girls to go hug them." The team charged into the stands and enveloped Ernie, Gregg, and Catharine with a heart-wrenching squeeze felt throughout the gymnasium. Mothers pulled tissues from their purses and dabbed their tears. Fathers raised their moistened eyes skyward.

The Founds, showing up for the first game, had a huge impact on the players. Some of them attributed the family's attendance as the genesis of their belief they would have the strength to play an entire season. "Seeing them there being so strong when they were in some of the worst moments of their lives made us strong. It was the first sense of, 'we can get through this together,'" Hannah said.

Before the first sets were played, the teams lined the court and there was a moment of silence for Caroline. The only noises were the sniffles from the crowd, players, and coaches. The Women of Troy tightly grasped their teammate's hands on either side of them and openly wept. In the *Press-Citizen* sports page the next day, an article by Ryan Suchomel ran with the headline, "We Really Missed Her" and featured a photo of teammates Olivia Mekies, Kelley, and Shelly standing next to one another, clutching hands—Olivia's head leaned on Kelley's shoulder and Shelly's eyes were skyward.

West started the tournament with a convincing 2-0 victory over Bettendorf High School for their first victory of the 2011 season. As the day progressed, emotions proved too much for the girls, and they dropped the following two matches to lesser ranked Pleasant Valley and unranked North Scott. The tournament concluded with West collecting a 1-2 record.

The two-setter experiment failed. Brez realized that the team couldn't afford to wait for someone to be completely ready. She simply had to decide on someone and have them learn on the fly. After the tournament, the coach made it official and declared Kelley Fliehler the team's setter.

Kelley had been a spot player the prior season, but Brez always liked her intelligence and quiet determination. When the coach initially approached Kelley about taking Caroline's spot, the senior turned her down. Knowing Kelley had all of the intangibles to be a decent setter, Brez went to work to convince her and explained she was the team's best option.

After a few meetings in Brez's office, Kelley slowly warmed to the idea. She eventually accepted the role, albeit begrudgingly. Kelley's final decision was based less on what the coach said and more on the thought of how excited Caroline would have been for her.

Brez put her expectations for Kelley on the table from the very beginning. "I told her that I was asking her to learn a position in a couple of weeks that normally takes me years to train someone to play. She would make mistakes, but I knew that she'd get it and reminded her of our new mantra, 'fake it 'til you make it.'"

Brez taught Kelley the crash-course version of the position. The two spent an excessive amount of time together. Some practices Scott took the rest of the team while Brez worked exclusively with her new setter. "I told the team that Kelley and I were best friends now," she joked. There were times when Kelley showed up to class and found Brez in her seat with her feet propped up on the desk.

Brez kidded she was moving into her house. When Kelley sat down to the dinner table later that night, there was an extra place setting. When she asked who was coming to dinner, her straight-faced mother told her, "Your new roommate." Later that evening, Brez picked up her ringing cell phone and heard Kelley screeching on the other end, "You're not moving in with us!"

Another running joke was that Brez was stalking Kelley. Brez's incessant teasing of her new setter had a purpose. The coach kept things light with Kelley because she came into the situation so uptight. Brez hoped all the good-natured ribbing would allow her to loosen up and not put so much pressure on herself to be perfect.

Kelley was a 4.0 student and a quick study. She had to be with the amount of information a setter must process in such a short amount of time. Just prior to the ball being served, the setter must choose one of about thirty plays based on the initial positioning of the opposing team's players.

Once the ball is served, the setter must anticipate what the blockers on the other team are doing and based on that decide which of the hitters to set. The setter must also keep track of what each hitter does when the ball comes over the net. If a hitter blocked or dove to dig a ball, they would be out of position to be set for a spike. The setter would have to recognize that and set the opposite hitter. If both hitters were occupied, she may have to drop a shot over the opponent's front line herself.

A good setter must also be a diplomat. There is no worse way to create tension on a volleyball team than for a hitter to feel they are being neglected. No hitter has ever felt they have had enough sets in a game, because every hitter wants to deliver the thunderous spike, or "kill," that causes the home crowd to go ballistic. The Women of Troy had the convenient problem of having two of the best hitters in the state—Shelly Stumpff and Olivia Fairfield and each enjoyed the excitement of being a hitter and so the role of setter was critical.

Chapter 10
She Lived Well, Laughed Often, and Loved Much

He has achieved success who has lived well,
laughed often, and loved much;
Who has never lacked appreciation of Earth's
beauty or failed to express it;
Who has left the world better than he found it,
Whether an improved poppy, a perfect poem, or a rescued soul;
Who has always looked for the best in others
and given them the best he had;
Whose life was an inspiration;
Whose memory a benediction.
— Bessie Anderson Stanley, "Success"

The things hardest to bear are sweetest to remember.
—Lucius Annaeus Seneca

At 6:30 AM, Pastor Matt Paul opened the unlocked front door of St. Andrew church and walked inside. He had arrived a few of hours before normal, he knew on the morning of Ellyn's funeral service a few hours of extra time would help.

The additional time wasn't just allotted to double check that preparations were in order, to review his words, or to make any last minute changes. The alone time would provide him an opportunity for personal reflection on the life of the person being memorialized. There was much for the pastor to consider about the woman who didn't just embrace the saying, "Live well, laugh often, love much," she'd lived it.

Expecting to walk into a dark and quiet church, he was surprised, and a bit perturbed, to find the sanctuary fully lit. He assumed someone had carelessly forgotten to shut off the lights after the previous night's activities. Leaving lights on overnight was an unnecessary waste of money for a church on a tight budget.

Pastor Matt reached for the light switches but withdrew his hand when he heard a muffled voice inside. He peeked in and saw Ernie standing alone at the front of the sanctuary. Matt watched in awe as the heartbroken man practiced what were sure to be the most important and difficult words he would ever speak in his life.

At 3 PM, the pews of St. Andrew filled with many of the same people who, just days before, attended Caroline's funeral. The feel in the sanctuary was different from Line's service. Many sat in silence staring out the windows. The unique set of circumstances leading up to Ellyn's passing left them emotionally exhausted.

People who knew Ellyn, like countless others who have a friend, family member, or spouse die after a long illness, had time to prepare themselves for this day. With Caroline's sudden death, their worlds were flipped upside down. They were still trying to work through the senselessness of Line's tragedy when Ellyn passed.

Pastor Kyle Otterbein opened the service by leading the congregation in the 23rd Psalm. Normally rock steady, Kyle's voice quivered, and his eyes filled with tears as he locked eyes with Ernie.

When Kyle was finished, Ernie walked to the piano and sat down. He accompanied his sister, Marilyn, who sang one of Ellyn's favorite songs, "Evergreen." Marilyn had also sung the song, originally recorded by Barbara Streisand, at Ernie and Ellyn's wedding.

Knowing the significance the song held for Ernie and Ellyn, some family questioned whether it would be too challenging for him to play. Ernie rationalized the reason the song was difficult to play was precisely the reason he had to do it. And he decided weeks ago he would play, "Evergreen" at Ellyn's memorial.

When Ellyn's condition worsened and it was clear she had very little time left, Ernie got up at 4:30 each morning before work and, little by little, learned the song on the piano. He felt a mixed bag of emotions each time he sat down at the piano in his living room. It gave him a warm feeling practicing it, yet the reason he was learning it was unsettling.

The painful association with playing the piano was caused, in part, by how he became the owner of the instrument. It was a birthday gift from Ellyn, and like many of the gifts she got Ernie over the years, the piano started out as an off-handed comment he made about how much he liked it.

Caroline's piano recitals and lessons were sometimes held at West Music. Going to West Music also meant Ernie could play some of the pianos for sale in the showroom.

There was one piano in particular that Ernie loved. Each time he returned, he made certain he sat down at his favorite and played. Once, while playing it, he mentioned to Ellyn he sure would like to own it someday. Ellyn pretended to ignore the comment, so Ernie dropped the subject.

A few months later Ernie came to one of Caroline's lessons. While they waited for Line to finish, Ernie played the piano he so badly wanted. He took the opportunity to remind Ellyn he sure would like to own the piano. Without looking up from the magazine she was thumbing through, Ellyn said, "Yes, you mentioned that; too bad it's sold." Ernie looked down and saw a neon yellow tag hanging from the instrument with the word "Sold" written in big red letters. His shoulders slumped at the thought. *His* piano had been bought right out from under him.

Months passed, and Ernie forgot about the piano. On the evening of January 14, Ernie walked into the entryway of his house, shook off his coat, and hoped the cold and brutal day in the operating room would come off with it. He had many things on his mind, and none of them were his fiftieth birthday. He wanted nothing more than to take off his shoes and relax in his chair.

As he walked into the kitchen, he heard beautiful piano music coming from the living room. He initially thought Ellyn had a CD playing in the stereo. Ernie listened more closely and suspected that the music wasn't prerecorded, so he padded to the living room to investigate. Ellyn and twenty of Ernie's closest friends surrounded the very piano he had coveted at West Music. They sang "Happy Birthday" to him while his favorite local concert pianist, Dan Knight, accompanied the singers.

Ernie put the piano to good use but rarely played for his own amusement. Throughout the years, Ellyn would hear a song somewhere and tell Ernie how much she liked it. He made a list of the songs and practiced them on the piano until he had them all memorized. He enjoyed playing for Ellyn, because she would generally sing along. She loved that her husband, a busy man, not only remembered her favorite songs, but took the time to memorize and play them just for her.

Since Ellyn's funeral the piano has sat in its original spot, mostly untouched. Ernie has only been able to sit and play it a few times. The instrument serves as a silent and sometimes painful reminder of the joyful connection he and Ellyn shared. "I guess to sit down and play those songs without her...I just can't do that very well. I'll get there one day."

Pastor Matt allowed Ernie and Marilyn to take their seats and then took the podium. He spoke of Ellyn's rare ability to inspire confidence and make anyone in her presence feel loved and cared for. "Such is the power of love, to direct our hearts to the needs of others." In the congregation, a Korean doctor and his sister nodded their agreement. They were living proof of Ellyn's giving heart.

Ten years earlier, Ernie was asked by Chairman Reg Cooper to travel to Korea and visit with a local physician about a possible international partnership with the University of Iowa Orthopedics Department. Ernie took Ellyn, and they met Dr. Han Chang. During their two-week visit, they struck up a friendship with the doctor and his family. For years after Ernie and Ellyn visited Dr. Chang in Korea and whenever the Changs came to Iowa, the Founds invited him to the farm.

When Dr. Chang's sister was forced to leave Korea due to the shame of her husband's suicide, Ernie's was the first phone number that Dr. Chang called. He sent his sister and her kids to the United States to make a new life. Ellyn's face was the first one they saw when they arrived at the Eastern Iowa Airport.

Ellyn took Iowa City's newest family under her wing and showed them the ropes. She helped Chang's sister assimilate to the new culture. She also helped her kids enroll at West High and then helped her enroll at the University of Iowa.

When Pastor Matt finished, Ellyn's brothers—Mark, Bob, and Joe Slocum moved to the podium together. Joe spoke about their family in baseball metaphors and described Ellyn as the star player. He spoke of the many championship seasons Ellyn had and how hard it was to know there would be no more chances for her to represent the team at the plate.

Joe talked about W.P. Kinsella, who graduated from the Iowa Writers' Workshop and wrote the novel *Shoeless Joe*, which was the basis for the movie *Field of Dreams*. He incorporated the most famous line of the book, "if you build it they will come," into a hope he had about Ellyn. He realized he could call her to the plate anytime he wanted through any number of wonderful memories.

Ellyn's sisters held hands and moved to the pulpit. The eldest sister, Mary, spoke of Ellyn's sense of humor. Once, when Mary told Ellyn she had ugly feet, her younger sister responded that if one had to be ugly somewhere that was the best place. Mary also talked about Ellyn's positive outlook on life. Even when she was in the middle of cancer treatments, she couldn't think of one unpleasant experience for an assignment given to her during a mindfulness class.

During the service, the family wanted Caroline's feelings for her mother shared. Ernie's sister, Grace, read a letter Caroline wrote to Ellyn on June 19, 2011, which happened to be Line's birthday. She wrote how her initial birthday wish was her mother be cured of cancer but knew that was asking too much. She settled for making sure her mom knew how much she loved her. Line attributed all of her good qualities to her, "We are told that we are wonderful, beautiful, kind, amazing, but that's you, mom."

Together, Gregg and Catharine came to the front of the church. Catharine remembered wanting guidance from her mother before she passed away, so she drafted a list of questions on how to live a meaningful life. Ellyn never got the chance to answer. Catharine admitted to initially being angry at not getting her questions answered. Upon further reflection, she realized that by living, laughing, and loving, Ellyn had modeled how to be a good wife, mother, and friend. She revealed the rewards of a selfless heart by reaching out to those less fortunate than herself, demonstrating that everyone had worth and deserved to feel loved.

Gregg spoke admiringly of his mother—how she started each of her days at 4 AM by hand-writing a letter to own mother when she became ill with Multiple Sclerosis. Ellyn's display of dedication and respect had a dramatic impact on him. When his mother became ill with cancer, he attempted to repeat the act, but his admiration for his mother grew when the task proved more difficult than anticipated—he switched to daily journal entries and a weekly letter.

Gregg and Catharine kissed their mother's casket and took their seats. Ernie was invited up by Pastor Kyle. Funeral Director Dan Ciha followed Ernie to the front and positioned Ellyn's picture on a stand facing Ernie so he could see her face while standing at the podium.

As Ernie moved to the podium, family, friends, and even the two pastors wondered whether the grief-stricken husband could maintain his composure while speaking.

At first Ernie turned away from the congregation, wiped his eyes, pulled his prepared speech from the pocket of his jacket, and took a breath. Then he turned and faced the congregation. Many of the eyes on him welled with tears. Some in the crowd were so overwhelmed with emotion they had to look away.

Ernie acknowledged the crowd. He recognized many of the same faces from Caroline's service. He knew they had the same broken hearts with the same unanswerable questions. He spoke of being surrounded by the same loving God, abundant in grace and mercy, who gives and takes away.

He unfolded the letter he had written to Ellyn, looked lovingly at his departed wife's picture, and smiled. Tears slid down his cheeks as he spoke, "Dear Ellyn, I love you." He paused to swallow the emotion filling his throat, then continued, "'I take you today to be one with me

92

for I feel that it's God's will.' This is the same opening line I used in our wedding vows 26 years and 52 days ago."

Ernie expressed what he called "OMG" (Oh My God) moments throughout his life with Ellyn, things that made him fall in love with her again and again, more deeply each time. He spoke of the first time he knew he was in love with Ellyn when they were both living in Boston. He was a surgery resident and she was an occupational therapist at a children's clinic.

While Ellyn was housesitting for the parents of one of her patients, she invited Ernie over for an afternoon of snacks, drinks, and a swim in the pool. For context, Ernie referenced the movie *Ten*, a popular '80s movie, starring Bo Derrick, that he described as a male chick-flick. He spoke of a memorable scene in the film, particularly for men, where Bo comes out of the ocean in a rather revealing bathing suit.

Ernie spoke directly to the picture of Ellyn again. "You went to the other end of the pool, dove in, and glided under the water to where I was sitting at the other end. You emerged with your long brown hair over your shoulders. You looked up at me, and I distinctly remember saying to myself, 'Bo, you got nuth-in,'" letting the "n" at the end run on for emphasis. The congregation exploded with laughter and applause.

Another OMG moment happened two-weeks later in Boston when he was at the hand clinic where Ellyn worked. Ernie, a self-described young, egomaniac resident surgeon, stood in the doorway and observed while Ellyn worked with a patient. He was shocked when Ellyn's patient, a big smile on her face, declared, "Thank you so much. You have helped me much more than my surgery has." He cherished Ellyn's compassion for her fellow man.

Ernie was wowed by Ellyn's determination. Running, as a sport, became increasingly popular in Boston during the 1980s, and she took it up. When she started she couldn't even run around the block one time without stopping. Despite that, Ellyn was determined she would run a marathon.

Ellyn trained and trained, and in 1986, Ernie was there to watch her cross the finish line at the New York City Marathon. He watched her celebrate the monumental accomplishment with exuberance like no other. "I fell in love with you all over again. I fell in love with you even deeper than before," Ernie said to the picture.

Ernie recalled their picturesque wedding day in New Hampshire and their self-written vows, which they agreed to renew every year at the same place. They also pledged to climb the scenic mountain filling the backdrop of their wedding each time they came back. Even if Ernie had kids riding on his back or Ellyn was pregnant, they climbed Mt. Monadnock every year.

Much like their life together, their trips to New Hampshire weren't always smooth sailing. One year they over extended their schedule which gave them little time to climb the mountain. When they finally had the time, the event seemed more like a chore than a time-honored family tradition.

With the three kids in tow, they shot up and down the mountain as quickly as possible, bickering the whole way. When it came time to renew their vows, although each was still in a huff toward the other and didn't really want to, something made them do it anyway. "I'm so glad we did. I think that day both of us began to understand what the meaning of the word 'forgiveness' is all about," Ernie admitted.

Ernie spoke fondly of his wife's affinity for games, which was a way for her to connect with those closest to her in a fun way. One game, he remembered, involved players describing the person opposite them with one word. He was thankful the game ended before his turn because he sat across from Ellyn and didn't think it possible to describe her in a single word. For years the question perplexed him, but he had finally come up with a word to describe her—Ellyn was a "fan."

Ernie explained that being a fan of something was short for being fanatical. Ellyn did everything in a fanatical and exuberant way. At school events she cheered for others' kids as loudly and strongly as she did for her own. "You would even cheer for City High as long as they weren't playing West," he quipped to the mixed City/West crowd.

She was a fan of quotations and clever sayings. She had a knack for finding ones that would stick with their recipient. "They stuck so much that you wallpapered the upstairs hallway with sayings—'Life is hard by the yard, but by the inch life's a cinch,'" Ernie said.

Ellyn loved celebrating birthdays. In typical Ellyn fashion, it wasn't her own birthday she enjoyed celebrating though, but others. One year for Gregg's birthday, she was torn between baking a basketball, baseball, or football cake, so she baked all three and served everyone a piece from each.

In the spirit of making each child's birthday unique, Ellyn refused to link Catharine's December 21st birthday with Christmas. She believed birthdays needed their own distinct celebration, so Catharine's birthday and Christmas were always two separate days for the family to celebrate.

Not wanting to miss out on any of the fun, Caroline—despite being a walking, talking birthday party—loved planning her party with her mother. They would spend several days together working out the details for Line's special day.

Ernie valued Ellyn being a fan of family, which was an extension of her being a fan of love. "You loved generating love, being loved, witnessing love, and encouraging love," he said. He referenced another '80s movie, *Love Story* and the line: "Love is never having to say you're sorry."

Ernie disagreed with the premise. "To me, love is always being able to say you're sorry, and I tried to love you in that way."

With his emotions overflowing, his post script was a letter he had placed in her hand, expressing how much he loved her. "P.S., there's a little note in there for Caroline. Please deliver it to her. I can't wait to be together with you and Caroline again. Love, Ernie." He closed his hand-written letter, walked to her casket, gently kissed the cross on the closed lid, and went back to his seat.

Ellyn's body was cremated and her ashes kept in a receptacle next to Caroline's. Ernie had a discussion with Gregg and Catharine, who agreed that Ernie should buy five burial plots in the Cathedral of the Pines cemetery. On the one-year anniversary of Caroline's death they would invite family and close friends to New Hampshire for a week-end memorial service to inter Caroline and Ellyn's ashes.

Chapter 11
Support and Honor

No person was ever honored for what he received.
Honor has been the reward for what he gave.
—Calvin Coolidge

After Ellyn's funeral, family and friends knew Ernie would need assistance but probably wouldn't ask for any, so they provided their unsolicited support for several months. Local restaurant owner Charlotte Nielson added cooking and packaging extra food for Ernie to her already crowded schedule. Neighbors showed up with tractors to help with the acres of mowing that Ernie normally did himself. Family members stayed with him in shifts and helped with day-to-day chores around the house, made sure he ate, or be home alone.

There was another issue Ernie had to address. He now was accountable for managing the day-to-day responsibilities of a household Ellyn had seamlessly handled for over a quarter century. Ernie needed help figuring out Ellyn's system for basic things like paying monthly bills.

Boyd Murray owned a local insurance company and offered to assist, and it was a good thing. "Ernie's initial method was to bring a stack of bills down to my office and my staff helped him," Murray said. Boyd didn't mind helping, but he quickly realized, in the long run, he was doing his distraught friend a disservice not helping him find his own method for personal finances.

Ernie took an indefinite leave of absence from work, but not to curl up in a ball at home, although no one would have blamed him if he had. Instead, he threw himself headlong into being with Gregg and Catharine, supporting West High's 2012 senior class, and especially the volleyball team. He was a fixture at the high school's concerts, plays, and sporting events. He became their biggest supporter through his enthusiastic cheering at events and generous financial contributions.

Ernie asked Principal Arganbright for the music and athletic programs' wish lists and then opened his checkbook. While attending a volleyball game, Ernie thought about how great it would be for the players and fans to have a state-of-the-art video board in the gym. The next morning, the principal was surprised to find a blank check from Ernie earmarked for the item.

The impact of the Founds' tragic events spread beyond the borders of Iowa down to Trinity University in San Antonio, Texas. Trinity is a tight-knit community with an annual enrollment of around 2,500 students. When word spread that one of their own had experienced such awful events, Catharine's losses became the entire Trinity family's losses, up to and including the university's president, Dennis Ahlburg.

As Trinity students, staff, and faculty returned for the 2011-12 school year, they were well informed about Ellyn's worsening condition by a steady stream of updates from Catharine while she was at home over summer break. When Catharine returned on August 9, everyone was relieved to hear her mother had made it through the summer. Although they were happy to have Catharine back on campus, they knew that because of Ellyn's fragile health, Catharine's return was likely just temporary.

When Catharine was absent from practice on August 12, her team-mates assumed she went home because her mother had passed. Team members gasped when Trinity head volleyball coach, Julie Jenkins, told them about Caroline's accident. "We knew that she was going to lose her mom, but losing her sister on top of that was too much for one family to bear. We had to do something very special to honor her family whenever she decided to return."

Since the team didn't know when Catharine would be back to school, they initially decided they would take a team picture honoring the family. "The family already had 'TEAM ELLYN' shirts made up, so we decided to have 'TEAM FOUND' shirts made in purple, which is the color for pancreatic cancer awareness. We'd have the number '9' on the back as that's both Catharine's and Caroline's volleyball number," Coach Jenkins explained.

The coach ordered twenty shirts, and the plan was to have the team wear them for a photo in front of the tiger statue on campus. They put the photo on the team's website and notified Catharine and Ernie so they could see it.

While it was a nice gesture, the team didn't feel it was enough, so they decided to wear the t-shirts during pregame warm-ups the en-tire season. When the players got their shirts, they wore them around campus, and much like the LIVE LIKE LINE shirts, classmates took notice, and the shirts became a commodity in high demand.

When the team found out that Catharine would indeed be back for the team's home opener, the coach spoke with Trinity's long-time ath-letic director, Bob King, about the potential for a surprise memorial honoring Catharine and her family. He loved the idea, but he needed to clear it with the university president.

Director King brought Coach Jenkin's memorial idea to President Ahlburg. King said it would be nice if the university would provide a purple "TEAM FOUND" t-shirt to every attendee of the game as a sign of the school's solidarity and support. He requested the school provide two thousand shirts just in case they filled the place, but he admitted to the president there was no way of knowing how many people would actually show up.

The new college president, on the job less than two years, found himself in a uniquely sad and terrible situation. He knew that conventional wisdom dictated he laugh such a ridiculous request out of his office. Purchasing two thousand printed t-shirts for the student body that may or may not show up to a volleyball game was a questionable expenditure at best.

Whether it was inexperience or blind faith, President Ahlburg approved the purchase without batting an eye, trusting that the outstanding students at the university would show up for one of their own. Anticipating that all of the members of the Slocum and Found families couldn't attend, the president took an additional step and had the game broadcast on the web. No matter where they were, as long as they had internet access, family members would be able to share in the evening.

With the September 2 game only three days away getting word out quickly was important. Notifying students proved tricky because the team wanted the memorial to be a surprise for Catharine. A campus-wide email would have been the most efficient method, but ultimately ruled out because the guest of honor would be included as an addressee. Most of the notifications were handled via Facebook.

Contacting students was only the first hurdle. Even if notifications were completed in time, it didn't guarantee attendance by the student body. The game was on Friday evening, a time historically reserved by college students for off-campus social endeavors.

When the team arrived at the gym on the night of the game, Catharine thought it odd her teammates rushed into the locker room. There was a good reason for their haste. Fans in purple t-shirts were already trickling into the gym and nearly spoiled the surprise. It was stranger still to Catharine that, despite everyone being ready to warm-up, Coach Jenkins kept them in the locker room. The coach gathered the team, and Catharine's teammates presented her with a "TEAM FOUND" shirt. The team explained their plan to wear the t-shirts over their jerseys during warm-ups. While this was a sincere gesture by the team, they were also stalling until the gym was full.

A lookout posted at the gym's entrance gestured to Coach Jenkins to come over and take a look. The coach peaked out the door, and what she saw astonished her, "I've coached here for twenty-eight years and never seen the gym that full for any event, and we've hosted some big ones."

The team gathered at the door and then charged in. The crowd jumped to their feet and cheered loudly as the home team ran across the floor.

By design, Catharine was last through the door. When the over-capacity crowd of 2,000 caught a glimpse of No. 9 the noise level surged and echoed throughout the gym. She smiled and waved to the rowdy fans, charging them up even more.

As Catharine scanned the crowd, two fans waving to her from the top row of bleachers caught her eye. Gregg and Ernie made the trip and were decked out in their matching purple t-shirts. Catharine was overcome with emotion at the sight of her family and disappeared behind the bleachers to regain her composure. When she reappeared, it spurred the still cheering crowd even more, and they responded by chanting, "Cath-rine Fou-nd, Cath-rine Fou-nd!" Tears streamed down Ernie's face as Catharine's name filled the air.

With the teams lined up on each side of the net, the PA announcer asked for a moment of silence for Caroline and Ellyn. Coach Jenkins looked at Catharine, whose eyes were elevated skyward. She wondered if her decision to allow Catharine to start the game might be too much for the twenty-one-year-old to handle so soon after losing her sister and mother.

When Catharine called Coach Jenkins expressing a desire to return, the coach suggested she take more time to be with her family, but Catharine was adamant about playing against nationally ranked Wisconsin-Platteville. Coach Jenkins divulged, "She knew what this game meant to the team and didn't want to let her teammates down."

Any concerns the coach had about her right side hitter's play quickly dissipated when the first ball was set for her. Catharine elevated and split the defenders with a laser beam spike for a winner. The point brought the crowd to full froth and set the tone for the team.

Catharine led the Tigers to a two games to zero win over Wisconsin-Platteville—Coach Bresnahan's alma mater—by playing one of the best matches of her career. She registered twelve kills, a team high of seven blocks, and a hitting accuracy of fifty percent (a banner night for a hitter is thirty percent).

The family was moved by the university's loving gesture. The spirit of Team Found lived on throughout the school year and purple t-shirts could be seen around campus on a daily basis.

As passionate as the Trinity Volleyball match was, it would pale in comparison to West High's first home dual match September 13 versus Cedar Rapids Prairie. The team knew, unlike tournaments, a dual match would bring out the home fans.

After the team's disastrous start at the MVC-MAC Tournament, the girls righted the ship and began playing championship volleyball.

They had won both the Marshalltown tournament and their own West High Extravaganza Tournament (now called the Caroline Found Extravaganza) for the first time in the twenty year history of hosting it. Going into their dual match with Prairie, the Women of Troy were ranked sixth in the state.

The night of the match, the stands bracketing the volleyball court were packed with students on one side and parents on the other. The majority of fans were sporting LIVE LIKE LINE t-shirts. The gym was filled with raw emotion the second the girls took the floor for warm-ups. Everyone cheered and chanted. The gymnasium was full of West students screaming. Many parents couldn't avoid looking at Ernie without crying.

The Women of Troy were dealing with a mixed bag of emotions. Each player faced her own individual feelings which seemed to be running on a loop. Several were sad, while others were nervous that without Line they would underachieve in front of the home crowd.

The team's mood shifted with each passing moment. Each high five between the West players was so forceful that a loud "smack" could be heard throughout the gym. Hip-hop music blasted from the speakers during pregame. Shelly Stumpff and a few of her teammates danced to the music. The gesture was a thinly-veiled charade designed to alleviate the pressure they felt and to keep them from emotional outbursts.

With clenched teeth, Kelley Fliehler wore the tension on her face. She had taken over at setter and was playing unbelievably well considering the circumstances. Kelley had improved each game but still made her share of mistakes. She still didn't feel like the position was hers, or a worthy substitute for Caroline. She was pressing to be perfect.

The season before, when Kelley made a mistake during a game, it was Caroline's encouragement to forget about it and move on to the next point that calmed her. She was now thrust into a position where each mistake was glaring because she touched the ball nearly every play. Kelley's teammates and coaches tried their best to encourage her. While she appreciated their efforts, the support somehow seemed inadequate compared to what Caroline used to provide her.

The pregame ritual of West High and their opponent lining up on either side of the net, honoring Caroline and Ellyn took place, but with one change. Instead of a moment of silence, the PA announcer asked for the spectators to "Live Like Line" and introduce themselves to someone they had never met before. While the crowd got acquainted in the stands, the West volleyball team went to the Cedar Rapids Prairie side of the net and introduced themselves to their opponents.

The Women of Troy were relieved when the first game finally began. West jumped out to an early lead over the unranked Prairie team and never looked back. Each point the home team scored brought an eruption of cheers from the student section and then a corresponding chant directed at their opponent's fans. When West's Laynie Whitehead got a kill, the students chanted, "She's a fresh-man, she's a fresh-man!"

Charlie Rogers and Anthony Brown were in the first row of bleachers, and the two West High football stars led most of the cheers. They became volleyball fans when Caroline made the varsity team as a sophomore. The previous season, the guys had been front-row-and-center when the volleyball team won the state title. Back then, they were both thrilled for Line and envious she had something they coveted in football. Once Caroline discovered Charlie and Anthony's jealousy, she, of course, dished out some good-natured teasing by wearing her state championship ring in front of them.

The Prairie match ended with a lopsided West victory. The student body flooded the gym floor to celebrate with the team. Hugs were distributed liberally in and out of the stands.

When the familiar introduction to "Sweet Caroline" filled the gym, the crowd of teenagers wrapped their arms around the shoulders of the people on either side of them, no matter friend or a foe. As the song blared and crackled on max volume, students, parents, coaches, and players sang along with the chorus: "Sweet Caroline, bumm, bumm, bumm, good times never seemed so good." Caroline's classmates shouted the words to the song as if to ensure that she could hear them.

Ernie remained in the stands thirty minutes after the match ended. He accepted a steady stream of hugs and handshakes from adults, students, and players, exchanging a pleasant word with each.

For the remainder of September, Ernie attended a series of school and community events. Every event turned into a Caroline and Ellyn memorial, and they all wanted Ernie there as the guest of honor. He never refused an invitation.

Chapter 12
Respite and Reflection

Keep close to Nature's heart and break clear away once in a while, and climb a mountain or spend a week in the woods.
—John Muir

The risk of love is loss, and the price of loss is grief—But the pain of grief is only a shadow when compared with the pain of never risking love.
—Hilary Stanton Zunin

Not everyone necessarily saw the continued homage for Caroline and Ellyn as a good thing. Those closest to Ernie were concerned about the potential emotional and physical toll exacted on him from being the constant center of attention wherever he went and the reasons for it. "Is it a good thing to have your tragedy be famous? Is it a good thing to have the names of your dead wife and daughter on t-shirts all over town?" Larry Marsh asked. "Most people live through tragedies in a more quiet circumstance."

The Marsh and Murray families worried Ernie wasn't as tethered as he was when Ellyn was alive, but they were forced to accept that it was an uncontrollable situation. They were hopeful he could get through the year and the memorial in New Hampshire without burning out.

Then, maybe, Ernie would be able to grieve properly and chart his new course.

Despite the concerns that the numerous events memorializing Caroline and Ellyn may be detrimental for his well-being, Ernie assured everyone he was fine, and in fact, the events were helping to keep him going. "Were there some things that I would have rather skipped? Sure, but it was honoring Caroline and Ellyn, so how could that be a bad thing?" If organizers of local events wanted to recognize and honor his family, Ernie felt he owed it to them to be there.

Family members from both sides encouraged Ernie to move back East. They worried about him being all alone and so far away from them. They reasoned that with Gregg and Catharine out of the house, being closer to family would help him with the healing process.

Ernie thanked those concerned, but he was exactly where he needed to be and doing what he needed to do. Besides, he wanted to keep the farm for Gregg and Catharine to call home until they settled down with families of their own.

However, Ernie couldn't deny the full schedule of events honoring his family was unsustainable and had taken an emotional toll. He needed a short break, and he knew the only way he would get one was out of the state. In his mind there was no better place to get away to than New Hampshire.

Ernie didn't want to go alone so he asked Paul Etre, his trusted friend and the long-time assistant to the chairman of the orthopedic surgery department, if he would accompany him. Paul agreed, but they couldn't leave until Ernie attended one more event honoring Caroline—the Ponseti Races.

The Ponseti Races occur every October in Iowa City. Organized by Paul in 2002, the annual running race is held to honor the legacy of the late Dr. Ignacio Ponseti. Dr. Ponseti, a legend in the field of orthopedic medicine, developed an alternative method to cure club foot in children. Despite the initial success of the Ponseti method, the medical community shunned the procedure for fifty years in favor of a more expensive and invasive surgical correction. Ponseti made it his life's work to teach his techniques to countless medical providers in the poorest regions of the world where surgery was unavailable. To date, the Ponseti method has helped hundreds of thousands of kids walk normally all over the world. The doctor, who gave so many children a new lease on life, lived an unassuming life, practicing medicine into his 90s.

Paul decided that in the 2011 Ponseti Races Caroline would be honored as someone who, like Ponseti, dedicated her life to improving the lives of others. On October 1, runners and spectators gathered in the chilly 40 degree air and together paid tribute to Line. The runners were then called to the starting line, where the West High volleyball team, Ernie, and University of Iowa football coach Kirk Ferentz prepared to initiate the race. Coach Ferentz raised the starter's pistol above his head and fired. Doves were released to honor Caroline and Ellyn as the race began.

Later that day, Paul and Ernie boarded a plane. They used a few days on the front end of their two-week sojourn to visit Catharine and Gregg. They planned to close out their trip in New Hampshire.

The first stop they made was in Memphis to watch Catharine and the Trinity volleyball team in action. Next, they hopped another plane to Bristol, Connecticut, to be with Gregg. He took them on a tour of the massive ESPN complex where he worked.

Their next stop was Ernie's hometown of Batavia, New York, to see his parents, Ernest Sr. and Eleanor Found. Ernie was the second child of four born in upstate New York.

During their stay with Ernie's parents, Paul was regaled by Eleanor of stories from Ernie's childhood. She told him about losing their youngest son, Danny. Paul knew Ernie had a younger brother who'd passed but never knew the specifics.

Danny was ten years younger than the eldest, Marilyn. Diagnosed with ADHD and other learning disabilities, Danny was a troubled boy who struggled to find his way. By the time he was eight, there was some concern whether or not he would even graduate from high school. Danny did ultimately graduate but not without significant help.

Danny hit his stride as a young adult and got himself into Alfred University studying electrical engineering. Danny loved fast cars, saved his money, bought an old Camaro, and dropped a big-block engine into it.

While on a nighttime cruise with a couple of buddies, a deer bounded across the road in front of the car. Danny swerved to avoid the animal and hit a pothole. A tire blew, and he lost control of the vehicle. The Camaro careened off the highway and struck a steel bridge support, killing all three.

Eleanor told Paul how crushed they were when Caroline died. Their pain doubled seeing their son lose a child suddenly, the same way they had. Eleanor expressed to Paul her concern for Ernie now that Ellyn had passed. She worried about her son not having his spouse to lean on when the really bad times came, and she assured Paul bad times would come. She thanked him for being such a good friend.

When it was time for the guys to leave, the pair packed up and said goodbye. Ernie merged the rental car into eastbound Interstate 90 traffic to go visit some of the Slocum family scattered around quaint New England communities.

With each stop, Paul learned, in detail, about Ellyn from the people who'd shared their childhood with her. Her siblings told story after story about young Ellyn growing up in Binghamton, New York, a mere three-hour drive from Ernie's hometown.

Ellyn was James and Helen Slocum's fourth child of eight. She always joked she was the Jan Brady of the Slocum family, the middle child, the neglected one.

K.C. described Ellyn as having loads of integrity and honesty. "Ellyn was the best of all of us, the shining star of the Slocum kids. She wanted to do the right thing even though it was fearful sometimes." The rest of Ellyn's siblings agreed that her best attribute was her generous heart. Her acts of kindness and compassion weren't for popularity or acceptance; she cared for people and took a genuine interest in others lives, even people sometimes marginalized by society, people like her Uncle Roger.

Uncle Roger had health problems most of his life and was mentally challenged. A man of little means, he lived for a time at the local YMCA. James and Helen invited Uncle Roger over every Sunday for brunch. Ellyn took an immediate shine to Roger and went out of her way to spend time with him each time he would visit.

"It was just in her nature to nurture," K.C. said. "She loved people. If she was your acquaintance, she wanted to know about you and what was going on in your life. She wanted to know about your kids and family."

When Helen was diagnosed with Multiple Sclerosis in 1974, she could have turned to an older family member or friend with more life experience, but it was nineteen-year-old Ellyn she turned to for counsel and advice. This may have been puzzling to those who didn't know Ellyn, but it wasn't surprising to the rest of the Slocum family. "With Ellyn being so compassionate and understanding people so well, mom relied on her," K.C. said.

Ellyn always placed a premium on her education. Her dedicat[
paid off in 1974 when she was selected salutatorian of her high school
graduating class. She chose to attend Utica College, a small liberal arts
school not far from home. Ellyn studied occupational therapy with an
eventual focus on the hand.

During Ernie and Paul's trip together, Ernie showed him some of the
natural beauty of New Hampshire during the autumn months. It was
at this point that Ernie exposed his ornery streak.

In advance of their trip, Ernie asked Paul if he would like to go for a
hike in the New Hampshire hills. He told Paul of a spot with amazing
berries they could eat right off the vine. Paul inquired about the eleva-
tion of the hills, explaining he wasn't a fan of heights. Ernie knew that
Paul understated his fear, and in reality the Lebanese-American was
terrified of heights. Ernie assured Paul it amounted to nothing more
than a "little hike."

What the acrophobic Paul didn't know was Ernie had pre-scheduled a zip-lining session for them at Alpine Adventures, the longest,
fastest, and highest zip line adventure in New Hampshire. The disclaimer on the company's website ominously read: "This isn't for everyone." Ernie, the adventurer, decided on the Sky Rider Tour which has a
series of zip lines, some of which propel riders hundreds of feet above
the forest canopy at speeds of up to fifty miles-per-hour.

Paul became suspicious that Ernie had misrepresented their "little
hike" when he was fitted with a full rappelling harness and helmet.
Paul's suspicion gave way to apprehension when they needed to be
transported by a four-wheel drive vehicle in order to go hiking. After
Ernie coaxed Paul up a sixty-foot ladder, he told his friend what they
were really doing.

Paul wasn't too happy. As a matter of fact, he was terrified, but he agreed to go along because Ernie was excited and his friend's happiness took precedence over his fear of heights. Paul looked up at Ernie, who placed his large hand onto Paul's shoulder, and smiled to reassure him. Paul realized this was just the sort of shenanigan Caroline had pulled in the past, and he certainly understood where she got it.

After some instruction on hand positioning and breaking, they were taken to the first line, hooked up, and began their adventure. The instructors told the men the most important thing to remember was maintaining their speed and breaking at the proper time. "Past riders who came into the platform too fast slammed into trees and were seriously injured." Conversely, riders breaking too soon ended up stuck, dangling from a steel cable hundreds of feet off the ground.

The whole process was easy enough in theory. Even Paul was moving along, albeit cautiously, and considering his circumstances, doing a great job. Then the guys came to the longest and highest zip of the excursion. Ernie went first. He completed the zip and stood on the platform and encouraged his bulging-eyed friend speeding toward him.

Paul was going much faster than on the previous zip lines. As he got closer to the tree at the end of the line, some of the instructor's words played louder and louder in his head, "too fast...seriously injured." Paul simultaneously closed his eyes and his break hand.

Once stopped, Paul opened his eyes and saw Ernie standing upside down on the platform about forty feet away. As he dangled helplessly from the wire, Paul mistakenly dropped his head and looked down. "I was looking down at the really tall trees," Paul said.

Paul shut his eyes tight and ignored the guide's instructions on how he could reach the platform safely. He prayed to God for a miracle, asked forgiveness for his sins, and then opened his eyes long enough to glare at Ernie, who grinned at him and said, "You can do it, Paul."

The prayer calmed Paul enough to pull himself towards the platform until his strength gave out on the last uphill section of cable. The instructor hooked up to the line, went out, and pulled Paul the rest of the way to "safety."

Once on the platform, Paul's legs shook as he hugged the tree and wouldn't let go. For ten minutes Ernie tried to talk Paul into releasing his grip on the massive cedar. The pair was in a real dilemma. Even if Paul let go, there wasn't a ladder for them to climb down. The only way down was to complete one more zip. Paul finally calmed down enough to remove his death grip on the tree and take one more terrifying ride.

When Paul's feet finally touched the ground, he dropped to his knees and kissed the earth. Only about halfway through the excursion, the guide told Paul they had two options from where they were, "We can rest a little bit and then continue on, or ..."

Paul cut the guide off mid-sentence, "No, that's not an option! What's the second option? It has to be better than the first one."

The guide laughed and said, "The other option is I call base and have a four-wheel drive come and pick us up."

"Yes, that's an excellent option! Call them right now," Paul said.

After their zip lining adventure, Paul and Ernie got back on the road. During their drive through the small New England towns, Ernie pointed out landmarks that were special to Ellyn—a restaurant, a bric-a-brac shop, or a particular house she had liked. He had to hold back his emotions frequently as they passed each one. He explained to Paul that each year during their visits, he would take Ellyn to some of these places. The prior year Ellyn had been too ill, preventing her from seeing everything one last time.

As they traveled a two-lane highway in silence, Paul asked Ernie to tell him how he and Ellyn met. He already knew much of the story, but he hoped Ernie talking about happier times might boost his spirits and be cathartic for him. Ernie happily obliged.

Despite Ernie and Ellyn both growing up and attending college in upstate New York, it would be years before they met. Before there was Ernie and Ellyn, there was Ellyn and Larry Marsh. Larry attended Colgate, and it was through a common acquaintance that he met Ellyn. They became friends and remained close during their time at their respective schools, but their relationship never advanced beyond friends.

Ernie chose to attend tiny Hamilton College for his undergraduate work. He graduated after a stellar four-year academic and basketball career, followed by his acceptance into Syracuse University medical school where he met Larry, and they quickly became best friends. Despite having a common acquaintance in Larry, the rigors of medical school kept Ellyn and Ernie from meeting.

While talking, Ernie signaled and turned into a parking lot at the edge of Lake Winnipesaukee. He would have to tell Paul the rest of the story later; they had a ferry to catch.

Chapter 13
Destiny Their Compass

The seeker embarks on a journey to find what he wants
and discovers, along the way, what he needs.
—Wally Lamb, *The Hour I First Believed*

All love stories are tales of beginnings. When we
talk about falling in love, we go to the beginning
to pinpoint the moment of free fall.
—Meghan O'Rourke

During the last week of their trip, Ernie and Paul stayed on Bear Island
at a lake house owned by K.C. and her husband, Barry. Bear Island is
part of an archipelago located on Lake Winnipesaukee. The island is
only accessible from the mainland via boat or helicopter during the
summer months. When the lake freezes in the winter months snow-
mobiles are used by the permanent residents to shuttle back and forth
from the island.

With top-notch amenities and access to a boat tied to a private dock,
Ernie and Paul spent the days traveling the beautiful waterways created by the islands dotting the lake. On the shore, they could see the
famed New England foliage ablaze with yellows, reds, oranges, and
browns.

In the evenings, the guys sat around in the cabin, sometimes late into the night, sipping wine by a crackling fire. For hours on end they laughed and cried as Ernie unfolded his family's life story, starting where he had left off, just before meeting Ellyn after moving to Boston for residency training.

After graduating from Utica College, Ellyn wanted to experience life in the big city, so she moved to Boston. She worked part time in a hospital as a hand therapist. To supplement her income, she also worked as a waitress in a trendy restaurant located in Quincy Market/ Faneuil Hall called Hoolihan's. Being a people person, the job suited her well.

Upon graduation from medical school, Ellyn's friend, Larry Marsh moved to Boston for his residency. A year later, Ernie followed him to Boston and entered the orthopedic surgery residency program. At the time, Larry was renting a house with his live-in girlfriend. He invited Ernie to move in as a roommate and third wheel.

Larry finally got around to a proper introduction of Ernie and Ellyn when she came to the house one day for a visit. Ernie was immediately floored by her. "I'd had girlfriends in the past," he recalled, "but she was—wow—she was striking."

Ellyn was involved with someone else at the time, but Ernie decided she was definitely someone he wanted to know better. He had two essential qualities that made him confident he would eventually win her over: persistence and patience.

It took six months before circumstances were right for Ernie to ask Ellyn out on a date. They were both working at the Lahey Clinic and sometimes shared patients and the occasional cup of coffee. "She had this pretty long hair, dressed in nice skirts that knocked me out, and it was just great to be around her," Ernie remembered.

As it turned out, Ernie wasn't the only physician with his eyes on Ellyn. "Her hand surgeon was infatuated with her, too," Ernie said. The poor hand surgeon, however, soon found himself out of his depth against the charming Dr. Found.

Ernie and Ellyn both suspected their relationship may turn into much more, so they took it slowly and really got to know one another. They learned they shared common interests, such as their affinity for Boston's professional sports teams. She was impressed to hear that Ernie was a Boston Celtics season ticket holder considering how difficult it was to become one. Figuring she would be less than impressed with how he secured the tickets; he conveniently left out that part of the story for a very long time.

Being a passionate NBA fan, one of the first things Ernie did when he got to Boston in August, 1981, was to march down to Boston Garden to buy Celtics tickets. The naïve young man told the ticket agent he would be living in Boston the next five years and wanted season tickets. The old Boston native was dumbfounded. He hesitated before responding to the ridiculous request, certain the appeal for one of the most sought after tickets in professional sports had to be a practical joke.

"Son, this is the Boston Celtics we're talking about," the crusty old ticket agent uttered.

"Great, I'm in the right place then," Ernie said with a smile.

"There's a waiting list for season tickets."

"If I get put on the waiting list now, will I have them by the start of the season?"

The man's jaw dropped. His patience was shorter than the stubby cigar he pulled from his mouth. "Look kid, you're number 1,011 on a list that averages only three season ticket holders turning in their tickets each year. So, no, you won't have tickets for this season or any other season," and slammed the window shut.

Dejected, but undeterred, Ernie developed a Plan B. He needed to find someone connected to the team. He didn't have to look any farther than his own department at the hospital. The chairman of orthopedic surgery, his boss, was the Celtics' team surgeon.

Ernie didn't feel comfortable walking up to the head of his department and asking him for Celtics tickets. But the chairman's long-time secretary, Margaret, was a different story.

It was common knowledge in residency circles that Margaret was single, lonely, and—most importantly to Ernie—had deep connections to the Celtics' front office. Ernie zeroed in on Margaret and cranked up his charm. After an appropriate amount of playful banter, he popped the question; "Margaret, would you happen to know where I could get my hands on Celtics season tickets?" Margaret's smile indicated he had come to the right place, but the tickets would come at a price.

Ernie took the news to his co-conspirators, Larry Marsh, and a colleague who shall remain nameless. Since their unnamed colleague was happily married, either Larry or Ernie had to befriend Margaret. "Larry was unwilling to complete the task, so it fell on my shoulders," Ernie explained.

As off-putting as it was for Ernie to use someone this way—and dangerous considering it was the boss's secretary—the start of the basketball season was rapidly approaching, and he was without an alternative option. "These were Celtic's season tickets we were talking about, and I'm 1,011 on the waiting list," Ernie said. Not surprisingly, he became a season ticket holder before 1,010 names ahead of him on the list.

When Ellyn learned of Ernie's exploits to acquire Celtics tickets years later, it turned out she had her own story about charming a season ticket holder to get Red Sox tickets.

An elderly and long-time attending physician at Lahey was a decades-long Red Sox season ticket holder. The elderly physician was very fond of Ellyn, and she knew it. "She could get Sox tickets anytime she wanted by simply batting her eyes at him," Ernie said.

Ellyn had a trickier time gaining admission to Celtics' games though. She didn't know any season ticket holders who would readily give them up, so she developed clever ploys to gain admittance. For instance, she presented herself at the entrance for players' wives and passed herself off as starting center Robert Parrish's wife. She persuaded the security guard that her scatterbrained husband forgot his lucky socks and she was dutifully bringing them to him. Ernie wasn't the only one with persistence and resourcefulness.

About half way through his residency, a requirement of Ernie's rotation took him ninety minutes outside of Boston to Springfield, Massachusetts, where he worked at a Shriners Hospital for children. Things were changing in both Ernie and Ellyn's lives, including their feelings for one another. They were in love.

Knowing he wanted to spend the rest of his life with this extraordinary woman, Ernie asked her to marry him, and she accepted. They wanted to marry right away but, considering the demands of a surgical residency, decided to wait until he was finished. The couple's love continued to blossom over the last two years of Ernie's residency, making the wait for their wedding that much more difficult.

In the spring of 1985, as Ernie neared the completion of his residency, the couple decided to wed over the July Fourth weekend. After their plans were finalized, Ernie was assigned to a spine surgery fellowship in Syracuse, New York. He was scheduled to start on the exact weekend as his planned wedding. "Before I went there I told them, 'I'm taking off July Fourth weekend to get married so fire me now if that's going to be a problem,'" he recalled. They did not fire him.

Ernie's last day in the residency program was June 30, 1985. One of the outgoing residents had to be on call, and Ernie and Ellyn were hopeful it wouldn't be him because they had last minute preparations to make before the big day. The entire department knew of Ernie's upcoming wedding that weekend—including Margaret, who set the schedule. He never found out whether it was bad luck or payback, but his name came up on the call schedule for the last day.

After an extensive search for wedding venues, the couple settled on a location on the outskirts of Rindge, New Hampshire, called Cathedral of the Pines. Positioned on a hilltop with panoramic views of Monadnock Mountain, Cathedral of the Pines is an open-air non-denominational house of worship and meeting place situated on 236 pristine acres.

Most of the wedding party and immediate family arrived a few days before the wedding. They stayed at the Woodbound Inn, a bed and breakfast on steroids. The Inn is located in the woods on the edge of Rindge. The main lodging is a grand white house with two floors of quaint bedrooms, a restaurant, and a bar. Additional lodging outside of the main house consisted of individual cabins. Wedged between the main house and cabins was a larger rustic cabin that served as an event room.

Positioned alongside Lake Contoocook, the inn had plenty of activities for everyone including a private beach, a nearby golf course, and was only a short drive to Mount Monadnock.

Ellyn had plenty to keep her busy before the wedding. She understood her future husband to be a wonderful man with a host of great qualities, but none of them would have helped with the multitude of logistical considerations to double check. So she excused her fiancé until the following day with one simple and clearly stated mandate before Ernie and Larry departed: "Don't be late for rehearsal."

The parting edict may have been communicated to both Ernie and Larry, but Larry knew he was the intended target. Ernie's on-time record was sketchy at best. Ellyn put her husband's punctuality squarely on Larry's shoulders.

With a day to kill, Ernie and Larry planned an overnight camping and fishing trip. They picked out a location deep in the Adirondack Mountains, five hours by car. The location, in the middle of nowhere had a pristine pond loaded with brook trout, which made the extended windshield time more than worth it to Ernie. They agreed to budget plenty of time to get back, well before the rehearsal.

The guys spent the day fishing the tranquil tarn surrounded by trees and fresh mountain air. They didn't see another human being in any direction.

The next morning, Ernie assured Larry they had time to climb a bit of the mountain before they had to leave. The higher they climbed, the later it got, but Ernie kept coaxing Larry higher despite his repeated protests for them to turn back. When they finally arrived back at the pond, Larry thought if they packed quickly they would only be fashionably late. Ernie had a different plan, and it involved catching one more trout. This carefree attitude was what made being friends with Ernie and Caroline so much fun. Unfortunately, it was the same carefree attitude which frustrated anyone expecting them to be on time.

By the time they got back to the car, they realized they weren't just going to be fashionably late, but extremely late. All the way back, Larry reminded Ernie of Ellyn's final proclamation before they left. Ernie tried unsuccessfully to reassure Larry, telling him it would be okay. "When we got back, it wasn't okay. It wasn't okay that night, or the next day. It wasn't okay for a long time," Larry said.

On July 6, 1985, the wedding party made their way over to the Cathedral of the Pines, nestled into a centuries old pine forest with postcard beauty. Visitors are frequently so overwhelmed by the unspoiled magnificence of the location, despite being outside and in the wilderness, they instinctively speak in hushed tones, just above a whisper.

The main cathedral is located in a clearing between two massive pines about thirty feet apart. An altar, built from local multi-colored stones and mortar, is wedged between them. Behind the cathedral the terrain falls away into a rolling forest which stretches to the base of majestic Mount Monadnock.

The splendor of the occasion, set against the misty valley backdrop, left a lasting impression on everyone in attendance, including the single, freewheeling best man. "Here they are surrounded by this perfect setting, professing these unbelievable self-proclaimed vows to each other," Larry recalled. "It was beautiful."

The cathedral and mountain were forever embedded in Ernie and Ellyn's hearts as the foundation of their lives together. The newlyweds promised to pay homage by returning to New Hampshire each year, renewing their vows and climbing Monadnock. From then on, no matter their circumstances, they did.

When Ernie finished telling Paul his story, it was well past midnight. The last of the wine was gone, and the fireplace was reduced to glowing embers. Paul thanked Ernie for sharing, and the guys returned to their rooms to pack for the trip home.

Chapter 14
They Visited, They Stayed

One's destination is never a place, but a new way of seeing things.
—Henry Miller

Home is the place where, when you have to
go there, they have to take you in.
—Robert Frost

The New Hampshire respite over, Ernie and Paul boarded a plane back for Iowa. Ernie couldn't help but think about the lonely existence that awaited him at the farm, and he dreaded the idea. Instead, he wanted to remember a happier time about his home. So, his mind flashed back twenty-four years to the first time he climbed aboard an airplane bound for Iowa. As he settled into his seat and buckled in, his thoughts drifted to the circumstances that led him to visit Larry in Iowa City.

It was the summer of 1985. Ernie and Ellyn had moved to Syracuse, New York, for Ernie's spine surgery fellowship. Ellyn, not one to sit idly by, took the opportunity to complete a master's degree in communications she had started in Boston. Once he completed the fellowship, Ernie took a position with a private practice surgery group in New Hampshire. The couple moved to Durham.

Ernie performed cutting edge spine surgery and made an immediate impression on his colleagues. His partners marveled at his innovative and extremely technical procedures. The downside to the surgery was it soon became evident if he stayed, he better be prepared to do this and nothing else for the rest of his career.

Ernie became a hot commodity at the teaching hospitals in Syracuse and Boston—both of which competed vigorously for his services. While Ernie was flattered by the attention from the academic hospitals, he also understood that working at one was very different from private practice.

In need of guidance, Ernie called Larry Marsh. After completing his fellowship at Oxford, Larry had come back across the Atlantic to take a position at the University of Iowa Hospitals and Clinics (UIHC) as an orthopedic trauma surgeon. During a lengthy telephone conversation, he provided Ernie with the pros and cons of being on staff at a university hospital.

While Larry welcomed any chance to talk to his friend, it was a well-timed call. A position had just opened up in the renowned orthopedic surgery department at UIHC. Larry took the opportunity during the phone call to see if he could coax Ernie to come for a visit. Ernie agreed to come and take a look, but first he had to consult a map. "The truth is, when you're born in the northeast, you don't even know where the hell Iowa is, just that it's in the middle of nowhere," Larry admitted.

Larry considered Ernie's visit a lark. The two surgeons' personal lives couldn't have been more different. Larry had no attachments, so it was easy for him to maintain a spartan's existence in a one-bedroom apartment in Iowa City. His plan was to build a résumé at the prestigious program and then move back to civilization on the east coast.

Conversely, Ernie was a happily married man, building a thriving practice on the east coast surrounded by family and friends. Larry figured, even if by some miracle Ernie did consider taking the position, there was no way Ellyn would agree. Among the other factors for the family to stay put was the arrival of their first born, Gregg, in August 1986. The way Larry figured it, his friend was not moving to Iowa City, but at least they would have a weekend of darts and beer.

Ernie climbed off the plane in Cedar Rapids, Iowa, during March. The best way to describe Iowa in March is cold and ugly in equal parts. The skies were mostly filled with dense and gloomy clouds. The roads were soupy, and every car was coated with layers of gray splatter. If you were to poll Iowans for their least favorite month of the year, March would likely win in a landslide. "It could not have been uglier," Ernie recollected. "It sleeted, rained, snowed, blew, and everything was wet and dirty."

On the surface, things seemed stacked against the Founds moving to Iowa, but there was plenty to make Iowa City appealing. Ernie was a college sports fan and liked that the UI athletic programs were having a nice run of success. The football team had just been to the Rose Bowl. The men's basketball team advanced to the Sweet Sixteen in the NCAA Tournament, and the women's basketball team had made it to the Elite Eight in their national tournament. The wrestling team had won multiple national championships under famed coach Dan Gable. "Larry told me that all of it happened within pissing distance of the University Hospital," Ernie said.

Another strong draw for Ernie was the orthopedics surgery department which was ranked No. 4 in the country. The department employed renowned doctors, including the famed Dr. Ignacio Ponseti, a trailblazer in the profession.

Ernie was so taken by the physicians, staff, and entire department he was ready to go to work immediately. He was captivated enough with the community, university, and hospital he sent roses to Ellyn, who was visiting her sister in Atlanta. In the attached note, he told her she had to come see this place because it was pretty amazing. Upon reading the note, Ellyn turned to her sister and said, "It looks like we might be moving to Iowa."

Five weeks later, Ernie brought Ellyn to Iowa City for a visit. The orthopedic department chair, Reg Cooper, wanted Ernie on the staff, so he rolled out the red carpet to impress Ernie and Ellyn. He scheduled a departmental dinner at a private club. During dinner, he gave the Founds a heartfelt speech that indicated he was making an offer to have the Founds join the U of I family.

On the last night of the visit, the Founds met with Larry and his colleague, Jim Nepola, over beers and a game of darts at a local pub. Jim blurted out, in the middle of the game, "Well, are you coming or not?" While Ernie ran down the pluses and minuses, Jim interrupted exclaiming, "I'll make it easy for you. Let's play a game of darts, Larry and me versus Ellyn and you. If we beat you, you're coming to Iowa." Larry and Jim won the game, and Jim still takes full credit for bringing the Founds to town.

Ernie had been impressed with Iowa City and all it had to offer on his first visit. Ellyn, however, was less enthusiastic about the prospect of moving where she would know exactly one person besides her husband.

Because she saw how enthusiastic Ernie was about the community and the job, Ellyn tried to persuade herself she would be fine if the move happened. Her sister, Mary, had lived in Omaha, Nebraska, for two years and survived, so Ellyn figured she could hack it. Ellyn told Ernie, "Honey, if you want to give it a whirl, let's go ahead. Just promise me that we get Larry settled down somewhere, because you seem to follow him wherever he goes."

With that, Ernie, Ellyn, and Gregg became Iowans.

Ernie and Ellyn returned to Iowa for a follow-up meeting with the university. The deal all but done, the department made arrangements with a realtor to show them places around Iowa City, but none were quite right. Realizing they were getting nowhere quick, the realtor asked what they were looking for.

One of the things that appealed to Ernie about Iowa was its rural landscape. His grandparents had run a dairy farm in New York, and he fondly remembered the summers he spent working there. "If you can find a place out in the country, I'd like to see that," Ernie asked.

"I've got just the place," the realtor replied.

They pulled up the lane to a hundred-year-old fixer upper with a huge dilapidated barn, an in-ground pool, and open farm ground as far as the eye could see. Ellyn said they would think about it. For Ernie, there was nothing to think about. He was sold.

"I may have beaten them out here by nine months, but I was still living in an apartment and not sure how much longer I wanted to be here. When Ernie saw that farm, he became more Iowan than I was," Larry admitted.

As they flew back to New Hampshire, Ellyn rested while Ernie sketched improvements to every floor of the old farm house on the back of his drink napkin. Ellyn opened an eye to see Ernie had scribbled the entire property on that dinky napkin. "You really like that Green Acres place, don't you?" Ellyn asked.

Ernie smiled at his exposed eagerness and said, "I really do."

She was a city girl and knew nothing about the country, but her husband's enthusiasm made her want to give it a try. "We literally moved to Iowa and bought the farm," Ernie said.

They were greeted back to the state by the blast-furnace heat of August. Ernie formally accepted his new position on staff with a firm handshake from Chairman Reg Cooper. "They didn't even have any paperwork for me to sign—the handshake sealed the deal, which I liked," Ernie said.

Reg accompanied the newest members of the orthopedic surgery family to the main branch of the First National Bank in downtown Iowa City. Ernie's new boss marched the couple past the bank receptionist, the president's personal secretary, and right into President Ralph Radcliffe's office without benefit of an appointment—or of knocking for that matter. He skipped a personal greeting and proclaimed, "These are my new friends, Ernie and Ellyn Found. They're buying a piece of ground out west of town. Take care of them." With that, Reg walked out.

After a few rudimentary financial questions and a quick discussion about the St. Louis Cardinals, a mortgage was issued to the couple without so much as a credit check.

The Founds arrived a couple of days ahead of the moving truck carrying their belongings. All they had with them on their first night in the house was a small suitcase of clothes and toiletries. The only air conditioning in the poorly insulated house was open windows, which provided no relief at all from the soaring daytime heat.

What made Ellyn really wonder what she had signed up for was the first time she caught a whiff of her neighbor's livestock. Hogs—or more specifically, what comes out of them—which created a pungent ammonia-like scent rural Iowans jokingly refer to as "Iowa perfume." The stench was intensified by the August heat and carried into the Founds' home on a steady westerly breeze, providing an inescapable invasion on their nostrils. Most native Iowans never come to appreciate the fragrance, so it was understandable the transplants from New England wouldn't either.

One of the selling points Ernie used to persuade Ellyn that farm living would be the life for her was the quiet. He told her how tranquil it would be without any cars or people, especially at night.

The first night they spent in the farmhouse proved Ernie partially right. With the sun down and the windows open, even without the benefits of air conditioning, they were quite comfortable. Lying on an old mattress left over from the previous owners, Ernie and Ellyn stared out the window at the brilliant stars shimmering against the jet black sky. It was so soothing that before long the exhausted couple's eyelids were too heavy to keep open.

Soon after Ernie and Ellyn faded into peaceful slumber, they were startled by a strange noise. It was outside, so Ernie got up and peeked out the window to investigate. He scanned the darkness but couldn't find the source. Then he heard it again. It sounded like metal banging against metal, a "clunk clunk."

"We couldn't figure it out. It went on all night long," Ernie said.

At first light, the red and blurry-eyed couple found the source of the mysterious noise. The drinking water for the hogs was kept in large, round, metal containers. Surrounding the bottom of the reservoirs were individual watering stations covered by hinged metal lids. When the hogs wanted a drink, which was often, they would simply drop their snouts under the extended lids, lift, and drink. When they had enough, they pulled out their snouts causing the metal lids to fall with such force they bounced off the metal frames before staying closed.

Feeling groggy, Ernie and Ellyn began to clean their long neglected house. The place was coated with a thick layer of dust and grime from ceiling to floor. They donned the grubbiest clothes they had, rearranged things, and vigorously wiped dirty surfaces. Cleaning what they could with limited materials, it was soon apparent they needed proper cleaning supplies and a mouse trap or two. They put Gregg in the car and drove to town.

The Founds packed a cart with supplies from Paul's Discount, a decades-old family-owned Iowa City store. The checkout clerk punched each item's cost into the register, finally the price of the last item entered, he announced their total was $80.34. Ellyn rummaged inside her purse for her checkbook but suddenly remembered she had forgotten it back at the house. The employee told them they would keep the items in the cart until they returned with a check.

As the Founds left the line and headed for the exit, a tiny elderly woman next in line offered to pay for them "Here's this complete stranger offering to buy this cart full of stuff for us. We were still in the same ratty work clothes from the day before, a dirty and sweaty mess. She probably wondered if we could actually pay her back," Ernie said. If she was concerned about being reimbursed, it wasn't enough to stop her from handing the clerk a check for the exact amount of the Founds' bill. The transaction complete, the older woman wrote her name and address on a piece of scrap paper and told the shocked couple to pay her back when they could. "We were just flabbergasted. This kind of thing would never happen in New York," Ernie said.

This random act of kindness had a profound impact on Ellyn and shifted her perception of Iowa. If Iowans were willing to open their hearts and wallets to complete strangers, this place had potential. To her, it was still a smelly and oppressively hot place, but the kindness of the people might just make up for the area's climatic shortcomings. Ellyn was intrigued enough to give Iowa City a chance.

Ernie and Ellyn settled into their new residence with one-year-old Gregg and went to work creating a family and a home. Ernie quickly established himself as a valuable addition to the orthopedic department. He loved everything about their new community. Iowa City had great restaurants, sports, entertainment, culture, and friendly people.

Making things more difficult for Ellyn was the location of their residence to the proximity of the city. Despite having an Iowa City address, Ernie and Ellyn lived in the country amongst farmers who were a bit leery of non-farming neighbors.

The Founds' closest neighbors were John and Janice Maier, who farmed the land to the west of them separated by a gravel road that was named after the Maier family. The Maier's initial apprehension of the Founds came from a disturbing trend of city slickers buying up acres of tillable ground because it was a trendy thing to do. This type of owner was generally a transplant from out of state and solely here because of a job relocation or promotion.

The outsiders bought up acres of property because they had high incomes and were looking for an investment. They had no intention of working the land like generations of Iowa farmers before them. This new breed of owner showed little if any respect for the land, some not even bothering to clean up downed trees or plant a garden.

The worst offenders bought the ground as nothing more than a way to earn a quick profit. They held the land until the ever expanding city got close enough for a developer to come calling with a generous offer. To a third generation farmer like John, selling farm ground for development was an unforgivable sin perpetuated by people with low morals.

John passed by the Founds' property several times a day during his daily routine and began to size up his new neighbors out of the corner of his eye. The farmer was cautiously optimistic when he drove by and, most times, saw Ernie toiling on the property wearing an old pair of jeans, a dirty t-shirt, and a worn and faded St. Louis Cardinals baseball cap. One time when John passed by he saw that Ernie had cleared brush and made burn piles. Another day, Ernie had chain-sawed, split, and stacked downed trees. The next day John's new neighbor mended fences.

Even if Ernie didn't plan on farming his ten-acres of land, in the farmer's eyes he at least had respect for it. That was enough to earn the doctor an introduction, so one day John pulled his well-used pickup into the Founds' drive.

Sitting in his truck, the weathered farmer gave Ernie the once over. The guy knew his way around a tool box and wasn't afraid to get his nails dirty, but until he proved otherwise, he was nothing more to John than the next pretentious doctor from out East to own the property.

The farmer's past experience with doctors led him to believe that they were self-important people who generally didn't even acknowledge neighbors with a wave as they drove by. In John's experience, if they did stoop to an introduction, they usually insisted the doctor moniker preceded their last names.

John slid out of his truck and crossed the yard. He would be just neighborly enough to extend his hand; the rest was up to Ernie. Ernie saw him coming and drove the post hole digger into the pile of dirt next to the hole. He pulled the ball cap from his head and wiped his sweaty brow with a rag dangling from his back pocket.

John strode up to the much larger man, stuck out his hand, and said his name. Ernie pulled his utility gloves off, tucked them under his arm, and smiled. "I grabbed his hand and shook it firmly," Ernie recalled. "Hi, John, I'm Ernie Found." A broad smile slowly spread across the farmer's rugged face, and he pumped Ernie's hand vigorously. "Goddammit, I had a feeling you weren't like all those other snooty doctors. It's good to meet you, Ernie," John said. From that moment on, a strong friendship was formed between the two families.

The Maiers became the best neighbors the Founds could ask for, offering an unsolicited hand in any number of situations. To Ernie and Ellyn, their neighbors' no nonsense, generous, nose-to-the-grindstone sensibilities represented everything unique and endearing about people from the Hawkeye state.

Found family atop Mt. Monadnock.

Ernie, Caroline, and Ellyn.

Caroline celebrates with teammates after a win at the state meet in 2010.

Caroline kisses trophy after winning Iowa City West High's first ever volleyball state title in 2010.

The 2011 volleyball team, in honor of Caroline, put her shoes under the first chair on the bench, which remained empty during the 2011 season.

Catharine Found at introductions with Trinity University teammates. The stands were filled with the remainder of the student body wearing purple, "Team Found" t-shirts provided by the university to honor Catharine and her family.

Caroline's volleyball teammates gathered around their leader's casket during her visitation. It was estimated that three thousand people came to the West High gym to pay their respects.

Volleyball teams from around the state came to Caroline's visitation, including cross-town rival, Iowa City High.

Ernie walks with Ellyn at Caroline's funeral. Pictured here, Ellyn is days from losing her battle with cancer. She ignored hospice advice to ride in a wheel chair and walked down the aisle of the church comforting others along the way.

Display at Caroline's funeral.

Teammates Shelly Stumpff and Olivia Fairfield embrace Ernie after winning the Spike.

Ernie and the seniors share a hug on senior night, 2011.

Aerial picture of the Found farm.

Gregg, Caroline, and Catharine in the back of Ernie's 1952 pickup.

Catharine, Gregg, and Caroline on the top of Mt. Monadnock, waiting with a special anniversary surprise for Ernie and Ellyn.

The painting was a gift from Ernie to Ellyn on their 25th anniversary. A special moment from each of their twenty-five years together was woven throughout the artwork.

Each time up the mountain, it was tradition for the Founds to kiss the US geographic marker, a brass disc embedded into the mountain to mark the top.

Ernie and Ellyn's wedding at Cathedral of the Pines in New Hampshire, 1985.

Ernie and Ellyn.

Ellyn's wedding photo.

Our group preparing to climb Mt. Monadnock at the one year memorial of Caroline and Ellyn's passing, August, 2012.

Ernie at the top of the mountain view.

Gregg, Ernie, and Catharine atop Mt. Monadnock during the one year memorial, 2012.

Memorials, Cathedral of the Pines, Rindge, New Hampshire.

Catharine and Gregg carry the cremated remains of Ellyn and Caroline to their final resting place, August, 2012.

Paying respects at the memorial.

Caroline at the Recker's being tutored by Mike.

Caroline at Camp Castaway, July 2011.

Players and coaches from the 2011 season gather by a bench dedicated to Caroline and Ellyn in downtown Iowa City, 2014.

Gregg, Catharine, and Ernie, Mt. Monadnock, 2014.

Crash site memorial for Caroline, 2012.

Found family

Caroline and Ellyn, 2011.

Live well
Laugh often
Love much

In Memory of #9
Caroline Slocum Found

Memorial stone beside the West High softball field.

Ernie with his hop vines, 2014.

Caroline "Line" on Mt. Monadnock.

Chapter 15
Ten-Acre Utopia

... But every house where Love abides
And Friendship is a guest,
Is surely home, and home-sweet-home:
For there the heart can rest.
—Henry Van Dyke, "A Home Song"

They who go feel not the pain of parting; it
is they who stay behind that suffer.
—Henry Wadsworth Longfellow

Nightfall, Ernie and Paul scooped their bags and walked through the maze of vehicles in the Eastern Iowa Airport parking lot until they located Paul's car. A dread filled Ernie's stomach when he realized it would be his first night alone at the farm since Ellyn's funeral. All that waited there was darkness and quiet. He filled the half-hour ride with a quarter-century of happy memories, hoping the mental images might ease the difficult transition waiting for him.

He thought about the first few years on the farm and the significant investments—monetary and sweat-equity—on structural and cosmetic improvements to the house. Many were just in time because in April 1989, Ellyn learned she was pregnant with the couple's second child. On December 21, Ernie, Ellyn, and Gregg received an early Christmas present when Catharine was born.

Ellyn settled into her role as homemaker and mother. While Ernie worked, she took care of everything either home or family related. She also became more connected to the community through their church, St. Andrew Presbyterian.

St. Andrew was where Ellyn met another couple new to the area, Boyd and Lisa Murray. Lisa and Ellyn had plenty in common. Lisa's daughter, Anna, was only five months younger than Catharine. "We both had kids in pre-school, and then we were pregnant at the same time with Leah and Caroline," Lisa explained. As it turned out, there was a group of five women at St. Andrew all pregnant. They watched, encouraged, and consoled each other throughout their pregnancies and eagerly waited to discover who would have their baby first.

Shared experiences created a special bond between Ellyn and Lisa. They got together after the older kids went to school so little Caroline and Leah could play while the moms had coffee. The families would get together in the summer for bonfires at the Found's and occasionally celebrated holidays together when both families stayed in town.

As their friendship flourished, Ellyn and Lisa became trusted confidants. When both of their mothers, at different times, battled long-term illnesses before they passed, each provided the other moral support.

Ernie, with the improvements inside the farmhouse completed, channeled his adventurer's spirit into fun outside activities with his kids. When six-year-old Gregg had his buddies over and they were looking for a place to play anything involving a ball, Ernie took them to the open field behind the pool. The rectangular patch of grass was shielded from the wind by trees on three sides and a five-foot high wooden pool fence on the other. Ernie told the boys it was their own

Field of Dreams, borrowing the title from the popular movie. He set up field parameters depending on whatever sport the boys played and even played with them from time to time.

The field became the unofficial sports arena. Gregg went to work with a can of green spray paint on the wooden fence. He officially christened the area "FIELD OF DREMS," writing as best he could in large block letter. "He took an awful teasing about his spelling, so he went outside with the paint can and squeezed in a skinny 'A,'" Ernie said.

By the time Gregg was twelve, the games on the farm became more complex and expansive. One day, he and his pals approached Ernie about transforming the ten acres into a golf course. Ernie loved the idea and told them they could use the mower if they wanted.

The boys mapped out a course, each hole unique with varying degrees of difficulty. They even had a water hazard—designing one of the holes to play over the pool. The hole they considered the crown jewel was a par four that ended in a freshly cut hay field some three-hundred yards away. To make greens, they dropped the mower deck to the lowest setting. The boys worked like fiends all day in the blazing sun.

Finished with their masterpiece, they toasted with glasses of ice water and started their inaugural round of the many they pre-scheduled over the course of the summer. The guys had planned tournaments, and at the end of the summer a champion would be crowned.

They used the mower as their golf cart and attached Ernie's grass catch, which was equivalent to a small hay bailer, to carry their clubs. The boys reached the tee box for the par four hole, lined up, and hammered their golf balls into the hay field. They piled onto the mower and headed down the fairway for their second shot. Going too fast over the uneven ground caused the grass catch to bounce violently up and down. As they argued with each other about whose tee shot went farthest, their clubs were jostled loose from their golf bags and fell on the ground in front of the weighty steel grass catch. The heavy attachment ran over their clubs, mangling them.

One of the boys finally looked back and was horrified at the sight of bent and broken clubs scattered on the ground behind them. "It looked like a tornado hit a golf club manufacturing company," Gregg said. Ernie, who had been working outside, watched as the dejected boys drove slowly past him. He raised an eyebrow at the sight of their ruined clubs tossed unceremoniously into the grass catch. As Gregg and his friends got older, Ernie would, for a chuckle, occasionally remind them of that day.

It wasn't all fun and games for the kids though. Ernie and Ellyn wanted them to learn responsibility and have a healthy respect for their environment. What better way to have them learn both lessons than to help with outside work. While Gregg spent countless hours on the mower cutting grass, the girls helped rake leaves and carry downed limbs to a burn pile. They helped split firewood, repair fence, and did some painting. Gregg and Catharine didn't always like it, especially when they got older and would have rather been with their friends, but Caroline never seemed to mind. "I think she rather enjoyed it," Ernie reflected.

To Caroline, the outside work meant time with her father. The chores could be hard sometimes, so Ernie tried to mix in a little fun. Occasionally a mound of leaves he gathered found their way onto Caroline's head instead of added to the pile. Sometimes they would dive into a pile of leaves before burning it.

Ellyn had to watch Ernie and Caroline like a hawk when they did any outdoor work together, especially after the fence incident.

During an otherwise normal autumn day, Ernie and Caroline had made countless leaf piles on the grass outside to burn. It was blustery, and the experienced Ernie knew a controlled burn could get out of control quickly in the stiff and shifting Iowa winds, so he took the necessary precautions, putting the piles in a field away from the house, on the leeward side of the barn so the structure would help block the wind. He had gathered the burn material, and it was Caroline's job to rake it into a tight pile and light it.

The fire sufficiently burning, Ernie and Caroline went about collecting more piles. While gathering leaves the wind shifted ever so slightly, not enough for Ernie to notice, but just enough to change the direction of the flames. The pair was having a great time until Ellyn charged out of the house yelling, "Ernie, the fence! Look at what you're doing to the fence!" Ernie looked over to see his brand new, expensive, synthetic fence warping and melting under the intense heat of the flames. Ellyn retold the story for a laugh many times after the incident, although it took a while for the incident to move into the funny column.

On the eve of the new millennium, while many people stacked provisions in anticipation for the world to shut down, fearing an unforeseen computer glitch, the Founds faced a much less complicated, but no less difficult decision. The huge barn next to the house was so run-down from years of neglect there were questions about its structural integrity.

At the time, the barn was only used to house Ernie's pickup, mower, tractor, and a small workshop. The rest of it was wasted space. "We either had to tear it down or put a ton of money back into it to build it back up to what it was," Gregg explained.

Ernie, a kid at heart, saw an opportunity to transform the musty old outbuilding into the ultimate teenage hangout. Ellyn saw it as a questionable use of their hard-earned money. Ernie's justification to his wife was sound. He wanted their home to be the official hangout spot for their kids and their friends. Gregg and Catharine were getting older, and he would rather they spend the money to fix up the barn a little bit and have the kids and their friends hang out there instead of in town where they could get themselves into trouble.

His argument swayed her, but she was still reluctant. When he asked her, "Why," she told him was the term, "a little bit." A little bit wasn't in his lexicon. She knew when her husband took on a project like this he had a tendency to do it big—and big in most cases meant expensive. She thought, specifically, of Caroline's request for a tree house. Instead of building a two-by-four ladder on the trunk of a tree leading to a platform supported by branches, Ernie had an actual miniature house built, complete with windows, a door, and furniture inside.

Ellyn ran the pros and cons of Ernie's barn idea. Although it would be expensive, on the upside, she knew if he designed the barn it would be fun and get significant use. So she ultimately gave her blessing.

Once she agreed and the project started, it moved along rapidly. Ernie had the outside of the two-story barn completely restored from ground to roof. Then he went to work on the inside. "Like any construction project, the second bill is higher than the first, and the third higher than the second," Gregg recalled. Since Ellyn was in charge of the family's finances, she was the one vetting the incoming bills, and her eyes bulged with each one she would get.

Ernie, true to his word, made full use of the interior and had something for everyone. On the first floor, Ernie transformed the workshop into a hybrid game and sports memorabilia room, a place to come and just hang out. He had a mixture of Hawkeye and Cardinals items— signed balls, bats, and replica rings from every Cardinals' World Series championship on display in cases. There were Hawkeye and West

High signs and posters on dark and inviting walls. For the winters, he had a wood-burning stove at one end of the game room stocked with plenty of wood.

At the top of a wooden staircase leading to the second floor loft was a rope swing roughly eight feet above the concrete level. Putting the wooden seat between the legs, one sits back and yells, "Clear out," and takes a leap of faith. The traveler moves in a downward arc through the air Tarzan style, on a rapid ascent towards a garage door opener suspended from the ceiling. For an added element of danger, Ernie attached a small bell to the back of the opener. Only the bravest release their two-handed death grip on the rope, reach out, and bang the bell before shooting back towards the jump off point. To this day, no one, young or old, hasn't been grinning from ear to ear upon completing their ride.

One of Ernie's fondest memories of the swing was when five year-old Caroline professed her desire to take a ride. Little Caroline stood poised at the jump-off point, which probably looked like jumping off of the edge of the Grand Canyon to her. Ernie released the seat, and Line sailed through the air, initially frightened out of her wits. The first ride complete, a now confident Caroline requested another one, then another. They spent an hour out there until she decided she had conquered the swing.

When Caroline became a teenager, she used the barn in much the same fashion as her brother and sister. She would have the volleyball girls over during the season or host her softball teammates after a big win. Line also used the barn as a fun and safe place for kids who otherwise had nothing but negative influences in their lives. Line appreciated she had loving and caring parents, a roof over her head, good food to eat, and a plethora of friends. She shared her blessings with those less fortunate than her, regularly bringing kids on the margins of school and society into her fold. "She wanted them to feel as blessed as she did," Brez remembered.

Ernie converted the second floor into a basketball court. Most dads would have stopped at a hand-painted basketball floor and a cheap Plexiglas backboard with a breakaway rim, but not Ernie. Surrounding the court, high on the walls were colorfully painted plywood cutouts of cheering fans.

When West High upgraded the scoreboard in the gym, Ernie bought the old one and put it in the rafters of the barn so the kids could keep score in style. To complete the court ambiance and to add a little flair, Ernie put up St. Louis Cardinals, Buffalo Bills, and Boston Celtics banners along with the 2010 West High Volleyball State Championship. He also honored Gregg and Catharine's colleges with North Carolina Tar Heels and Trinity Tigers flags.

The Found Farm became more than just a home—it was transformed into an institution. It became, for many, a refuge and a symbol of friendship, safety, companionship, acceptance, adventure, exploration, fun, and even love.

On September 3, 1994, under the overhanging branches of a towering silver birch, Larry Marsh took Linda as his wife. "It was Larry's idea to get married at the farm," Linda declared. Ernie and Ellyn unanimously agreed to his request, joking with him that they would do anything to marry off their friend.

While a local magistrate performed the ceremony, Larry smiled and reflected on the profound impact the Founds' place had on his life. Prior to dating his wife, the farm became the one constant in Larry's otherwise untethered existence in Iowa City. He had never committed to the community and spent his first few years with one foot out the door. "I came here as a thirty-one-year-old, exclusively for the department's reputation. When they came and put down roots, it made my life here more than just a sojourn. I had no grounding here. When they came, I did," Larry said.

Paul slowed his car and exited Highway 218. When Paul applied the break, Ernie's body moved forward and brought him back to reality. Paul negotiated the gravel road and finally turned into Ernie's drive, the vehicle's headlights illuminating the farm house. Ernie shifted uncomfortably in his seat as Paul stopped by the back door. Worried about his friend, Paul offered to stay the night. Ernie breathed deep, thanked him, and said he would be fine. Standing on the rock drive, he watched as the tail lights on Paul's vehicle faded into the night.

Ernie stood alone in the darkness and stared at the back door. He always knew what made this place special was not how it looked outside or the furnishings inside, but who occupied it with him. With that premise in mind, the full weight of walking into the empty home pressed down on him and rooted him where he stood. The place that used to be so warm and inviting was now cold and lifeless. All that waited for him were memories of a happier life. He wasn't sure if he could bear to face them.

After what seemed an eternity, Ernie mustered the courage to walk through the entry way to the kitchen. As he walked in, two questions entered his brain: "What do I do now? Where do I go from here?"

Knowing he couldn't stand in the kitchen all night, he reluctantly forged ahead. He decided to go directly to his bedroom and not look around for fear of being noticed by his happier past. "It was like I was picked up for DWI, and I didn't want anyone to recognize me as they led me away in handcuffs," Ernie admitted.

Ernie moved through the house as if his own sadness were in hot pursuit. He thought if he could just get to his room and shut the door before the rush of emotion caught up, he would be okay. He soon discovered that no matter how fast he moved, his grief, an unwelcome intruder, caught up with him.

Ernie sobbed as he sat alone in the bed he had shared with Ellyn for so many years. It was a perfect time for him to question God's motives. Who would have blamed him? It seemed if anyone had the right, it was him.

"The first night was very, very hard," Ernie admitted. "I wasn't feeling as lonely as I was feeling ripped off. It felt surreal, like it really wasn't happening. It seemed like any minute they would come through the door talking and laughing."

Ernie did converse with God on that first night, but not to question the Almighty's plan. He looked skyward and asked, "Who am I crying for?"

The answer didn't come right away, but as Ernie sat there in the dark, sadness engulfed him. God did reply. He wasn't just crying for himself. There were many people saddened by Caroline and Ellyn's deaths, and he was crying for all of them.

Chapter 16
Hopeless Romantics

You and I will make each night a first
Every day a beginning
Spirits rise and their dance is unrehearsed
They warm and excite us, cause we have the brightest love.
—Paul Williams, "Evergreen"

Romance is the glamour which turns the dust
of everyday life into a golden haze.
—Elynor Glyn

Daybreak was a welcome sight for Ernie. He hoped sunlight would make being in the house tolerable. The interior was Ellyn's domain, and therefore her stamp was on everything. He walked around from room to room as if he were in a museum. Everything—family pictures on the wall, the kitchen wallpapered with her favorite sayings, even the furniture—reminded him of her and why he loved her.

Ernie and Ellyn were often described as a fantasy couple by those who witnessed expressions of their love. That label can be a lot to live up to, even for hopeless romantics. "It wasn't a fantasy in the make believe sense, in their eyes they were meant to be together—to marry, have kids, and to live on a farm in Iowa," Larry explained. "So the few times they had difficulties were tougher for them because they almost felt like they weren't living up to the fantasy their lives together was meant to be."

It takes a group of hopeless romantics to understand what Ernie and Ellyn had together. Caroline's teenaged female friends viewed the Founds' marriage as the model by which all other marriages should be judged. "Out of any of our parents' marriages, that's the one you would want," Kelley confessed.

While in the kitchen, Ernie opened the cupboard looking for tea and smiled when he saw stacks of canned vegetables. Most had at least one companion can. Ellyn ran the family's finances like they were living on a pauper's salary, not a surgeon's. She was an eagle-eyed bargain hunter, always looking for the best deals on everything from gas and clothes, to school supplies, or groceries. They had so many cans because she waited until a grocery store had two-for-one sales and then stocked up.

Ernie changed his mind on the tea and shut the cupboard. Once the cupboard was shut, he looked through the window and noticed the barn door was open. Through the doorway, he caught a glimpse of the front end of his red 1952 Chevy pickup.

The pickup was one of a few extravagant gifts Ellyn had bought him. It was out of character for the couple of some means to lend themselves to excessive spending on each other. When they did spend money it was usually in the form of gifts and normally the result of some milestone or accomplishment—which was the case when, shortly after they arrived in Iowa, Ellyn bought Ernie the vintage truck.

It was well known by Ellyn, and anyone else who listened to Ernie, he wanted a 1952 Chevy pickup. It had to be a 1952 because that was the year he was born. Chevrolet trucks visually appealed to him more than others.

Ellyn even had his sales pitch memorized about why she should buy him the truck. He asked her to imagine all the wonderful times their family could have with it. In the summer they could jump in, go to town, and get ice cream from their favorite ice cream parlor. It would come in handy for tailgating before Iowa Hawkeye football games. On crisp autumn days, they could bundle up and jump in the back and go for a spin around the gravel roads, sipping homemade hot apple cider.

As wonderful as Ernie made it sound, Ellyn outwardly dismissed the pickup as frivolous, all the while biding her time until she found the exact truck and the perfect moment to give one to him.

The perfect time presented itself when Ernie prepared to take his orthopedic surgery oral boards. While Ernie spent months studying, Ellyn found a 1952 Chevy pickup advertised in the paper. She went to a classic car dealership in Cedar Rapids to check out what she hoped was the perfect gift for her husband.

While Ellyn inspected the pickup on the showroom floor, a salesman sauntered over. Confident he had an easy sale, he wished the price on the sticker was higher. The salesman clearly didn't know who he was dealing with and was about to get a lesson in underestimating a person based on first appearance. Ellyn may have been charitable in other aspects of her life, but negotiating the price of products and services wasn't one of them.

The self-assured salesman told Ellyn, in a tone indicating he was doing her a huge favor, he could let her have the truck for $1,500 and not a penny less. He watched with great anticipation as Ellyn reached in her purse. She pulled eight crisp one-hundred dollar bills out of her purse and countered, "Listen, I'd like to buy the truck from you. I've got $800 with me. I'm either leaving with this fixer upper that still needs a paint job or the money, you choose." The flabbergasted salesman didn't know what hit him. After a few futile attempts to get her to come up in price, he grudgingly relented. She handed him the $800, got her paperwork, and left with the truck.

After Ernie took the boards, the family decided to get out of town in order to peel away some of the stress they were feeling waiting for his results. They went for a mini-camping trip in upstate New York.

Ellyn had asked her neighbor, Janice Maier, if she would take in their mail while they were gone, which she happily agreed to do. She also asked if an envelope from the American Board of Orthopedic Surgery arrived, if she would please open it and call immediately with the results. Janice called Ellyn later in the week and said Ernie passed the boards with flying colors. Ellyn made a few phone calls to put operation "Chevy Surprise" into action.

The family drove sixteen hours from New York back to Iowa. They arrived home around dinner time, exhausted and hungry. Ellyn said she was too tired to cook, so she would go get them a pizza if Ernie would unpack.

She jumped in her well-used Mazda and headed to town. About ten minutes later the phone began ringing. Ernie answered the phone, and it was Ellyn saying when she got to Godfather's Pizza, smoke started rolling out from under the hood of her car. There was also a strange hissing noise, and now it wouldn't start. A ten-year-old car with high miles, Ernie had expected something like this to happen for quite some time. He loaded Gregg into the more reliable car and went to pick up Ellyn.

Ernie pulled into the lot behind the pizza place and found the Mazda with the hood up and his good friend, Ted Wernimont, checking the engine. Ted had grease smeared on his face and was holding a wrench. When asked, Ted said he had stopped in for pizza and saw Ellyn having car trouble, so thought he would lend a hand.

Ernie had no way of knowing this was all a well-crafted ruse. Ted was a willing accomplice recruited by Ellyn from the outset. Ernie's gift had been stored in Ted's garage five months. It was Ted who drove the vintage vehicle, at Ellyn's behest, to the parking lot before Ernie's arrival, and parked it in a conspicuous spot.

Ted's prognosis for the Mazda was dim at best. Ernie feigned interest, but he wasn't really paying attention. His focus was drawn like a magnet to a shiny, red pickup parked across the lot. Try as he may to concentrate on the problem at hand, Ernie's eyes were involuntarily pulled back to the pickup.

Ernie wasn't going to let the opportunity slip by to remind his wife this was the very type of truck he hoped to own. "Ellyn, you see that pickup truck? That's just the kind of truck I'd like to have some day."

Ellyn pulled a set of keys out of her purse, tossed them to Ernie, who snatched them out of the air. "If you really like it that much, the truck's yours," she said.

Once Ernie had his '52 Chevy, he made good on his promises, explaining, "We had more damn fun with that pickup truck. We would take the kids for ice cream. Ellyn's mom was an invalid, so when she came to visit, we put her in the back of that thing and drove the back roads. We used it for tailgating."

Once this memory faded, Ernie found himself sitting in the driver's seat of the truck, no idea how he made it from the house to the barn. He climbed out and opened the hood, a cracked engine block in 2006 rendered the truck unusable. Though he hadn't gotten around to getting it fixed, it didn't stop him from pushing the pickup into the front yard each December and having the kids help decorate it with lights and a stuffed snowman driver.

Ernie went back into the house to answer some emails. Walking through the living room, he passed the painting of the *American Gothic* on the mantle above the fireplace. He turned on the silver tract lighting to illuminate it. His eyes welled with tears.

Try as he might, Ernie always felt his gifts for Ellyn never quite lived up to her gifts to him. 2010 was their 25th anniversary, and he really wanted to step up his gift-giving game. Twenty-five years of marriage is a milestone that not many couples experience. Because of the magnitude of this anniversary, along with the quarter-century of amazing gifts Ellyn had presented to him, Ernie wanted to get his wife the gift of all gifts, and more than anything, he wanted it to be a surprise.

Ellyn was an art enthusiast, so Ernie decided on a piece of art to commemorate their anniversary. The self-admitted procrastinator was proud of himself. In February, a full five months before his anniversary Ernie called a Cedar Rapids artist. "I checked out his website, and all I saw were motorcycle tanks that he'd painted. The work was extremely intricate though so I set up a visit," Ernie said. The artist asked Ernie to bring along a wedding photo album for possible inspiration.

During their first meeting, the artist recommended he pick out a wedding photo for him to spray on an aluminum canvas he had built. The men poured over the Founds' wedding photo albums, but nothing really jumped out at either of them.

Although uninspired by the photos, he was captivated with all of the wonderful stories Ernie told him about the couple's lives together. The artist told Ernie they had such an iconic marriage and family that maybe they needed to go in another direction. He had an *American Gothic* print by Grant Wood in his workspace and floated the idea of painting Ernie and Ellyn's heads in place of the farmer and spinster daughter. Ernie was concerned it would end up looking like a caricature, and the artist agreed. They settled on the Grant Wood classic, but with twenty-five special moments from their marriage discreetly blended into the painting.

Ernie is a man of ideas. Because his ideas are grand, the planning and implementation of them are where he sometimes runs into obstacles. The painting was no exception.

Obstacle No. 1—Ellyn was in charge of the checkbook. The artist needed to be paid as he went along. Canceled checks for large amounts to someone Ellyn didn't know would bring questions.

Ernie told her to not worry about it, so she promptly Googled the name on the canceled check and found an art gallery. Ernie anticipated this and hoped she would gain just enough information to realize that her anniversary gift would be some sort of art piece and leave it at that, which she did.

Obstacle No. 2—time. Ernie woefully underestimated the amount of time this type of project required. He assumed starting an anniversary gift five months prior to the date put him way ahead of the game. In most instances that would be true, but it wasn't nearly enough time to complete a large piece of art, sprayed to completion on a blank aluminum canvas the artist hand built.

When July came, all Ernie had to give his wife for their anniversary was a promise that something really good was coming and he was hopeful it would be ready any day.

"Any day," turned into weeks and months. Autumn arrived and leaves changed colors, then fell from the trees. The weather grew colder, Thanksgiving came and went, and Ernie still had no gift. Snow flew, and the '52 Chevy was towed to the front yard and decorated with Christmas light. Gifts were exchanged on Christmas morning, none of which was Ellyn's anniversary present. The Founds' rang in the New Year at home. As they sang "Auld Lang Syne," the irony of the translated song title, "Days Gone By" wasn't lost on Ernie as he stared at the blank wall where Ellyn's painting was supposed to be.

Around Valentine's Day, Ernie got a call that the painting was about a week from completion. He put silver track lighting on the ceiling in preparation. Unfortunately, he forgot to consider the amount of time and effort Ellyn had spent picking out the perfect brass accents for the room. The clashing lights would be referred to by Ellyn for the rest of her days as, "Those ugly lights that go with nothing."

This brought Ernie to his third and final obstacle, getting Ellyn out of the house so the painting could be hung. He recruited fellow art enthusiast and family friend, Jennifer Whitmore, "I filled her in and even took her to Cedar Rapids to see the painting. She assured me that Ellyn would be out of the way."

As the completion date of the painting drew near, Ernie was on his way home from work one night and feeling pretty good about himself. He was going to pull off the surprise, albeit seven months late. It would be payback for all of the great gifts she got him without his knowledge.

He thought all his hopes were dashed when he got home and saw an 8-inch-by-12-inch framed picture of *American Gothic* conspicuously placed on the mantle of the fireplace. It was right on the wall where he planned to place the painting. The track lighting was even on, highlighting it. Ernie was fuming because the only person who knew about his gift besides Catharine, who would never let Ellyn know, was Jennifer Whitmore.

He stifled his anger and played it cool when asking Ellyn about the framed picture. She told him she thought it looked nice there. "She knew she had me, and now she was busting my balls about it. The whole time I'm thinking, 'Damn you, Jennifer Whitmore,'" Ernie admitted.

He wasn't going to give Ellyn the satisfaction of discovering another gift before she got it. In reality, she had no idea. It was just a coincidence, and he was being paranoid. The only thing she knew was she hated the silver track lighting and she was letting him have it. "Why silver? Didn't you even bother to look around the room? It goes with nothing in here," she kept reminding him. This did nothing for his confidence as the arrival date got closer. His only thought was, "This painting better be worth it for the cost and the dozen or so fifty-mile round trips to Cedar Rapids and back."

The day arrived, and after numerous assurances that Jennifer could be trusted, Ernie allowed her to get Ellyn out of the house. To make the unveiling extra special, he went to a florist and grabbed a box or two of rose petals, creating a beautifully fragrant red walkway right to the painting. Everything in its proper place, he phoned Jennifer, who brought Ellyn back to the house.

When Ellyn came home, she was completely surprised. After a brief explanation from Ernie, she went to work looking for the hidden treasures in her new piece of art. "I was so excited and impatient for her to find the twenty-five things that I kept giving her clues. She finally shooed me away. She wanted to find them on her own," Ernie said.

Ellyn closely studied the painting. There were times she had to do a double take to find a particularly well-hidden hidden item. Upon first glance, the farmer's shoulder looked as if something has been spilled on it. She leaned in and saw the outline of the crescent shaped island of Santorini, Greece, where the couple celebrated their 10th anniversary. A funny looking shadow in the spinster's smock was actually a picture of the 1952 pickup truck. Korean writing shown sewn into the sections of the farmer's bib overalls represented the trip they took to Korea. Ernie translated it for her, "It says, 'Happy 25th wedding anniversary' on this one, and 'May our love last forever' here." She drew her focus on the three tines of the pitchfork in the farmer's hand and saw the children's names and birth dates, one on each. After finding each hidden item of significance, Ellyn said it truly was the perfect anniversary gift and worth the wait.

Chapter 17
The Easter Bombshell

When we meet real tragedy in life, we can react in
two ways—either by losing hope and falling into self-
destructive habits, or by using the challenge to find our
inner strength...I have been able to take this second way.
—Dalai Lama

Loving a child doesn't mean giving in to all his
whims; to love him is to bring out the best in
him, to teach him to love what is difficult.
—Nadia Boulanger

Ernie didn't know on Easter Sunday, 2011, that in less than five months
he would lose both his youngest daughter and his wife. Ernie sat in
front of the congregation with the rest of the St. Andrew Presbyterian Church Brass Choir and felt gut-punched. Try as he might, he
couldn't draw a proper breath to play the French horn as he had since
junior high school. Each time he looked at Caroline and Ellyn sitting
in the pew, tears blurred his vision and a growing lump closed his
throat. The best he could do was press his lips to the mouthpiece as
his mind rambled.

A sideways glance at his wife, and Ernie remembered she had encouraged him to be involved with the brass choir in the first place. A dozen years earlier, Ernie's parents had visited and brought his old French horn. Coincidently, the very next Sunday, a little blurb in the church bulletin mentioned St. Andrew was seeking players for a new brass choir. "Ellyn circled it, nudged me, and said, 'Here's your chance to play again.'" Admittedly, he never would have done it without a push from her.

Ernie's thoughts flashed forty-eight hours earlier to Good Friday. He and Ellyn sat together in Dr. Don McFarland's office, arguably one of the best oncologists in the area. Dr. McFarland splayed his fingers across Ellyn's medical chart and confirmed Ernie's worst fears—Ellyn had pancreatic cancer. He explained they would start treatments right away, but realistically ninety-eight percent of people diagnosed with this type of cancer died in months, not years.

As they walked into the waiting room after the appointment, Ellyn was thankful no one else knew, because it would allow them to tell people on their own timeline. The consoling thought disappeared when she saw their friend, Vicki Burketta, sitting in the waiting room. The minute their eyes locked, Ellyn knew her strong-willed friend would need to be told something.

"What are you doing here?" Vicki asked.

Ellyn stumbled and mumbled her way through a half-hearted excuse.

Vicki cut her off, "Don't give me that. What are you doing here?"

The Founds were first introduced to Vicki when they took Catharine, and later Caroline, to the University of Iowa math professor for tutoring. Vicki cultivated a fast friendship with Ernie and Ellyn. When Vicki had been diagnosed with cancer six months earlier, Ernie, Ellyn, and Caroline were right there to help. Vicki was a proud woman and, like the Founds, was a much better giver than receiver. Each time Ernie mowed her yard or Ellyn and Caroline helped her rearrange the Mickey Mouse collection that filled her basement, she vowed to pay them back.

A sudden crescendo from the brass choir snapped Ernie back to the present. He saw the agony spread across his wife's face and felt completely helpless. She was suffering from a disease that would probably take her life in months, and there was nothing he could do about it but pray. His eyes shifted to Caroline, who smiled back at him. His heart ached at the thought of his sweet little girl getting the life altering news about her mother. What made things even more sad was that mother and daughter had endured a couple of rocky years and now were closer than ever.

2011 started very promising for the whole family. Caroline was midway through her junior year, and the volleyball team had won the state title. Gregg excelled in his analyst job at ESPN, where he fed statistics into the ears of the on-air talent, making them seem much smarter about sports than they are in reality. Catharine was in her junior year at Trinity University in San Antonio, Texas. Not only was she an excellent student and stand-out volleyball player, but she was a productive and philanthropic member of the local community. She was also a front runner to win the college's prestigious Community Service Award.

However, the most glaring improvement for the Founds in 2011 was between Ellyn and Caroline. The pair had spent most of Caroline's first two years of high school in an assortment of disagreements. They argued about phone usage, driving habits, her boyfriend, and Caroline not being where she was supposed to be.

Their average-level teenager/parent differences paled in comparison to the disagreements about her grades. Ernie and Ellyn both came from highly educated families and placed a premium on their children excelling in the classroom. High school came easier for Gregg and Catharine. Caroline struggled in her studies, particularly with math. Combine her learning obstacles with a preference for social life over studies, and it was not surprising she brought home B's and C's on her report cards rather than the A's her parents expected.

Ellyn's determination, that there is a solution for any problem, sent her on a dogged quest for any motivational tools, medicine, tutoring, or therapy to get Line as enthused about academics as she was about life outside the classroom. Ernie was okay with the tutoring, and even with the medication for her attention deficit, but only in moderation. Initially these methods created an uptick in Caroline's grades, but eventually they slipped again when her priorities shifted back to being friend-focused. The emotional roller coaster Caroline and Ellyn were on caused a larger and larger divide between them. "It hurt Ellyn deeply," Ernie said. "She sometimes felt like the only thing she was doing was harping on Caroline."

Ernie became an intermediary between mother and daughter. From Caroline's perspective, her mother placed more importance on academics, where she felt inferior to her brother and sister. She would often say to her father that when her mother always compared her to Gregg and Catharine, she felt like the dummy of the family.

Caroline thought her efforts in athletics, where she decided to make her mark, were largely under-appreciated by her mother. Caroline conveniently ignored the fact that Ellyn never missed even one of Line's athletic contests and was always directly involved with her teams. From Ellyn's view—which was confirmed by many of Line's teachers—Caroline had tons of potential, but she seemed to let exterior distractions get in her way.

When Caroline earned poor grades, Ellyn and Ernie removed the distractions by grounding Caroline from her phone and the computer. Caroline saw this as taking away the lifeline to her friends, some of whom relied on her for advice with their problems. She thought the punishments were less about her grades and more an attempt to control her personal life. She felt her parents' actions forced her to go behind their backs just to get some quality time with her friends.

What never wavered between mother and daughter was their love for one another. Their relationship was strained, but never in jeopardy of shutting down. "I heard them in Caroline's room many nights talking together, yelling at each other, and crying together about things that there was no way I could talk to her about," Ernie said. "Ellyn always made sure Caroline knew she was in her corner. There were several times I heard Ellyn empathize with Caroline by saying, 'I can imagine that must have been very difficult for you.'"

Caroline's relationship with her parents took a bigger hit when they forced her to stop seeing her longtime boyfriend. She and Josh Anderson had dated since the eighth grade. When the couple got to high school, Caroline embraced new experiences—taking in as many music, club, and sports offerings as her schedule would allow. Through extra curricular activities, Caroline made more and more friends with both genders.

Josh, however, focused all his attention on Caroline. Even worse, he translated her growing crop of friends into an unfounded fear that he was losing her to another boy. He countered with the only weapon he felt he had—control. Josh wanted to know where and whom she was with at all times. If she said she would be at work, he would drive by and check. He checked her text and email messages. Innocent correspondence with guy friends and workout partners were misinterpreted as romantic intentions. "He became obsessed with Caroline," Ernie said. "When we found out, we became concerned about Caroline's safety. We had a meeting with his parents and told them that we didn't want Josh seeing Caroline any longer."

Josh wasn't willing to give up Caroline easily. They continued to stay in touch electronically, so Ernie and Ellyn had Caroline's cell number changed and made her create a new email address. During all this, Line's grades took another turn downward.

When conventional methods of improving her daughter's grades failed, Ellyn looked into mental and emotional aspects. Ellyn suspected her daughter was depressed and wanted the family to attend therapy.

There were several issues going on in her daughter's life that supported Ellyn's depression theory. In addition to lower grades and losing her boyfriend, Caroline was not where she wanted to be athletically. She received only sporadic playing time on the softball team, which had more to do with her missing softball games because of family summer vacations than her ability as a player. The coach benched her two games for every practice she missed, no matter the reason. "While we understood Caroline was committed to the team, at the same time she was on summer break, and we liked to travel as a family," Ernie said. "I thought it was a bit heavy handed on the coach's part."

Line had a bumpy ride her sophomore year with volleyball too. She was thrilled when Coach Brez brought her up to varsity. It was a mixed blessing, however. She was kept on the lower squad of the Iowa Rockets volleyball club that summer. The Iowa Rockets are a regional club pulling from four eastern Iowa counties. The club's top team is nationally ranked every year and a feeder program for Division One volleyball programs around the country. Caroline wanted to get a Division One volleyball scholarship and knew the Rockets would be the best way to do this.

Graduation had created a vacancy at the back-up setter position on the Rockets top squad, and the coaches had to make the difficult decision about which setter to bring up. It came down to Caroline or her close friend, Erin Muir, who played for cross-town rival City High. Both sophomores were loaded with potential, but the club ultimately decided Erin was farther along at the position. So the Rockets brought her up instead of Caroline. Adding to her bumpy year.

The rift between mother and daughter spilled over into Ellyn's relationship with Ernie when he disagreed with her assessment of Caroline's emotional state. "Ellyn thought she was depressed. I wasn't so sure," Ernie said. "She would sometimes criticize me that I didn't look into it as much as I should have." This caused some of the strongest differences between Ernie and Ellyn during their marriage. "We all went to counseling, but I think it was pretty evident it was really for Caroline and Ellyn."

The therapy may not have necessarily helped with Ellyn's intended purpose, but it paved the way for mother and daughter to find some common ground on issues standing in the way of the close relationship they were used to. Each had to give a little, which is particularly difficult for teenagers.

After Ellyn's cancer diagnosis, Ernie and Ellyn put their own feelings aside and were more worried about the best way to inform the kids. They understood, just one stray email or text message, and their children might hear about Ellyn from someone other than themselves. In the interest of expediency, they considered telling each of them, one at a time. This strategy presented one main problem, whoever they notified first would immediately want to call the others. They decided to wait and tell all of them at the same time. This strategy would be easier said than done—with Catharine away at college, Gregg working in Connecticut, and Caroline still at home.

This plan had several complications. Catharine was on break from school, kayaking with a group of friends in the Gulf of Mexico. Gregg had flown to the West Coast to link up with some high school buddies, a trip he had planned months in advance. They decided to wait Sunday evening and contact each child one at a time.

When the time came, Ernie and Ellyn first sat Caroline down at the kitchen table and told her about her mother's condition. She understandably fell to pieces. One at a time, they called Catharine and Gregg and gave them the news.

Caroline was distraught and called Mike and Barb Recker. At Ernie's request, they were also the first place she went, outside of her own home, for consolation. Ernie drove Caroline, and her friend, Adrienne Jensen, to the Reckers. "We pretty much hugged them for two hours," Barb said.

When they got news of Ellyn's illness, the Recker kids came to the house. Charlie was the last to know. When he arrived it only took one look at his adoptive sibling's face to know something was wrong.

Two days later, Ellyn was having a liver biopsy, and Caroline wanted to be at the hospital for the procedure. Unfortunately for her, hospital policy denied someone her age admittance. "I got a call that day from West High that Caroline was having a really hard time not knowing anything. She asked me to come get her from school. I cleared it with Ernie and then gave Amy Kanellis a call," Barb said.

When Barb pulled up in front of the school to pick up Caroline, Charlie was right there with her. Barb immediately knew why. The prior April, Charlie had lost his favorite cousin. A fifteen-year-old shot in the head by a gang member in Chicago. The death crushed Charlie, and he was thankful to the Reckers for being there to help soften the blow. Determined to pay it forward, Charlie insisted on coming with them.

When it came to riding in the Recker's car, Charlie always occupied the front passenger seat. On that day, however, Charlie opened the front door for Caroline to sit in the front. His gesture wasn't lost on Barb, and she spent much of the drive to her house wiping her eyes. Charlie consoled an emotional Line with reassuring pats on the back. "He kept telling her, 'It's okay, we'll get through this together,'" Barb recalled.

Barb made the pair lunch and afterward pulled some recorders out of a long forgotten bag in a closet. She wanted to do anything to get Caroline's mind off of her mother's condition. Barb knew all she had to do was introduce the idea of something as goofy as playing a recorder to Caroline and she would turn it into some kind of an imaginary adventure.

Soon the two elite athletes, leaders on varsity sports teams at one of the premiere high schools in the country, each the epitome of cool, were playing goofy tunes on a glorified child's toy. Once they had their timing down, Charlie suggested they start a band and take their act on the road. Caroline agreed and, as was customary with her, took the idea to a whole new level. She said, "Big E" (Ernie) could play the keyboards. Line even named the fictitious band: Big "E" and the Nuggets. Barb let them down gently when she suggested that the one song in their repertoire, "Hot Cross Buns" probably wasn't enough material to start a world tour.

As Ernie and Ellyn notified family and close friends, the waves of worry and sympathy began—which was exactly what Ellyn wanted to avoid. Concerned people in her life continually asked what they could do for her. She didn't want people hovering over her, so in typical fashion, she politely declined any help for herself. She asked people to look out for Caroline, who was wallowing in the uncertainty of her mother's future.

With family and close friends notified, Ellyn began a fierce battle with cancer. When Ellyn started treatments, Vicki got her chance to pay the Founds back for all of the assistance they had given her, and she delivered. She was by Ellyn's side every step of the way offering encouragement, jokes, even scheduling her own treatments at the same times. The support Ellyn received from Vicki was invaluable because she wasn't going through it alone. She had someone right there who understood all the physical, mental, and emotional challenges.

No matter how miserable the treatments were, Ellyn refused to reduce her schedule and wanted life to go on as normally as possible for her family heading into the summer of 2011.

Chapter 18
Soul Searching

You never know how much you really believe anything until its
truth or falsehood becomes a matter of life and death to you.
—C.S. Lewis, *A Grief Observed*

For the meaning of life differs from man to man, from day
to day and from hour to hour. What matters, therefore, is
not the meaning of life in general but rather the specific
meaning of a person's life at a given moment.
—Viktor E. Frankl

After learning of her mother's diagnosis, Line searched for a reason
why Ellyn was suffering from cancer. She knew it couldn't have been
anything her mother had done. In Caroline's eyes, her mom was a role
model, mentor, and friend. She was a loving, giving, and spiritual person, the picture of health and beauty both inside and out. Try as she
might, Line couldn't think of a single thing her mother had done to
invite the disease. She became desperate and grasped at any explanation that might have fit into her distraught teenager dominion. She
examined who or what could have done this to her mother, and the
only Being with that kind of power was God.

Caroline was raised to believe God was merciful and good. If people were bad, they were punished. Conversely, obedient servants of the Almighty were rewarded. Since her mother was as close to being a saint as Caroline could find, she reasoned that God must be punishing her for not honoring her mother the past few years. Cancer seemed entirely unfair, especially since they had reconciled their differences. This perceived injustice angered Caroline. It didn't make sense to honor a God who operated in such a way, so she stopped. Ellyn became concerned and asked the adults closest to Line—the ones she knew her daughter would turn to—to encourage her to keep God in her life.

Line went to Amy Kanellis for hope and encouragement. Amy tried to talk with Caroline about rejecting her faith, questioning God's motives, and blaming God for taking her mother from her, but Line refused to discuss any of it. Amy decided to save the topic of Caroline reconciling with God for another time. Instead, they searched high and low for survivor stories. Sadly there weren't many, but it was important for Amy and Caroline to keep hope alive.

By late May, Caroline slowly and reluctantly accepted the fact that her mother may succumb to cancer. Amy prepared both of them for the very real possibility of life without Ellyn. Amy's pledge to Ellyn was to help soften the blow for Caroline during her senior year.

Ellyn wouldn't speak to Caroline in terms of life expectancy. Ellyn spoke to her about the activities they could look forward to sharing together. As she got sicker, Ellyn continually readjusted her timeline. Line's graduation in May 2012 turned into Christmas of 2011. Christmas turned into Caroline's volleyball season, which then became the start of her senior year in August. Ellyn reinforced all of the fun events they had planned for the summer. She reminded Caroline of the upcoming Cardinals game over the Fourth of July and their annual trip to New Hampshire.

Ellyn's difference between life expectancy versus the events she would be around to attend may have been nothing more than semantics, but it was a perspective Caroline connected with. Her primary focus shifted from concentrating on the dwindling amount of time they had left to what they did with the time they did have. Caroline realized the bitterness she felt, when she thought about all of the experiences they wouldn't share, blocked any possibility of creating quality moments while her mother was still with her. The new perspective may have been the best gift Ellyn ever gave her—reinforcing the depth of her mother's wisdom and how fortunate she was to be able to call her "Mom."

Line expressed this in a letter she wrote to her mother in June, on her 17th birthday: "All I asked for, for my birthday was a cure, or the lifestyle we had on April 20. But I'm asking for too much when I say that … All I want is for you to know how much I love you. I will never, ever love anyone, or anything more than our family, the Found Five. I think when a family is very close, every thing, every quality, every value that a family holds reflects upon the mother. And for our family, we are told we are wonderful, beautiful, kind and amazing; that's you mom. You are the best woman I could ask for to be my best friend."

Chapter 19
So Much to Do, So Little Time

Don't walk behind me; I may not lead. Don't walk in front of
me; I may not follow. Just walk beside me and be my friend.
—Lyrics to a Jewish children's song

To us, family means putting your arms
around each other and being there.
—Barbara Bush

Summer was typically a busy time for the Found family, yet they were
also the most enjoyable times of the year. The summer of 2011 was anything but joyful. They were consumed by uncertainty and stress due to
Ellyn's rapidly deteriorating health. The cancer had advanced, and she
required longer and longer stays at the hospital.

As difficult as it was on the rest of the family to watch, wasting
away in a hospital bed was especially agonizing on the normally active
Ellyn. It wasn't the physical toll cancer took on her as much as the
activities she was missing while cooped up in a hospital room. She
was a doer, and her deeds were performed almost exclusively for the
service of others. She volunteered at school events whenever she could.
She worked at the Steindler Orthopedic Clinic, and she hosted new
families to town, especially families who spoke English as a second

language. She was a fixture at church and other volunteer opportunities around town.

The one thing she did for herself, and really missed, was her morning walk. Ellyn had taken a morning walk the past twelve years. They started after a proclamation she made to Ernie one night before they went to sleep, that she was setting the alarm for 4:30 AM. When Ernie asked why, she told him that she was going to start walking with Liz, the neighbor lady down the road. Ernie was accustomed to getting out of bed at 5:30 AM, not by choice, but as a requirement for work. He was baffled by anyone who would voluntarily get up to exercise at that hour. He thought to himself, as he rolled over to go to sleep, "I'll give this a week."

Good on her promise, Ellyn popped out of bed with the alarm each and every morning, Monday through Friday at 4:30. The ladies walked for an hour from 5 to 6 AM. After Liz developed a health issue that prevented her from walking, Ellyn recruited Lisa Murray.

Whether the dead of winter with blowing snow or August under sweltering heat, they walked. They walked in weather that would cause many to pull the comforter over their head and fall back to sleep. "There were maybe two mornings a year that the weather kept them from walking," Ernie said.

In the winter time, Ellyn bundled up with multiple layers of sweatshirts, winter coat, snow pants, winter boots, and a hat. She would throw a shoulder into the door, besting the biting wind, and trudge, sometimes through deep snow, into the pitch black morning. The pair would start by 4:50 AM. "We'd do two miles out and two miles back and be done just in time to buzz home and get the kids up, ready, and out the door," Lisa recalled.

When asked, the ladies listed "exercise" as the official reason for their morning treks, but it wasn't the only one. As two mothers with young kids, the reason was just as much for their mental health as physical health. "They had that hour to themselves and didn't like to miss it because it was their link to sanity while raising the kids," Boyd Murray explained.

Ernie wasn't the only one who admired Ellyn's dedication. Ken O'Keefe, then offensive coordinator for the University of Iowa football team, lived close by the ladies' route: "I'd be headed to work at 5:30 in the morning thinking, 'I must be the most dedicated person on the planet,' until I saw those two every morning. It didn't matter if it was raining, snowing, sleeting or anything in between. I'd pass by in a nice warm car with my morning coffee and there they'd be."

A few years into Ellyn's morning exercise routine, her mother's health began to fail from Multiple Sclerosis. From that moment forward, Ellyn set the alarm at 4 AM instead of 4:30. She used the extra half-hour to hand-write a letter to her mother each and every morning.

By June, Ellyn had become much sicker. The battle that raged inside her body required every ounce of her energy, leaving no reserves for her precious morning walk. "They really wanted to walk together. They'd plan it, and it wouldn't work; plan it again, and it wouldn't work. I remember how thankful both Lisa and Ellyn were when they were able to finally sneak one in," Boyd said, choking back tears.

The ladies were able to get out one last time in late June. What could Lisa say to her best friend during what she suspected would be their last walk together? Over the years, the ladies' discussions typically would be centered on kids and family. As they wore the tread off countless pairs of tennis shoes, they became each other's cheerleaders, therapists, fashion consultants, and confidants.

One topic they certainly tried to avoid on their last walk was Ellyn's cancer and treatment. They each had their own reason to sidestep her illness. For Lisa, speaking about Ellyn's illness was too sad a subject to end such a cherished tradition. Ellyn's reason for not discussing her disease was more intrinsic; that's just not how she was built. She never allowed herself or anyone around her to focus on her cancer for too long because that led to pity, and Ellyn Found didn't desire or accept pity, ever. The idea that her hardship would cause anyone sadness was unbearable for her. The Founds were, and still are, much more comfortable in the giver rather than receiver role.

As the ladies padded down their familiar route, they talked about the upcoming summer events the Founds had planned and how excited Ellyn was for them. There was Lauren Hansen's wedding the Founds were planning to attend because Caroline was slated to be a greeter in her club volleyball coach's wedding. They also discussed the annual St. Louis trip to see the Cardinals play over the July Fourth weekend and the annual trip to New Hampshire, which Ellyn was very much looking forward to. Her disease, however, dictated what she was able to do, when she was able to do it, or if she could even do it at all. "She was worried that the fluid buildup in her stomach would prevent her from going back East, which was her immediate goal. She really wanted to see her family one more time in a place that held so much meaning for her," Lisa said.

Fighting cancer was an exhausting proposition, and Ellyn struggled to finish the walk. Once they were done, Ellyn went right back to her hospital bed.

July 1st is a busy time for Ernie at work. New residents start their orthopedic residency program, and current residents advance another year. The rule of thumb for faculty at a teaching hospital is not to be on vacation or sick during this time because the residents are all dealing with a new set of responsibilities. Everyone will have questions and need supervision.

On this particular July 1st morning, Ernie awoke and climbed out of bed to excruciating pain in his downstairs region. "I couldn't stand up without feeling like a ten-pound weight was attached to my scrotum," Ernie said. "As soon as I'd lie down, the pain would go away." Ernie tried time and time again to rise up, hoping the pain would clear up, but it always returned and persisted until he would lie back down. He couldn't stay down long, he had a surgical case that morning.

The slightest movement caused Ernie intense pain, even getting to the hospital was monumental. Once there, he struggled to put on his scrubs and meet with the eager new senior resident, thrilled at his shot to work with Dr. Found. "This kid is excitedly trying to go over this X-ray with me, and I can't even stand up straight to look at it," he said.

Ernie started the surgery, which required him to be on his feet. He was in agony, but he strained through to a point where he could take a small break while the other staff took an X-ray. He scrubbed out and went outside the room to lie down. The pain disappeared as soon as he did. Lying pain-free on the floor outside of the operating room, he tried to persuade himself that he could continue. He managed, by sheer will to stand and went back inside the operating room, but by now the pain was excruciating. "I was seeing stars and about ready to pass out," he said. Ernie sat down for a bit. He stood again and nearly fell over. A dedicated surgeon, Ernie reluctantly admitted to the worried surgical staff members what they already knew—he wouldn't be able to finish. He would need to call in a replacement.

Meanwhile, Ernie laid back down to relieve the pain. He suspected the inguinal hernia he had been dealing with for quite some time had become strangulated and he would need surgery. He reached out to a fellow surgeon, Joe Cullen, for confirmation. After examining Ernie, Dr. Cullen told him he could probably wait, but he would be smart to take care of the situation right away. Ernie heartily agreed, and the surgery was set for the afternoon.

As Ernie lie prostrate on a table being prepped for hernia surgery, he contemplated the inescapable irony. "At 8 AM, I was the surgeon in room 19, and at 12:30 I was the surgery patient in room 17."

The surgery successfully completed, the next prescribed step was rest and recovery. It would have to wait. "Ellyn had tickets for us to go to the Cardinals' game over the July Fourth weekend. Her health had been up and down, but she really wanted to go. Gregg was coming home for this, so it wasn't something that I felt like I wanted to skip out on," Ernie said.

These were not just baseball games to the Founds. Ernie passed his love of Cardinals baseball on to his family, taking them on trips to St. Louis for a game or two every summer. It was especially meaningful to Gregg, who always got much more from the trips than just quality major league baseball games. The trip was an adventure, educational, and a real bonding moment with his dad. Ernie passed along not only the genesis of the Found family's love of Cardinals baseball but weaved into the stories great advice for living a happy, meaningful life. One of Gregg's favorite stories was the 1968 Hall of Fame game in Cooperstown, New York, Ernie attended with his father.

By the mid-60s, fifteen-year-old Ernie Jr. knew every Cardinals player and could rattle off their career stats from memory. He was thrilled when, in 1968, his father took him to the Hall of Fame weekend in Cooperstown. It was tradition, then, for the two World Series participants from the prior season to play an exhibition game during the weekend. The reigning world champion St. Louis Cardinals were scheduled to play an exhibition game against the Boston Red Sox.

Ernie was excited. He would finally get to see his favorite Cardinals player, Bob Gibson, pitch in person. Just prior to the weekend, the

Red Sox inexplicably pulled out and were replaced with the Minnesota Twins. It didn't matter to Ernie which team faced the Cards, Gibson was the draw.

The day of the game, Ernie was crushed when he learned that St. Louis was sitting Gibson in favor of some tall, lanky, left-handed minor league prospect he had never heard of. In protest, the devastated teenager refused to watch the game each time the minor league upstart took the mound. Ernie Sr. intently observed the unknown pitcher for the Red Birds as he carried a no-hitter through three innings. "Dad kept asking me, 'Are you watching this kid on the mound? He's really good,'" but Ernie Jr. wasn't watching because he was too busy fuming about the injustice perpetrated on him by the organization. He couldn't understand why his father wasn't as indignant as he was that the Cardinals played some guy not even fit to wear a St. Louis uniform in lieu of Gibson, a Cardinals' legend.

As the game progressed, the unfamiliar hurler had pitched six shutout innings. "My dad was gushing over this guy, and I'm thinking, 'Screw you, dad. He's not Bob Gibson, so I don't care.'"

Ernie Sr. wasn't the only one impressed by the minor league pitcher. The Cardinals called the big lefty up that season, and he went on to have a great major league career. It turned out they, well at least Ernie Sr., had been watching future Hall of Famer, Steve Carlton.

Carlton was inducted into the Major League Baseball Hall of Fame in 1994. At the induction ceremony, a mutual acquaintance of Ernie and Steve's told Carlton the story of the disgruntled boy at the '68 exhibition game. Carlton was so entertained by it he signed a bat for Ernie: "From the Hall of Fame Game in 1968 to the Hall of Fame, Steve Carlton." Ernie still has the bat in his office at work.

Many life-long lessons materialize in unexpected places. This one came at a meaningless exhibition game, but he got it from the man he respected more than any other, his father. Ernie Sr. probably was equally disappointed about not getting to see the legendary Gibson pitch, but he had the wisdom to accept his disappointment and turn it into a positive, allowing him to appreciate a future great at the genesis of his career. It was one of an extensive list of lessons Ernie learned from his father and passed along to his kids. They were lessons that gave him strength during the most difficult time in his life.

After the difficulty with his hernia taken care of, Ernie was discharged from the hospital that evening and headed home. Any movement he made sent stabbing pain signals to his brain, a constant reminder this would be an extremely difficult weekend. Complicating matters further, his high pain level and fresh incision closed with stitches caused him concern about moving his bowels, so he didn't. "I was worried that an exertion like that might rip the sutures out," he said. The good news was that Ernie had a couple days of recovery time at home before they left. The Founds planned to leave the morning of the Fourth and arrive in St. Louis for the night game, watch the fireworks afterwards, and then spend the night in a hotel.

Sunday night came, and Ernie's pain from the surgery hadn't subsided. He dreaded the drive he faced the following day and didn't think he would be able to endure it. Just as he was about to make an announcement to his family that he wouldn't be joining them, he looked at Ellyn, who was also fighting agonizing abdominal pain. "If she wasn't going to let the pain she was in stop her from going, how could I?"

Monday morning, the Founds climbed in the car and headed south with Gregg in the driver's seat. After the five-hour trip, which seemed like twenty-five hours to both Ernie and Ellyn, they checked into the Millennium Hotel, perfectly situated a block from Busch Stadium to the east and the Mississippi River on the west. The hotel was so busy on the holiday weekend it took them an hour-and-a-half just to check in. Ernie and Ellyn spent every one of the ninety minutes in misery until they could finally get to the room and rest a bit before the game.

They went to Busch Stadium and watched the Cardinals take on the Cincinnati Reds, which was a nice distraction from their physical ailments. "We had great seats, and it was a 1-0 game so it moved right along," Ernie mentioned.

After the game, they returned to the hotel so Ernie and Ellyn could regroup before going to the fireworks scheduled to take place right outside the hotel. Ernie knew that he wouldn't be able to watch the fireworks, because he had an unfinished issue to address. "I was constipated and didn't feel that I could ignore it any longer." With the rest of the family at the fireworks, he was thankful for the privacy to confront his issue. Suffice it to say that, with the assistance of a suppository or two, there were simultaneous fireworks going on in St. Louis that night. With his mission accomplished, an exhausted and relieved Ernie watched the colorful finale through the hotel room window, lying on the bed.

Chapter 20

Castaway

Take the first step in faith. You don't have to see
the whole staircase, just take the first step.
—Martin Luther King, Jr.

Every tomorrow has two handles. We can take hold of
it with the handle of anxiety or the handle of faith.
—Henry Ward Beecher

The winter of 2012 hung on as long as it could, but ultimately it was pushed aside by spring. Spring is a time when Iowans reconnect with the outdoors. Ernie stepped outside the house in nothing more than jeans and a t-shirt. He donned his Cardinals cap to shield his eyes from the sun and surveyed how much spring cleaning would be required around the property.

A breeze enveloped Ernie with the smell of freshly churned soil. To him, the smell of the black dirt was as aromatic as any flower. He closed his eyes and drew the earthen scent deep into his lungs.

When Ernie opened his eyes, he was staring directly at the tree house across the yard which made him think of Caroline. He thought about when she asked him to create the structure, and he, being Ernie, went way over the top in its construction. Although most tree houses have a ladder to reach it, this one had a tiered stair case. The garden variety tree house has square openings cut for windows, but Ernie's had paned windows with actual glass. He basically had a solidly constructed and fully furnished miniature log cabin built in a tree.

Ernie wandered over, climbed the stairs, and with some effort, bent and contorted his large frame into the tiny structure. Once inside, his fond memories quickly shifted to regret. He wept thinking about a promise he made to Caroline—they would camp out in the tree house one more time before she went away to college.

When Caroline returned from a camp or vacation she been at without her parents she typically would regale them with a day-by-day account of her time away. But in the summer of 2011, with their focus on Ellyn's failing health, Line told Ernie she would tell him all about her week at Camp Castaway later. He assured her they would squeeze the activity in before school started. Regrettably, they never had the opportunity.

Ernie had to rely on Caroline's camp counselors, Shannon Harris and Stephanie Onder, to hear about Line's time at Castaway. In the spring of 2012, he invited them to the farm, and they told him all about Caroline's week. He was appreciative to hear how impactful the camp had been for her.

That summer Ellyn pushed Catharine, and especially Caroline, to get their fall schedules and associated activities in order for the upcoming school year. Perhaps she sensed the end was near, or maybe thinking of schedules and tasks provided her with some normalcy during a summer of uncertainty and worry. Whatever the reason, it was important to her the kids maintain their regular activities and continue on with their lives, no matter what their future held.

Ellyn knew, despite Caroline putting up a strong facade for her friends, she was struggling. Ellyn asked Amy Kanellis to continue her conversations with Line to prepare her for the upcoming school year and, eventually, life without her. Ellyn drew great comfort knowing Amy would be there for Caroline when she was gone.

"Caroline was very concerned that things would just hit her [during the school day]. She would ask, 'What if it just hits me in math?'" Amy explained, "I would tell her, 'Well, then you are going to text me, and I'm going to come get you. We will work it through, and then you go back to math.'"

Amy had to help Caroline realign her thinking when faced with the loss of her mother. She needed Caroline to understand it was important for Ellyn to know Line could move ahead with her life. "I had to convince her that's just how life is when you lose someone, and that there was never going to be a day when she didn't think about her mother. There would never be a day that her mother wouldn't be there to tell her exactly what to do. She wouldn't physically be there to do it, but that her mother would live in her heart forever."

At Ellyn's gentle, yet persistent, urging Caroline agreed to revisit her own relationship with God. Enough time had passed and she had accepted the reality of her mother's situation without blaming God, but unanswered questions still lingered. She was ready to start a dialogue with the Lord because acceptance and coping with her mother's condition were two different things and she needed help beyond what any of her friends or family could offer.

Line talked to Leah about her desire to reconnect to God. Leah mentioned Camp Castaway was coming up later that month. Caroline touched base with Gregg and Catharine, and they both encouraged her to go. Caroline always wanted to attend Camp Castaway, the same Christian summer camp that her brother and sister raved about, but as a member of the varsity softball team, her schedule always conflicted with the camp. The Iowa City chapter of the Christian youth group,

Young Life, was slated to attend Castaway from July 17 through 24. Caroline vowed to be there if possible.

Pending a week at Camp Castaway, her summer schedule included the New Hampshire trip the day after Castaway ended and then leaving New Hampshire early for one of the premiere volleyball camps in Iowa at Central College in Pella.

Caroline's attendance at Castaway hinged on when her softball season ended. The squad was on a winning streak and had a realistic shot at the state tournament for the first time in a while. Their remaining schedule was tough so there was no way to predict ahead of time if they would make the tournament. Her dilemma—if the team made the postseason, Caroline would feel obligated to skip camp yet again.

Although a spot player on the softball team, Line was a valuable teammate. She gave her normal hundred percent, whether on the field or in the dugout, providing moral support. During her mother's illness, her priorities shifted. She focused more on supporting her family and figuring out what her role would be without her mother. She felt as though some of those answers might be waiting for her at Castaway. For the first time in her athletic career, she secretly pulled for the team's defeat.

God must have wanted Caroline at Castaway more than in the state tournament because the softball team faded in the stretch and was knocked out of contention for the last tourney spot. The camp leader, Stephanie Onder, got a text message from Caroline after her last softball game: "We lost, but I'm going to Castaway!"

The week leading up to Castaway, Caroline questioned aloud whether or not she should leave her mother for so long. Ellyn reassured Caroline she would be here when she got back and it was her wish that she go. Internally, Caroline was allowing God back into her life, but she still had lots of unanswered questions. Ultimately she decided Castaway was the perfect place to try to get some answers.

The morning of July 17, Caroline said her goodbyes and climbed aboard a vehicle with the Iowa City Young Life group consisting of ten City High and West High girls and their two volunteer leaders. They headed north for Castaway and arrived late afternoon to a welcoming committee of enthusiastic volunteers who helped them check into their cabin.

Camp Castaway is nestled in the heart of Minnesota lakes country in Otter Tail County. Set on a strand of ground separating Little Pelican and Pelican lakes, it has been the summer refuge for countless high school students from around the Midwest and world since 1963, when a local family donated the private property to Young Life.

The donation had one stipulation for the new owners—the property was to be used for the betterment of young people through Christian education. It was a perfect way for them to honor their patriarch, Sydney Smith, who had purchased the land for a summer home at the turn of the twentieth-century. Throughout the years, Mr. Smith and his son, C. Gordon Smith had shared Bible stories with local kids and taken them for boat rides on the lake.

True to their word, Young Life transformed the private property into an amalgam of summertime fun and faith-affirming activities for teenagers transitioning from their formative years into adulthood. For decades, Castaway has improved the lives of countless teenagers.

With the number of activities offered by the camp, in and out of the water, boredom at Castaway would have to be a camper's choice. In any given week, a camp attendee can climb a twenty-five-foot rock wall, fly through the air on a zip line, ride a giant tandem swing, or play disc golf, soccer, tennis, or any table game imaginable. For campers interested in water activities, Castaway offered water skiing, wake boarding, parasailing, tubing, banana boat rides, and a hot tub to relax in after a full day of activities.

The evening they arrived, Caroline attended an activity called "Club"—a nightly opportunity for all 450 high school campers to get together in the main lodge. They played games, sang songs, read scripture passages, and then listened to a speaker brought in for the week from Kansas City named Bill. He talked about what a huge impact his relationship with God had on his life. Once he was finished, the campers went back to their cabins, reflecting on Bill's stories and their own lives.

With everyone back in the cabin, the leaders asked the girls to share the scariest thing that had ever happened to them. Stephanie went first and shared the scariest thing for her was her mother passing of cancer when she was seven. By design, the leader asked Caroline to share next. "I was really nervous when the week started. We obviously knew about Ellyn being sick and wondered how open Caroline would be about it," Stephanie said.

A silence fell over the room and all eyes locked on Caroline, whose cheeks were moist with tears. She took a deep breath and said to Stephanie, "I know what you mean." Line confided in the group. She didn't know how to talk to God and didn't much want to. She was angry and wondered aloud how her mother could be taken away from her. She felt she was being punished for something she had done.

One at a time the girls revealed their fears to the group. Both leaders were amazed Caroline, despite sharing such a serious issue in her life, was able to set it aside and give equal value to the other girls' fears and problems no matter how trivial they may have seemed by comparison. One girl talked about her father remarrying and having a baby with another woman. Caroline was right there with caring words of support,

"That must be really hard for you." To Caroline, each girl's concerns were serious to them and deserved her respect and compassion.

The first night at camp was a seminal moment for the group and really set the tone for the cabin. When Caroline shared such a personal and impactful situation in her life, it made it okay for the rest of the girls to let their guard down and share their lives too. It allowed them to recognize there were other people with similar angst and problems. The leaders were hopeful by the end of camp the girls would understand by turning to God in troubled times they could unload their burdens.

Camp wasn't all reflection and deep thoughts. Campers spent most of each day split fairly evenly between high energy individual activities and group competitions, such as relay races and obstacle courses designed to promote team building and cooperation. Each evening there were social gatherings like dances and carnivals.

Pelican Lake, so named because it is shaped like the bird, has a 4,000-acre surface area and is surrounded by the opulent summer homes of Minnesota's affluent. During a boat ride around the lake, Stephanie convinced Caroline, who was certainly afflicted with a serious case of Bieber fever, that a particularly large home on the lake belonged to Justin Bieber's grandparents. "Caroline, of course, jumped right on it," Stephanie said. "She was screaming, 'I love you Justin Bieber!'" The puzzled elderly couple gardening in their backyard offered a civil wave. When Caroline learned that Stephanie had just had some fun at her expense, the expert practical joker plotted her revenge.

A few nights later, after lights-out, all campers were accounted for except Caroline. The leaders called for her, inside and outside the cabin, but got no response. As they searched for Line, Stephanie thought she heard a male voice coming from a different room inside the cabin. One hard and fast rule clearly spelled out to campers at Castaway is that boys are strictly forbidden in girls' cabins and vice versa. Stephanie couldn't believe her ears until a wide-eyed Shannon verified her suspicion. "Do you think Caroline is in there with him," Shannon asked. Whoever the intruding boy was, his next declaration made his intentions crystal clear, "Come on baby, just one little kiss."

The leaders rushed into the other room to break up the romantic interlude, the rest of their intrigued charges close behind. Stephanie hurried into the room and found Caroline alone with a Cheshire cat grin spread across her face. With the same baritone voice that initially alerted the leaders, Line asked, "Hey, how you doing?"

Stephanie rolled her eyes and let out a relieved groan, "Oh, Caroline," she said. Line roared with amusement at her successful lark. Soon everyone was laughing until their sides hurt.

Caroline was the linchpin of the cabin and went out of her way to ensure everyone was included, even camp veteran Amber, a high maintenance and, at times, annoying member of the group. "Amber was sometimes really hard to love," Shannon said. Caroline realized early on that Amber might be marginalized by the rest of the cabin, so she befriended her. "Caroline was a kid at heart, and Amber was like a forty-year-old woman," Stephanie said, "but the pair was joined at the hip all week."

Amber was at Castaway the prior summer, and despite the leaders' best efforts, she had generally refused to participate and meet new people. The summer of 2011 was different—Caroline made sure of that. All week long, Line dragged Amber from activity to activity, ignoring her cantankerousness. Amber tried every trick she knew to be miserable and make everyone else around her miserable, but her new BFF, Caroline, simply wouldn't allow it. In spite of her persnickety attitude, Amber warmed to Caroline as the week progressed. Line was the first of her peers to see past her bristly exterior and be a true friend.

Caroline's compassion for others was on display throughout the week. One of the activities the camp hosted was a dance party. While most of the campers took the opportunity to meet and dance with a variety of people, Caroline zeroed in on a boy who was blind and had no one to dance with. Throughout the evening, a multitude of handsome young men asked Caroline to dance, but she turned them all down. "She danced with that little blind kid all night long," Shannon said.

The last day of camp started early for those who chose to take the Believers' Walk—a chance for campers to walk down to the beach, find a stone, and heave it into the water. "The rock represents your old life, and you are throwing it away for this new God-centered life," Stephanie said. An exhausted Caroline rose early. It was time for her to decide if God had a place in her future.

As Line walked the beach hoping for answers, a morning zephyr blew in over the water. The gentle breeze blanketed Caroline with such warmth and nostalgia that she stopped to soak it in. The warm breeze carried her mind away to the living room with her family on Christmas Eve. The lights on the Christmas tree shimmered in the front window. Flames crackled in the fireplace. A steaming cup of her mom's homemade apple cider warmed her hands. The solemn sounds of howling wind and driving snow outside were no match for the cheerful noises of Ernie playing the piano to "Up On The House Top" while the rest of the family enthusiastically sang along.

The breeze subsided, and Line opened her eyes. She felt instant relief and was no longer anxious about her mother or the future. It was like a ship's anchor had just been lifted off her shoulders. Everything fell into its proper place: her circumstances weren't God's fault, they weren't anyone's fault, so she could quit looking for someone or something to blame. Gone were the burdens of trying to carry everyone's concern about her mother's illness, including her own.

Caroline dropped to her knees, closed her eyes, and revived the line of communication between her and the Creator. She asked for better understanding. Caroline asked for her mother's full recovery, but understood if God called Ellyn home, she had the strength to carry on. She prayed for her family and those impacted by her mother's condition. Finally she asked for guidance and direction for her future.

When Caroline opened her eyes, she saw something protruding from the sand. She reached down and pulled up a smooth red rock. She worked the stone around in her fingers, a perfect size and weight for her hand, as if God had crafted it just for her. She turned it over to be sure "Line" wasn't engraved on it. As she rolled the rock around in her hands, she concluded God wasn't being cruel or punishing her, but had been right there by her side all along waiting, patiently, to be accepted back into her heart.

With her path to enlightenment clear, Line took an outfielder's hop step, reared her arm back, and launched the stone into the air. She smiled as it sailed high above the water. The rock splashed down in the water and drifted slowly to the sandy bottom of Pelican Lake, a final resting place for Caroline's life without God. The symbolic gesture meant she had committed herself to a new journey with the Lord—a faith-based quest in search of the Almighty's purpose for her.

The last night of camp during the final Club meeting was the "Say So"—where campers are allowed the opportunity to give their testimony to their peers. Those who desired grabbed a handheld microphone and spoke to the campers about their faith journey. Caroline had learned about the "Say So" a few days before and was very motivated to participate, she just wasn't quite sure what she would say.

When the microphone was passed to Line, she took a deep breath and before she spoke, thought about her journey. Her mother's persistence and a favorable softball schedule may have gotten her to Castaway, but she had taken the final steps on her own. She smiled at the thought and said, "Hi, my name is Caroline Found, and I'm from Iowa City. On April 20th, 2011, my mom was diagnosed with stage IV pancreatic cancer and spread to the liver and lungs. Before this week, I hadn't talked to God in a long time. This week I prayed, so that's a start."

The significance of Caroline's brief public declaration was probably lost on the room full of campers, but for the people that knew her and everything she had been through, it was clearly a huge step in her life. Relief washed over Stephanie. She knew from personal experience that Line still had some tough times ahead. Although many would be there for her every step of the way, she had opened an avenue to help unburden herself. Caroline once again walked with the Lord.

Chapter 21
Ellyn's New Hampshire Goodbye

We do not remember days, we remember moments.
—Cesare Pavese

If one suffers we all suffer. Togetherness is strength. Courage.
—Jean-Bertrand Aristide

Ernie pulled a tin pan marked, "Charlotte's," from the freezer and made some lunch. He took his warmed plate of food into the living room and sat on the sofa. A red photo book on the coffee table entitled *Our Mountain* caught his eye. He grabbed the year-by-year account of their time climbing Mount Monadnock and opened the cover.

Ernie flipped through each page: many pictures had them on top of the mountain holding a hand-made sign signifying the year they made the climb. When he flipped to the page for 2005, a booklet fell out from between the plastic page protector. The hand-written book was titled: "*My Mountain,* by Caroline Found." In the book, a fifth-grade Caroline had written how, when she was little, she couldn't climb the mountain at all. As she got older, she could make the climb, but it was tough. Now she easily made the climb. She spoke of how special it was because she shared it with her family.

When Ernie got to the last page of the photo album he saw the photo of Gregg, Catharine, and Caroline in an embrace atop the mountain. Ellyn and he were noticeably absent which took him right back to the summer of 2011, their last trip to New Hampshire as a family.

The last family trip started when Caroline got home from Castaway. She barely had time to clean a week's worth of laundry and repack before the family was packed and leaving. Ellyn had become so ill by then the rest of the Founds would have preferred to cancel, but they couldn't. Ellyn made it known that as long as she was still breathing they would be going East as a family one last time. It could have been argued it was her sheer will to take this trip which kept her going. She was determined to get back to the place which had meant so much and provided so many wonderful memories over the years.

Travel took every bit of energy Ellyn had, which wasn't much. While in the security line at O'Hare in Chicago Ellyn had to sit whenever possible to keep from passing out. When they arrived, she vomited while waiting for their rental car. She was so weak the following morning they took her to the Dartmouth-Hitchcock Medical Facility in Lebanon, New Hampshire. Ernie had planned for such a contingency before they left home by reaching out to a former colleague at the University of Iowa, Dr. Jim Weinstein, who was CEO of the medical facility.

Members of the Slocum family rented a house on Bear Island for six nights. The house was large enough to accommodate everyone. "Ellyn's condition was so fragile that we spent all but a couple of nights in the hospital," Ernie said. The rest of the family tried to have a good time, but they were constantly worried which dampened the mood on the otherwise picturesque setting.

On the eve of the fifth day of their vacation, Ellyn was well enough to stay at the lake house. Ernie and Ellyn had been encouraging Gregg, Catharine, and Caroline to climb the mountain all week, but it just didn't seem right to climb Monadnock without their mother and father. Realizing they still hadn't ascended the mountain, threatening the annual tradition, Ellyn insisted the rest of them climb without her. Ernie bowed out in case her condition deteriorated, but told the kids they should go.

The following morning, Gregg parked the rental car in the lot at the base of the mountain. The three kids gathered some supplies in a backpack and reluctantly started up the familiar white dot route to the top of Monadnock.

In years past, the two-mile trek up the mountain ended in a race between the three physically fit siblings. There was no interest in racing this day. Instead, they took the easiest route, stayed together, and talked the whole way up. They reflected on their childhood, on their family, and their mother. They talked about their futures and how different it would be without her.

For the first time, Caroline spoke seriously about her future. She was no longer going to be a superhero or Santa's apprentice. She spoke of college and her desire to play volleyball at the next level. While she hadn't zeroed in on a career, she was certain it would be in the service of others. "When we started the climb, she was still my kid sister. By the end she was my equal, my friend," Gregg said.

They stayed on the top for a while, took in the panoramic view, had some lunch, and posed for a picture taken by another friendly hiker. While they enjoyed each other's company, they talked about how strange it was on the mountain without their mom and dad.

Caroline and Catharine had to leave the lake house a day early for prior commitments. Caroline had a volleyball camp to attend with her

West High team. The camp was held each summer on the campus of Central College in Pella, Iowa. Brez took her teams each year, which served several purposes: the girls could brush up on their skills while bonding and the team could get some preseason work done.

When camp started, the Women of Troy's play sputtered, and it made perfect sense why. When Line played well, so did the team, but if she played poorly, they were terrible. The normally rock solid Caroline had been distracted all summer, and her mother's illness made her mood unpredictable. The entire team walked on eggshells around her and was off-balance at the beginning of camp.

The distracted team needed an attention getter, so the coach benched her two best players: Caroline and Shelly. "It broke my heart to have to do it. Caroline had a ton on her mind, and with all that was going on with her family she hadn't set all summer," Brez admitted. "That being said, if she was going to be with the team, she had to focus, at least while on the court."

The rest of the team got the message, and even with their best two players on the bench they nearly beat rival City High. It was just the boost the team needed. Their first day disaster behind them, the 2010 state champs soon put the other teams at camp on notice—if they wanted a state title in 2011 they would have to go through West High.

A few days into the camp, Caroline received a call on her cell. Since all the girls hung out in the same room Line stepped into the hall to take the call. The lively girls fell silent. Eleven sets of eyes were on Line when she walked back into the room. The smile she had left the room with was gone, and her face was now twisted with worry. Line's teammates instinctively knew it was about Ellyn, and the news wasn't good.

Ellyn's cancer had worsened causing a dramatic increase in her abdominal pain. Hearing this worried Caroline, so she pulled Brez aside and updated her coach. Brez offered to drive Line the two hours through the night so they would be home by 1 AM. Caroline refused to leave the team. "They need me. I need to be here," Caroline said. The coach pleaded with her to go home. Line wouldn't do it.

The next morning, Brez went to the girls' rooms to wake them for breakfast. Because the dorm rooms were cramped, she had paid for six rooms so her players could pair up in relative comfort. "Room after room was empty, and I'm freaking out," Brez remembered. When she got to Caroline's room all twelve kids were in there. They had dragged their mattresses into Line's room, and covered every square inch of floor with them. One of the mattresses was even perched atop a dresser.

The coach struggled with a swell of emotions as the girls shifted in fitful sleep. She admired how the team chose to support Caroline the only way they knew how, by being there. The veteran coach would later describe this team as the closest she ever had.

Chapter 22
An Unbreakable Bond

Life is not a solo act. It's a huge collaboration, and
we all need to assemble around us the people who
care about us and support us in times of strife.
—Tim Gunn

Ernie and the volleyball team were inescapably connected by their loss
and sadness. They formed a resilient bond forged through mutual em-
pathy and vowed to be there for one another.

Despite this bond, the girls still struggled to control their emotions
on the court. Sometimes their emotions manifested with inappropri-
ate outbursts. Coach Bresnahan tried to allow their behavior as part
of the grieving process, but she was forced to address the issue after
they completed a first match drubbing of highly ranked Pella Christian. One of the West players said something unrelated to the match,
which triggered hysterical laughter from the rest of the team. The Pella
Christian team members, coaches, and fans, assuming they were being
made fun of, were visibly offended. When Brez sensed what happened,
she was mortified at the misunderstanding, "I apologized to the coach
who understood."

The following Monday at practice, Brez addressed the team about the incident. "I told them that the other team thought they were showing them up." As a school that prides itself on good sportsmanship, the girls were devastated at the thought of being perceived as poor sports and assured their coach they weren't laughing at the other team. Brez stressed the importance of them controlling their emotions when they were on the court. The situation was an eye-opener for the team, and they promised their coach they would work hard to do just that.

Controlling their emotions during games wasn't the only topic on the coach's agenda. She knew how much this season meant to the girls, but she told them if they didn't stabilize emotionally and have meaningful practices, they would surely fall short of their expectations. "It's time to pick it up. No more pity parties. No one we face on the court is going to care that we lost our setter and best friend. We need to start playing like we know we can."

Assistant coach Scott Sanders pulled Brez aside after the girls left for the night and said, "Welcome back."

The pep talk worked. Over the next month, the Women of Troy only gave up three matches, and by the middle of September the team had built an 18-5 record. They were ranked No. 2, right behind No. 1 ranked City High.

Whenever the team was confronted with a wave of grief during a match, they had a secret weapon—Ernie. If, for a series of points, the balls weren't bouncing favorably for them and the other team built momentum, the girls looked at Ernie in the stands. He would shoot them a quick fist pump and mouth an encouraging, "You can do it!" He was inspirational and comforting and put them back on track.

The team needed their secret weapon more than ever on September 20th when they traveled across town to take on City High. Led by senior all-state-setter, Erin Muir, City High had steamrolled their way to an impressive record and rode a wave of confidence into the home court showdown with West.

Players, students, parents, and even the coaches settled into the gym that night anticipating a war of attrition. Everyone expected the matchup to go the distance before a victor could be declared. City High head coach, Craig Pitcher, in an *Iowa City Press-Citizen* article earlier that week said, "It has all the possibilities," of being a five-set marathon.

Local bragging rights always played a role when these two teams got together, but the spotlight would be much brighter this particular Tuesday night. The match-up was only the second time in the history of the rivalry that No. 1 was squared off against No. 2. It was a matchup the entire state volleyball community would be tracking. All of these factors came together to create an energy level that, by game time, had an ear-piercing buzz of intensity.

The top spot in the rankings may have been on the line, but there was something both teams coveted even more, the Spike. The rivalry trophy, a bronzed railroad spike set on a wooden base, was nothing special to look at, but for the two teams it signified the chance to boast and one of the things that made the decades-old competition so exciting. The only piece of hardware with more significance was a state championship trophy.

The prior season City High had traveled to West, and in an epic back-and-forth contest, City won the Spike. After the game, a fuming Caroline stormed into the locker room and reminded her teammates how much she despised losing. "She actually punched her locker and hurt her hand," Hannah Infelt recollected. "It was bruised really badly. At first we thought she broke it." With the memory of Caroline's locker room tirade burned into their brains, the team was desperate to win the Spike for Caroline this year.

Before the start of the match, Caroline and Ellyn were honored with a moment of silence. After the national anthem ended, Ernie found his way through the rowdy crowd to the first row of bleachers where Brez was waiting. Crying as she hugged him, she said, "Caroline would have loved this."

Ernie could only nod his agreement and mouthed, "I know."

The ball was served, and the battle underway. The teams went back and forth, knowing each other's strategies so well they anticipated and countered instinctively. Long volleys made points tough to come by. Thunderous spikes and seemingly impossible digs showed everyone in the state these two teams were appropriately ranked at the top. The teams split the first two sets and the built-in break was welcomed by everyone in the gym.

West took control in the third set winning it 25 to 16. The Women of Troy rode the momentum of a 2-1 lead into the fourth and deciding set winning it 25 to 19. The team's Libero, Anna Pashkova, made the victory official when she sprung straight up into the air—nearly kicking herself in the behind with the heels of her own shoes. The leap was accompanied by a scream that was as much relief as joy.

If this were any other victory over City, the elated girls would normally take turns embracing the Spike, but not tonight. Trophy in hand, Shelly Stumpff and Olivia Fairfield went into the crowded stands, which parted like the Red Sea. Shelly handed the trophy to Ernie, who hoisted it to the heavens. The girls wrapped the sobbing father in a group hug. The weight of the scene in the stands overwhelmed Coach Bresnahan too. Just as she released her emotions, a local reporter for the *Gazette* asked her to describe what this victory meant to her. The only reply she could manage was, "I just miss my player."

Despite the team's success, an outstanding forty-four assists against City, and half of the season gone, Kelley Fliehler still hadn't claimed the setter position as her own. She lived with the nagging feeling she was only filling in for Caroline and at any moment Line would come back. Fliehler played every point for Line, and each unforced error felt like she was letting her friend down.

Even with Kelley's sporadic play, Brez refused to chastise her during timeouts. Instead, she turned upon her senior hitters, Shelly Stumpff and Olivia Fairfield. "I'd say things like, 'You're all-state hitters, and Kelley is brand new to the position. I don't care where it's set, you're good enough, just hit the damn ball!'" Kelley knew the mistakes were hers and felt like the team and coach were holding back on her, which made her feel even worse.

Kelley's intuition served her well. The team was indeed holding back at the coach's insistence. When Brez decided that Fliehler would be the team's setter, she secretly pulled Shelly and Olivia aside and left standing orders that if Kelley made a bad set they weren't to get down on her, not to even roll their eyes.

Kelley was frustrated the coach would go easy on her considering how rough she had been on Caroline. When the team played poorly in the 2010 season, Brez was known for calling a timeout, and instead of verbally tearing into the collective, singled out Caroline.

What the rest of the team didn't know was this was a ruse orchestrated by Brez and Line. Just prior to a timeout the coach would get Caroline's attention and then tug her ear, Carol Burnett-style. It was a signal she was about to get an earful. Line could predict when the indicator was coming, because it would be precipitated by a run of poor play by the team. Brez would call timeout, and even before the players reached the sideline, she would storm towards them. The team would brace for a well-deserved butt chewing, but the coach would bypass them and read Caroline the riot act. Line, for affect, put on her Poor Pitiful Pearl face. The befuddled team stood by helplessly as the coach unjustly scolded the only player performing well at the time. When Brez was done with Line, the team rallied around their wronged setter with words of encouragement. They would return to the floor and play inspired volleyball.

Brez understood the psychological tricks of motivating an under performing team, and she used everything she knew depending on the circumstances. Some involved positive reinforcement, while others required reverse psychology. The more complex involved self-reflection and a hope the individual would come to a realization they could perform better.

Singling out Line may have worked the prior season, but with the current team she had to use a different tack. Brez felt compelled to protect Kelley and bring her along slowly because she had come into the position reluctantly. She was still trying to encourage Kelley to loosen up and not dwell on mistakes. "I think the team thought that I couldn't adjust, wasn't ready, or just couldn't handle the criticism yet," Kelley stated.

Although amnesia is a setter's best friend, it takes time to acquire. Time was a luxury neither Kelley nor the team had. The coach kept a close eye out for indicators that Kelley was bothered by her errors. "I could tell when she was pressing to make up for a mistake. She'd set her jaw and get this grim look on her face," Brez explained.

When Kelley tightened up because of a mishap, the team followed suit. When a mistake occurred, Brez's prompt to her was always the same—she told her to smile. "Coach said that I had one of the best smiles and that our team relaxed and played better when they saw it," Kelley stated. Kelley tried smiling, and the results were immediately positive. When she smiled she relaxed and started having fun. As a result the team became loose and made fewer mistakes.

The victory over City gave the team more confidence. The seniors met and discussed their role as leaders. Each figured out how they could carve out a role. This seemed to immediately help with team cohesion and evened out their play and emotions for the rest of the season.

When the team struggled in high intensity matches, Olivia Fairfield, nicknamed "Eunice" after the nerdy Amanda Bynes character in the movie *She's the Man*, was a calming influence. Exclusively a front row player, she would come in the game with a joke to try to loosen everyone up if they were playing tight.

If Olivia was having a bad game, she would blame and criticize herself harshly. As a result the whole team's positive vibe would suffer. Some joking or small talk to get her mind off the last play would normally pull her out of the funk and back into the game. If that didn't work, someone would drop a curse word in front her. She never used cuss words and would blush when she heard one. This sent the others into hysterics, which loosened her up as well.

Olivia Mekies, in previous seasons, was known to struggle with bouts of frustration over her play. She responded to mistakes with anything from throwing her hands into the air and yelling to pulling her own hair. However, the loss of Line had transformed Olivia into a calming influence on others. If she saw someone else lose it and have to leave the gym crying, Olivia followed them into the hall to administer a comforting hug accompanied by encouraging words.

Anna Pashkova assumed two roles on the team. Off of the court she was the team's rock, never letting go of her emotions publicly. "She never cried in front of people," Kelley revealed. During games though, Anna's personality changed. She was a ball of fire on the court, the team's motivator. The other players fed off of her energy. When West would win a pivotal point, teammates waited in anticipation for Anna's signature celebration jump.

Shelly Stumpff was the wild and fun one of the bunch. She usually was the instigator of practice hijinks. "One time, when we were supposed to be hitting back and forth, she hit the ball into the bleachers," Kelley described. "She went to get it, stayed up there, and hid, lying flat in the foot-well where no one could see her."

Shelly may have been a bit of a screw-off and sometimes had the attention span of a gnat during practice, but when the first serve cleared the net during games, no one was more focused and determined. With her steady play, she became Kelley's security blanket when they needed a quick point. "She was the one I'd go to," Fliehler said. "I knew she'd adjust no matter what set it was."

Hannah Infelt not only settled into her new role on the inside, she and Olivia became such a formidable force on defense that the duo forced opponents to change their offensive strategies. Hannah was a cool customer on the floor. She used her intelligence to quickly recognize patterns and adjustments in an opponent's offensive strategy which allowed her to anticipate and be in the right position.

Winning the Spike was a milestone and a crossroads for the team. On one level, they had accomplished one of their goals, but it was the combination of self-reflection and seniors stepping up into leadership roles that allowed them to at least entertain the idea they could actually win it all without Caroline's physical presence. The revelation couldn't have come at a better time because both the Mississippi Valley Conference tournament and perennial powerhouse Dubuque Hempstead loomed on the horizon.

Chapter 23
The Title Run

Determine that the thing can and shall be
done, and then we shall find the way.
—Abraham Lincoln

A champion is afraid of losing. Everyone
else is afraid of winning.
—Billie Jean King

The West High volleyball team had come a long way in less than two
months, but there was no time for celebration. The swift pace of the
2011 season would gain momentum as they moved into the last month
of the regular season.

October was a good month for the team. They were rolling and
playing so well that on October 13 they popped up on PrepVolleyball.
com's Century Club with a national high school rankings at No. 98.

The national ranking came in spite of an October 8 hiccup in which
the girls lost the Westside Volleyball Invitational tournament. Hosted by Cedar Rapids Jefferson, the tournament was always one of the
toughest on the schedule each season, and the 2011 lineup was a real
murderers' row, boasting fourteen ranked teams in the field of twenty-four, including three top-ranked teams in three different classes.

West waded through the competition into the championship. They expected to see another ranked 4A school and were surprised to square off against tiny 1A Tripoli High School with a total enrollment of 246.

Most at the tournament figured West would be one of the teams to play in the championship match, but no one, short of the Tripoli players and their small contingent of Panther faithful, anticipated their tiny school could compete with the big ones. It's very possible that deep down even some Tripoli players and fans didn't figure on their squad making it to the championship against nationally ranked Iowa City West.

If the Panther players were intimidated, the fear wasn't reflected in their play on the court. The championship match ended with West playing Goliath to Tripoli's David. The loss was not the result Brez was looking for heading into the Mississippi Valley Conference tournament which West High was hosting.

The week of the MVC tournament should have been an amazing one for the volleyball team. They sat atop the state 4A high school volleyball world. Despite all of the good news, the girls had a particularly down week. The players were run down, and it couldn't have come at a worse time, especially when most teams were ramping up for sectionals and state.

The closer their goal of winning back-to-back state titles became, the more the pressure mounted. Despite their promise to the coach they wouldn't play for Caroline, each knew, in reality, they were. The only acceptable conclusion to the season was another state title. Brez knew what these girls wanted to accomplish and how good they could be, but on occasion, they still struggled without Caroline on the court. "I told Scott it was time for a 'Come to Jesus meeting,'" Brez said.

Friday, before the MVC tournament, was their last opportunity to game plan. Brez met the team at the locker room door before practice, and instead of having the girls dress for practice, sent them to her classroom. "You could see it on their faces. They knew when they didn't dress for practice and had a meeting they were in for it," Coach Sanders said.

The uninspired team slumped in chairs and waited for the coach to let them have it. Instead of being animated, Brez started with a rhetorical question, "Why are you afraid to be good?" Then she handed out pencil and paper and had the girls make a list of things that they thought were holding the team back from reaching its fullest potential. Time would tell if the coach's plan would work.

On October 15, the doors of West High's gym were flung open and the crowd of parents, family, and students filled both the main floor and the balcony bleachers. West played sluggishly in pool play but still managed to do enough to advance as one of the top seeds in the championship bracket.

Their lackluster play continued throughout the day, but it was just enough to get them into the MVC title game. West's opponent in the title game would be a familiar foe, City High.

The sight of their adversaries across the net in their red, white, and black uniforms spurred the sluggish West team out of their day-long stupor. They became like a bull seeing red. Kelley Fliehler explained the team's transformation in a postgame interview, "We knew we hadn't played well all day, but we're always pumped to play City."

The ten-hour tournament day concluded with West, encouraged by a rowdy student section, prevailing over City High in a spirited battle and winning their third MVC championship in a row. While the team played well in the match against City, Olivia Fairfield elevated her game to new heights. The following day in an *Iowa City Press-Citizen* article, reporter Susan Harmon described Fairfield as, "a one-woman wrecking crew, blocking shots and firing kills."

Brez had three short days to prepare the team before No. 4 ranked Dubuque Hempstead came to town. It was the last regular season home match and senior night. The team decided they wanted Caroline recognized with the rest of the seniors.

The girls were also distracted by scuttlebutt in the media and around Iowa City that local resident, Lillie Williams, would plead guilty to setting a September house fire that claimed the life of her great nephew and West High ninth grader, Raymone Bryant. In anticipation, the local media inundated the community with back stories of the circumstances surrounding the September 4 fire, including any new information on what might happen in court.

October 17, on the eve of the Hempstead game, Lillie Williams did indeed plead guilty to setting the fatal fire. Her reason for admitting what she had previously denied was to protect her six-year-old grandson from having to testify against her in court. The young boy was the lone witness to Williams dousing a pillow with accelerant and, despite knowing that Raymone was inside the house at the time, lighting it on fire, and throwing it into the garage.

Although most of the girls on the team didn't know the freshman who died in the fire, they did know his older brother, senior, Richard Bryant. Raymone's senseless death had an impact. It reminded them of the same senselessness which hung over Caroline's death.

As one might expect, Ernie invited Richard out to the farm. The two men who had each lost family members to tragic circumstances embraced, consoled, and cried together.

With regionals only a week away, the team had reached the part of the season Line loved most. She would get giddy with anticipation and annoy her teammates with hourly reminders of how many days remained until state. This fond memory of Caroline, like so many others, was followed with the cold and lonely realization of her absence. The awareness reintroduced the pain back into their hearts and took some of the luster off the headway they had made since October.

Hempstead showed up Tuesday evening ready to perform. The Mustangs level of play was peaking at the right time. Hempstead was hungry to keep rolling into regionals. Beating top ranked West High and winning the divisional title would go a long way in achieving that goal.

Despite the carnival-like atmosphere in the student section singing along to pre-match classics like "Tiptoe Through the Tulips," dancing to the "Macarena," and "YMCA," the Women of Troy were tense during warm-ups.

The seniors were individually called onto the floor and presented with a rose. When Caroline's name was announced, the group of seniors accepted her rose and presented it to Ernie, who hugged them tight. There wasn't a dry eye in the place while fans gave Ernie a standing ovation.

There was one more person to honor before the first serve cleared the net. Brez had secured her 600th win with the team's September 10 victory over Dubuque Wahlert. The girls gave her a plaque, flowers, and a poster with a collage of her career entitled: "600 Career Wins, West vs Wahlert, September 10, 2011."

West matched Hempstead's energy and came out on fire to start the match, taking the first two sets. Then the wheels came off when they squandered a 15 to 9 lead and gave away the third set. When they dropped the fourth set and let Hempstead right back into the match, Kelley blamed herself. The truth was, everyone, including Olivia Fairfield, the "one-woman wrecking crew" from three days ago, had an off couple of sets. "Eunice [Fairfield] and I just weren't connecting," Kelley recalled.

By the end of the fourth set, Kelley wanted nothing more than to curl up in the corner of the gym. Brez called a timeout between sets and immediately went after the team for not providing better passes for Kelley to set. Then Brez pulled Kelley away from the team and into a stairwell. Kelley, angry and crying, asked the coach to replace her. Brez told her to quit crying and pull herself together. "Fake it 'til you make it, you can do this, Kelley," Brez demanded. Kelley said they both knew if Caroline hadn't gotten to those passes, the coach would have been all over her. Kelley no longer wanted the coach to blame her teammates for her mistakes, saying, "Good passes or not, I have to get there. I have to make the plays."

Before the timeout ended, Kelley joined the team huddle on the floor and told the girls they shouldn't have to change their level of play to adjust to her. She said the only way she would get any better was if they were honest with her, "Hitters, you've got to tell me where you want it set," Kelley demanded, "I'll get it there."

West improved their play and won a tightly contested fifth and deciding set 20 to 18. They were promptly engulfed by the West High student body as they rushed the court to celebrate. In a massive group hug, students and players alike sang along at the top of their lungs to "Sweet Caroline."

With Kelley's declaration, she absolved her coach and teammates of their self-imposed restrictions on criticizing her mistakes, and the team took another huge step forward. "The Hempstead game was when it [the setter position] became my spot," Kelley proclaimed.

Kelley's revelation came at the perfect time. West hosted the first round of regionals on October 27 against Des Moines Roosevelt. West supporters had grown in numbers and enthusiasm. The fervent West students came decked out in their Halloween costumes. The Women of Troy, charged by the liveliness of their fans, dispatched the Roughriders from Des Moines in a 3 to 0 sweep. Ghosts, zombies, superheroes, and even a Lady Gaga or two crowded the floor after the match to celebrate with the team and sing "Sweet Caroline."

West took their show on the road for the next round of regionals, visiting Cedar Rapids Washington. West was focused, determined, and firing on all cylinders. They completely dominated the only team standing in the way of a return trip to the state tournament, defeating Washington in less than an hour.

The host team was nice enough to have "Sweet Caroline" cued up after the match and happily joined the West team and fans on the gym floor for the sing-along. Standing amongst their supporters, the West players finally understood their goal of winning back-to-back state titles was now in sight. The rejuvenated and reenergized reigning state champions were on their way to the state tournament to defend their title.

The week between regionals and the state meet was when Brez started to worry. She had been around long enough to know how the Iowa Girls High School Athletic Union (IGHSAU) worked when it came to the state tournament. She speculated City High and West High would be placed on opposite sides of the bracket. The IGHSAU would bank on the No. 1 and No. 2 ranked teams meeting in the finals. The organization and the sport would then reap the benefits from media attention normally reserved for football, boys' basketball, and wrestling.

When the state championship bracket was released Brez's suspicion about the seeding was confirmed. City and West were indeed on opposite sides of the state championship bracket. Brez knew after sweeping City in the regular season, the Little Hawks' collective chip on their shoulder would have developed into a granite boulder.

Chapter 24
2011 State Tournament

No man ever steps in the same river twice, for it's
not the same river and he's not the same man.
—Heraclitus

One man can be a crucial ingredient on a
team, but one man cannot make a team.
—Kareem Abdul-Jabbar

April 2012, Ernie's dining room tabletop was still buried under memorabilia from the 2011 volleyball season. He looked at the various team posters given to him from high school volleyball programs in the Mississippi Valley Conference. Some of the teams had incorporated Spiderman into their posters out of respect for Caroline and her love of the superhero. He found City High's poster, and there was the web crawler woven into their poster as well.

As he went through the stacks of volleyball mementos, he saw one photo after another and each brought a smile to his face. Ernie thought about how much more there was to the story than just the photos.

The 2011 High School Volleyball State Tournament was scheduled for November 9, 11, and 12 in Cedar Rapids. The original venue was the

US Cellular Center, but because of renovations to the facility, for the first time in the tournament's history, the games would be played at the Ice Arena. There was some head scratching among the volleyball community over the new site selection.

The concerns weren't without merit. The Cedar Rapids Ice Arena is a 3,800-seat venue and home of the Cedar Rapids Roughriders, a hard-nosed junior hockey club in the United States Hockey League. The high energy Roughriders' fans can expect to see beer advertisements all over the walls, hear loud ringing cowbells and colorful language, take advantage of nightly booze specials, and watch scantily-clad cheerleaders affectionately nicknamed the Rider Girls. During the hockey season the venue wasn't exactly a family friendly atmosphere.

The day before the opening quarter-final matches, the beer advertisements were covered, the netting used to keep the pucks out of the stands removed, and rowdy Hockey fans a distant memory. The cowbells were locked in a storage closet, the beer taps shut off, and the Rider Girls given the next few nights off. The ice was covered with three layers of laminate and topped with a volleyball playing surface.

The substitute venue ended up being a blessing in disguise because it was much more intimate and fan-friendly than its larger counterpart. At the US Cellular Center, spectators sit high above the action and all the noise goes up to the ceiling and stays. In the Ice Arena, the fans are ten feet from the players, and their noise and energy stays right on the court. The IGHSAU benefited financially because the venue waived the fee for the four-day event. The $27,500 it would have cost the organization to rent the US Cellular Center would stay in their coffers, putting next year's budget in the black.

While the smaller site was great for atmosphere, it didn't come without challenges—the chief one being there just weren't enough seats. The lower seating capacity created constant bottlenecks between matches. Knowing that seating was limited, fans of upcoming matches arrived early and packed the entrance/exits waiting for the preceding match to end. When a match ended, the exiting fans had to squeeze through a narrow exit, past long lines of people waiting to enter.

The thirty-two teams were separated into four classes. Wednesday's quarterfinal matches and Friday's semifinal matches were played two at a time. Since there was limited playing space, two courts had to be squeezed in, end-to-end. With simultaneous matches being played in such small environs—and four separate cheering sections right on top of the action—the lines between school spirit and chaos were blurred more than a few times.

The early part of state tournament week was used by Brez to get a few more practices in and game plan for their first opponent, Council Bluffs-Abraham Lincoln. Lincoln had overcome some early season hiccups but played their way back into contention with a late season charge through regionals.

To offset the mounting tension, some of the seniors attempted to keep the mood light. One of the ways was a practical joke with Brez as their intended victim.

The prior season, one of the many ways Caroline boosted team morale and camaraderie was to pick a day and have all of the teammates dress in a certain theme. Once they all came to practice wearing snow pants in honor of assistant coach Scott "Snow Pants" Sanders, a moniker Caroline saddled the coach with for a reason that only made sense to her. Another theme was western day. The seniors remembered how excited Brez, a former rodeo barrel racer, was to pull her authentic cowgirl gear out of mothballs. They figured there was no way she could resist donning her barrel racing outfit again, so the team declared the following day's practice Western Day.

The next morning, Brez woke early and packed her old rodeo regalia from boots to cowboy hat. Complete with leather belt and her championship belt buckle. After school, Brez sauntered into the gym in her cowgirl duds to find she was the only one in Western attire. The team had dressed up imitating how their coach normally looked for practice. Brez didn't mind being the butt of the joke. She was thankful for the laugh.

Noticeably absent, however, was the team's star hitter, Shelly Stumpff. Inquiries of her whereabouts got the coach nowhere closer to finding her. Just as her frustration was about to boil over, Shelly came waddling out of the locker room dressed exactly like Brez, from head to toe. She had on tennis shoes, blue gym shorts, and a gray t-shirt. There were a couple of items on her costume that Shelly embellished for comedic effect. Including black horn-rimmed glasses with a piece of white tape over the nose bridge. The other exaggeration was ana-tomical—a couple of large balloons filled with water inside the front of her shirt, not in the normal spot, but down by her stomach. The humor was well received by everyone on the team and a pleasant dis-traction from the pressure of the looming state tournament.

On Wednesday afternoon, Ernie and Paul Etre squeezed their way into the Ice Arena for West's quarterfinal match. During pre-match warm-ups, the Iowa Girls High School Athletic Union piped music over the loud speakers. Team requests for certain songs are always flat-ly rejected by the organization to maintain their impartiality. So it was happenstance when "Sweet Caroline" blared over the loud speakers before the West High match, but a welcome accident embraced by the Women of Troy and their fans. The significance of the song was well known. The players and a majority of the crowd sang the familiar chorus with gusto, an impromptu tribute to Caroline.

The game underway, West High fans panicked when Lincoln charged out to an early lead. The Lincoln coaches had done their homework. Game film revealed the only chance Lincoln had was to avoid West's powerful blockers and outside hitters.

Lincoln's plan was to serve to West's front line in an attempt to keep the ball from being set for a thunderous kill from Shelly Stumpff or Olivia Fairfield. In addition, Lincoln didn't set up to spike. Instead they would tip the ball over the heads of the front line to an open space in West's defense. Brez suspected this might happen going into the game and recognized the strategy from the outset. She didn't call for adjustments right away, waiting to see if the girls would adjust on the fly. They should have but didn't, something Shelly readily admitted to *Press-Citizen* sports editor Ryan Suchomel after the game, "We should have been ready for that."

Compounding West's early problems was that Kelley Fliehler was wound tight with nerves. The regular season was one thing, but this was state. Try as Kelley might to calm herself, her nerves impacted her play. Anna could tell that Kelley was struggling, so she pulled her aside. "She told me to take some deep breaths," Kelley said. The controlled breathing worked—Kelley calmed down and played much better.

When Lincoln built a 5-0 lead, Brez called out rudimentary adjustments from the sideline, saving her timeouts. The coach's adjustments forced Lincoln into a more traditional offense, setting up their hitters, which played right into the teeth of West's strength. The front line was an impenetrable wall, sending Lincoln's spikes right back at them.

West swept the team from Council Bluffs 3-0. Pashkova did her victory leap, Shelly threw her arms into the air and screamed at the top of her lungs, and Kelley looked skyward paying tribute to her friend. Brez smiled at Ernie in the stands, and he replied with two thumbs up.

The victory moved them into a semifinal matchup with Cedar Rapids Kennedy, who had managed to upset Dubuque Hempstead.

On the opposite side of the bracket, City High overcame a second set letdown to dispatch Cedar Falls from the state tournament in four sets and advance to the semi-finals. The Little Hawks would face off against third ranked Ankeny, a team they had beat earlier in the season. As the tournament progressed and both Iowa City high schools were still playing, local interest skyrocketed at the prospect of an all-Iowa City showdown in the championship match.

On Friday, just before the noon matchup between West and the Cedar Rapids Kennedy Cougars, the Ice Arena stands were filling up. These two teams met often, and because both school's colors are green and gold it can be tough to delineate West High from Kennedy fans, but this season was different. Many West fans were decked out in a mixture of blue LIVE LIKE LINE and purple TEAM ELLYN shirts.

The teams warmed up to the pre-selected music piped through the loud speakers. The West High players and fans, including the Founds, were thrilled and amazed when "Sweet Caroline" played once again. Even though no official would admit it, the music was no accident, the organization was breaking their long-standing rule of not playing songs for individual teams.

A sing-along commenced and when the song ended, a seamless transition of "Live like Line! Live like Line!..." exploded through the rafters. The touching display even brought the IGHSAU leaders to tears and validated their decision to bend the rules, proving some rules were meant to be broken.

West played inspired volleyball, dominating the strong Cougar team led by Allie Hutchinson and Alexus Rogers by identical scores of 25-18 in the first two sets. West continued its strong play into the third set, and with a 23-20 lead, was poised to sweep Kennedy and cruise into the finals.

Then something happened, a seismic shift in momentum from West's side of the net to Kennedy's. Different people gave different reasons. Kennedy's Hutchinson would later describe the realization they were two points from elimination as a wake-up call for the Cougars. Brez's perception was that West let its guard down. "We took our foot off of the gas."

The truth is, no one knows or can accurately predict when, where, or why momentum shifts happen. The only certain thing is they are fickle and don't play favorites and can change sides from one point to the next.

Kennedy, now armed with the momentum that had eluded them in the first two sets, went on a 5-0 run and won the third set 25-23. Even though they still led two sets to one and only needed to win one more to advance to the finals, dropping that third set unnerved the Women of Troy.

West carried their anxiety and tension with them into the fourth set. With their game plan not working, they pressed even harder, taking unnecessary chances. Everything they tried failed.

Even West's mighty front row lost their confidence and withered. The front four of Stumpff, Infelt, Whitehead, and Fairfield who normally kept opposing coaches and players up at night with visions of their lightning bolt spikes and impenetrable defense, seemed lost and confused. The Cougars took full advantage of West's derailment and crushed them 25-15 in the fourth set and carried all the momentum into a deciding fifth set.

The dejected West team came to the sideline looking for answers and perhaps a little sympathy from their coach. What Coach Bresnahan gave them instead was tough love. "Where's my front row? When do we ever tip for scores? Spike the damn ball!" Brez demanded. "Kelley, take control out there and get the sets where they belong. You're better than this!" The coach slowly scanned the team, pausing to lock eyes with each player. "This is your team! Together you better figure out how to get your swagger back, and right now!"

The girls huddled on the court without their coach and the seniors took over.

"It's a new game. Let's put on new faces and get this done," Pashkova said.

"Front line, let's go out with some cockiness and come out swinging," Shelly said. "If they block it, they block it, no more tipping."

Kelley assured the hitters the sets would be there for them and to be ready. They were about to become extremely busy.

The Women of Troy came out playing aggressively and with the confidence they had lost back in the third set. Utilizing commanding accuracy, Stumpff and Fairfield overpowered Kennedy with devastating spikes on perfect sets from Fliehler. The middle hitters were once again a defensive force the Kennedy offense couldn't penetrate.

West ripped the momentum away from Kennedy early in the decisive set. The Women of Troy smashed the gas pedal to the floor, never looked back, and left the Cougars in the dust.

After Stumpff's rejection of a Kennedy spike ended the match, the team's reaction was a mixed bag of emotions. Shelly was so overwhelmed with a surge of excitement when she swung her arms to celebrate, her momentum sent her tumbling to the floor. Others hugged anyone in arms reach.

Their coach stood on the sideline, and emotion overcame her as she watched her players celebrate their advancement to the finals. She was filled with pride at the thought of how far they had come as a team in the face of seemingly insurmountable adversity.

Brez couldn't afford to jump on and ride the unbridled wave of confidence like her players did, especially after learning they would have to beat City High to repeat as champions. City High had easily dispatched Ankeny High School in their own semifinal match and now waited in the wings at their chance at redemption.

The much anticipated all-Iowa City state title match was now a reality, set for the following morning. With endless storylines, it was the kind of matchup local sports reporters might wait a career for but never have the opportunity to report on. The deluge of local and state press coverage for the title match ramped up the excitement level.

In the semi-final postgame interviews, the West girls' expressed their excitement for the matchup against City. They anticipated a tough battle but felt confident. Brez was more tempered in her responses to the media, "We've said all along that we won't get any pity points because we lost Caroline. No one is going to take it easy on us. I don't suspect City will either." The coach's statement wasn't just intended to give the reporters something to write. It was a reminder to her players they needed to stay focused and not give in to the emotion which was sure to build before they could get on the court the following day.

Brez was a seasoned coach, and like most upper-echelon coaches at any level in the profession, she was a realist. Victories were always short-lived, and reality never extended beyond the next opponent.

"If it had been any other team but City, I would have been very confident, but there was such a mystique about a City-versus-West title game," Brez admitted. "Couple that with the emotion of the girls wanting it for Caroline and it just seemed like everything was stacked against us."

Chapter 25
The Epic Final

A constant struggle, a ceaseless battle to bring success from
inhospitable surroundings, is the price of all great achievements.
—Orison Swett Marden

The fight is won or lost far away from witnesses—behind the
lines, and in the gym, long before I dance under those lights.
—Muhammad Ali

Saturday morning, November 12, was cool enough that Ernie donned
a coat, closed the backdoor to the house, and once again climbed into
the car with Paul for the thirty-minute ride to the Ice Arena. He
placed a favorite framed photo of Line playing volleyball in his lap.
Earlier that week, Ernie asked Brez to include the picture of Line in
the postgame state championship team photo. She told him if they
were fortunate enough to win, she would come get the picture from
him herself.

Anticipation and knowing the match would be well attended, they
left the house a half-hour before they needed to. The media hype
brought an over-capacity crowd to the arena for the 4A championship match between City and West—which headlined the day's slate

of title games. Ernie squeezed into a bleacher section among the West faithful.

During pre-match warm-ups, Shelly was surprised with a "Happy Birthday" serenade from the West student body, fans, and teammates. Even though it was off key, it was appreciated by the eighteen-year-old who playfully bowed to the crowd. The song was a nice gift, but there was only one thing that she wanted on this birthday, and it wasn't something she would be given as a present.

With warm-ups out of the way, the game started with a fired up City High team jumping out to an early lead. Led by powerhouse spikes from their star hitters, sophomores Michaela Nelson and Rachel Rinehart, City took the first game 25-23. The second set was much like the first, a back and forth battle. West High's front row had no answer for Nelson, who repeatedly hammered spike after spike with pinpoint accuracy. "Michaela really came out swinging on us," Stumpff confessed.

When another Nelson spike found its mark and City took the second game 29 to 27, gasps leaked from the West stands. The stunned West fans sat in silence, some with hands covering their mouths. They contemplated the implausible realization—the Women of Troy, the team of destiny, was one set away from being swept in the state finals by City High.

The excitement among the City High fans following the second set was tempered by what a Little Hawk victory meant for West High players and fans. Emotions were complex. They may have been rivals, but they were also neighbors and friends. There were several people wearing the red and white of City High who had been touched by both Caroline and Ellyn. City High setter, Erin Muir, sometimes rode with Caroline and her parents to tournaments when they played on the Rockets together. "It was never a City versus West thing with her, we were just friends," Muir said. "She would sometimes tell me West's plays and strategy. I'd have to tell her, 'Caroline, you can't tell me that, we play for different teams.'"

Brez called a timeout. Her fear of a letdown was now a surreal truth unfolding in front of her eyes, and on the biggest stage. "I looked up and thought, 'Don't do this to them. Let them win at least one game, please.'"

As the girls gathered on the sideline, the coach took a moment for herself before addressing the team. During her life the word "fairness" never factored into her lexicon. Hard work and results were what mattered, but it occurred to her, if there was ever a time unfairness fit, they were now in that moment. This team had overcome so many emotional obstacles to reach this seminal instant, and she couldn't bear the thought of what a loss would do to her players' psyche. This wasn't how the title game was supposed to go.

While West fans fretted about being on the cusp of losing the state title, the Women of Troy confidently huddled. They blocked out the fact they were behind zero sets to two in the best of five final. If any of the girls had known in the last ten years of the state tournament not one 4A team down 0-2 had rallied to win, it didn't show.

From their perspective, they had suffered and sacrificed and simply had more on the line than their opponents. They set out to win this, not for themselves, but for Caroline. They would hand the championship trophy to Ernie to hoist skyward because of what it would mean to him and to Caroline.

Certain West teammates felt they held a one-player advantage. Some might call it spiritual, while others would attribute it to metaphysics, but more than one of the girls said Caroline was on the court with them. "I could feel her presence. I was looking for her all through the match," Shelly said. From their perspective, they needed to step up their play and take what belonged to them.

West took the floor for the third set and fell behind early, but soon Shelly's inspired play spurred the team on, and they eventually broke away from City, winning the set handily.

In the fourth game, the West front line put on a blocking clinic. Infelt and Fairfield sniffed out the City High hitters and barred scoring lanes with brutal rejections. West took the game from City in lopsided fashion, 25 to 15. Their dominance in the third and fourth sets gave them the momentum heading into the final and deciding set.

The bulk of the fifth set saw the familiar foes trying to establish some advantage over the other. It turned into a back and forth chess match between equally matched teams, countering each other move for move. The girls on both sides played brilliant volleyball, making one incredible diving save after another to keep a point alive.

As play tightened, the energy and noise level in the arena dramatically increased. During the action, Ernie asked Paul if he would go to the car and grab the picture of Caroline. Paul, without a word, excused himself down the bleacher row and scurried down the stairs and out of the arena.

As the conclusion drew closer, something very uncharacteristic happened. The normally accurate City players started missing serves. West took advantage of City's serving errors and grabbed match point, 15 to 14. City fought back, knotting the contest at 15-15. West took the lead back just as quickly as they lost it, 16-15.

The tension and excitement of each point became too much for the squeamish in the stands to handle. Several fans, on both sides, held their neighbor's hand. Some cried, others covered their eyes, unable to watch as the excitement of the epic match unfolded.

City's defense stiffened once again, and they tied the set at 16. All of the advantages were now stacked in their favor. They seemed to have made great line adjustments, and it was team captain Erin Muir's turn to serve. The senior was already good on 17 of 19 service attempts for the match. The Little Hawks were in a perfect position to take the next two points and win the state title.

Muir toed the end line, tossed the ball high in the air above her head, and flat-handed it toward the net. After repeating this act thousands of times in her years playing the game, serving came as naturally to Erin as breathing. She normally had pinpoint accuracy and a knack for finding the soft spot in the defense. But for some unexplainable reason, Erin misplayed the ball which caught enough of the net to keep it on City's side of the court. Little Hawk teammates watched helplessly as the ball dropped to the floor for a West High point.

It was City's fifth serving error of the game and opened the door a third time for West. Just like the previous two times, the Little Hawks evened the score, but West grabbed a quick point and went up 17 to 16. It wasn't a big secret to anyone in the building who Fliehler would set for the attempted game winner. Shelly was on fire with twenty-one kills. City's plan was simple—concentrate their best defenders in front of her.

West served, and City volleyed. City's spike was dug by Pashkova and, as expected, Fliehler lofted the set high above Stumpff's head. She elevated to meet the ball and hammered it down the line, but no immediate signal came from the referee. The crowd held its collective breath. Ernie clutched Caroline's picture with anticipation. After a split second of reflection to determine if the ball was in or out, the ref threw his hand toward West's side of the court.

A rush of joy spilled out of the West High stands. The explosion of noise in the arena burst beyond jubilant cheers. The uproar was earsplitting, raw emotion bounced around the rafters of the venue.

As if triggered by the push of a button, the West players' screamed simultaneously. Guttural shrieks emerged from deep inside them. Their contorted almost painful faces were emotionless at first. Joy would come later. The girls' passionate expressions were a snapshot of everything they had been through over the prior three months. It was stress relief, a necessary response to such monumental, life-altering events. It was losing Caroline and Ellyn. It was witnessing Ernie, Gregg, and Catharine's heartbreak at the funerals. It was the team's heartache and not wanting to play volleyball without their friend and leader. All of which had built up inside them, but now they were finally able to let everything out.

The prolonged screams were the girls' declaration to everyone in the arena—they had come full circle. They had clawed their way out of the depths of sorrow and climbed to the top of the mountain to accomplish their ultimate goal, winning the state title for Line.

Once the initial jubilation cleared, happiness filled their hearts, and the team rushed Shelly at the net, tackled her, and landed in a heap on the floor. The embrace was short-lived. Realizing the City High players were waiting at the net for the customary postgame handshake, the girls sprung from the floor. The last thing they wanted was their actions to be misconstrued as disrespect for their opponent. Heartfelt congratulations were given by the Little Hawks to the Women of Troy.

Meanwhile, Brez had climbed the three-foot rail and into the stands. She scanned the crowd for Ernie. When she zeroed in on his location, she made a nonstop jaunt to him. She gave the Found patriarch a long, tearful embrace and happily accepted Caroline's picture from him.

State tournaments usually run like clockwork due, in large part, to the rigid schedule between matches. At the conclusion of each title game, there are a series of tightly scheduled post-game events followed to keep the tournament on schedule. The teams shake hands, the 4A all-tournament team and team captain announced, and medals given. The runner-up trophy is presented, the state champions awarded their trophy, and finally, team pictures taken. With three games remaining after theirs and each contest potentially lasting two hours, few expected "Sweet Caroline" to be played.

As Brez made her way back down to the court to be with her team, she was pleased to hear the now-familiar "Sweet Caroline" played over the loud speaker. Everyone in the arena, including the 3A teams waiting to warm-up for their match, sang along.

At the conclusion of "Sweet Caroline," the all-tournament team was announced. Of the six positions, four were selected from the two Iowa City schools. City High's Michaela Nelson and Rachel Rinehart made the team along with Olivia Fairfield and Shelly Stumpff. When Shelly was announced as captain of the team, enormous cheers erupted.

The Little Hawks gathered at the edge of the court and were called to receive the runner-up trophy. Led by Erin Muir and Rachel Rinehart, the team walked out with their heads held high and graciously accepted the trophy. They took it and acknowledged the applause from both sides of the stands by raising the trophy into the air. They were a relatively young team and felt confident they had a good shot to get back to the title game next season.

The Women of Troy anxiously awaited their turn. When the public announcer proclaimed them 2011 state champions, the crowd stood and provided raucous applause as the six seniors: Anna Pashkova, Hannah Infelt, Olivia Mekies, Olivia Fairfield, Shelly Stumpff, and Kelley Fliehler walked out together and accepted the trophy.

The remainder of the team waited a beat then charged out to join the seniors, and together they raised the trophy. Ernie was moved to see the City High players leading the cheers for their opponents. "It's a shame a team had to lose. Those City girls were cheering right along with our girls. You would hardly know they lost the state championship."

In a show of appreciation, the West players ran to the West High student section. The lively bunch had been there for the girls every step of the way. As far as the players were concerned, this championship belonged to them as much as the team. Tears flowed as the players walked the rail shaking hands and hugging their fellow students in the first row.

As they celebrated, there was only one detail which would have made it better—if Line would have been there to share the moment with them. "It was a bitter-sweet moment. I broke down in tears thinking how much she would have loved it," Hannah Infelt said.

The sensational ending to the 2011 West High volleyball season was fitting considering its start. With the players' and coaches' constant tension and emotion throughout that season, how could there be any other conclusion? In the *Press-Citizen* the following day, Susan Harman put it best when she ended her column with, "Oh Hollywood? Your script is ready."

Indeed.

There was no easy way to fully describe the 2011 volleyball season. Brez probably covered it best in a postseason booklet she compiled and distributed to the team. "The season became bigger than us … students, friends, and the community seemed to turn to the volleyball team to help them cope with their pain of losing Caroline and Ellyn. How this team found the strength and fortitude to defend and win a state championship is almost beyond belief."

Admittedly, the coach hadn't had time to comprehend what happened. She wouldn't fully understand the season until she stepped away from the game, quieted her mind, and kicked her feet up on the back of a houseboat with a fishing line or two in the water. "It was an amazing journey, and I'm not sure that I'd change it. If I had to do it again, it would be with the exact same group because every kid contributed to help us survive," Brez said.

For many of the players, the 2011 season was more difficult and more meaningful than the prior season, despite each ending with a state championship. While their feelings may have varied, those who placed extra significance on the 2011 state title were similar in spirit to Kelley Fliehler in sentiment: "We knew how badly Caroline wanted to win back-to-back state titles. She wanted it more than anything, and we would have been disappointed in ourselves if we didn't get it for her. After everything that Ellyn did for this team and everything she taught us, we wanted to win it for her as well."

The West High volleyball team's championship lit a fire under other West High varsity teams. Most of them played their respective seasons with some tribute to Caroline on their uniform, warm-ups, or accessory in their hair. By the end of the 2011-12 school year West High had racked up a record setting six state championships—volleyball, boys' and girls' basketball, boys' soccer, boys' tennis, and boys' track and field.

Chapter 26
Good Things from Something So Bad

Our human compassion binds us—the one to the other—not
in pity or patronizingly, but as human beings who have learnt
how to turn our common suffering into hope for the future.
—Nelson Mandela

The dramatic conclusion to the inspirational and emotional volleyball season brought both relief and confusion. Ernie held a postseason bash for the volleyball team at the farm and then, in December, continued his travels with a family trip to Las Vegas.

With the stress-filled season completed, the media stopped asking for quotes from Ernie and those associated with the volleyball team. Understandably they all felt a bit forlorn. For three months they had a direction, goals, and purpose along with a huge support group encouraging them. With the season over, feelings of emptiness crept into their everyday lives.

Some of the teammates wrapped themselves up with friend-based activities, music, or other sports. Kelley and Shelly traded their volleyball gear for basketball uniforms and helped win another state title.

True to her word, Brez reached out to the girls on a daily basis. She paid special attention to the seniors who had so many plans for their final year at West, many of which had included Caroline. "I felt like the seniors got cheated," Coach Bresnahan said. "It was a harsh reality." Kelley and Shelly started eating lunch in their coach's room every day. They talked about their daily lives and future plans with her—she encouraged, supported, and promoted but mostly she listened.

The 2012 senior class vowed not to forget Caroline's death. They wanted to make sure her legacy lived on by setting a shining example for the underclassman to follow. They were nicer to each other. Petty differences were set aside, and new friendships forged in their places. They reached out to underclassman and filled up the mentoring program Caroline was so fond of. They got involved in civic causes like cancer research and how to raise money. One way was creating and buying all sorts of rubber wrist bands relating to cancer research. They bought more LIVE LIKE LINE shirts.

Although it was important for the administration to allow the students to honor Caroline, it was vital it was done positively and in moderation. At the beginning of the school year, when the sadness of losing Caroline was fresh, some of those close to Caroline developed an unhealthy competition of who-was-a-better-friend-with-her and who had the right to mourn and honor her more. "I find all that a very distressing part of human nature. It was a wakeup call for me," Amy Kanellis revealed.

With each school activity, the students tried to weave honoring Caroline into it. The administration felt it was necessary to be selective. "We were looking for ways to keep her name and memory alive in a positive 'I love life and people' message, at the same time realizing that she wasn't here and we had to move on," Amy explained.

One example, early in the school year, occurred when two members of the Homecoming Committee, social studies teacher, Mitch Gross, and Amy vetoed the idea of nominating Caroline as homecoming queen. The committee members who came up with the idea were angry and went out of their way not to talk to either Mitch or Amy. A compromise was devised instead—a "Live Like Line" award would be presented to the student who best exemplified Caroline's spirit.

Honoring Caroline took shape on a much grander scale when, in January of 2012, three West High seniors—Olivia Lofgren, Leah Murray, and Caroline Van Voorhis—were presenters during a Transportation Subcommittee meeting at the state capitol in Des Moines. They were there speaking in support of Senate File 2085 (SF2085), a bill proposing that riders of two-wheeled motorcycles and mopeds under the age of eighteen be required to wear a helmet while the vehicles were in motion.

The trio spoke eloquently to the legislators about the benefits of helmet laws, citing statistics to support their argument. They talked passionately about their friend Caroline and pointed out had there been a helmet law in August, chances are she would still be alive. Their presentation made quite an impression on the generally unimpressed government officials. "They had the legislators eating out of the palms of their hands," Boyd Murray gushed.

It was surreal for the high school seniors to sit in front of prominent state senators and present their ideas. The genesis of the proposed legislation started as an idea floated to Olivia Lofgren by local attorney Joe Mooreland during a neighborhood party.

Olivia was intrigued by the idea and reached out to her friend Leah Murray who loved it. Leah's parents saw it as a perfect cause for her since she struggled so mightily with her friend's death. "It was a great place for the girls to place their energy in a positive way," Boyd explained.

Joe Mooreland organized weekly meetings with the girls to strategize how to get a helmet law passed. Olivia and Leah drafted a "Letter to the Editor," making a case for helmet legislation which ran in the *Press-Citizen*. Classmate Caroline Van Voorhis read the article and was so moved she called her friends to see how she could be involved. She was immediately brought into the fold.

The group met with Mary Mascher, their former elementary teacher and a member of the Iowa House of Representatives. That meeting led to another meeting with David Jacoby, also a member of the Iowa House of Representatives from Coralville. This led to a meeting with state Senator Bob Dvorsky, who contacted fellow Senator Joe Bolkom. The group of legislators set the proposed helmet legislation in motion.

Later in October, Olivia, Leah, and Caroline were invited to the state capitol in Des Moines to present their helmet legislation to legislators from every corner of Iowa. Another person who listened to their passionate plea was Geoff Lauer, Executive Director of Brain Injury Alliance of Iowa, a citizens' lobby group concerned with trying to enact helmet laws in the state. Lauer contacted the girls just days after hearing them speak and told them he was interested in supporting them. Brain Injury Alliance of Iowa had many legislative contacts and a lobbyist designated to work on enacting a helmet law. With Brain Injury Alliance of Iowa support, the girls' efforts gained momentum.

By late January, senators Bolkom and Dvorsky had enlisted help and support from fellow senators Rob Hogg, Liz Mathis, Herman Quirmbach, and Pam Jochum, all of whom co-sponsored SF2085. The senators walked the bill to the Transportation Committee, who sent it to the Transportation Subcommittee for study and a return recommendation. The subcommittee invited the girls back to Des Moines to present their case on the record.

To garner support, the girls started a Facebook page: "Hope for a Helmet." Olivia, Leah, and Caroline used the page to educate the public with statistics on how many lives were saved by simply wearing a helmet and to inform them on the status of SF2085. They sold Carolina Blue key chains for $2 with "Hope for a Helmet" and Caroline's volleyball number "9" imprinted on them. West High students visited the page, purchased key chains, and liked the page.

Before they presented to the subcommittee, the girls were prepared by senators Bolkom and Dvorsky, mostly that they should manage their expectations regarding passage of the bill. There were a couple of issues that made it a longshot.

There are many bills proposed each legislative session, but few make it through the multi-step vetting process and become laws. The Transportation Subcommittee was only the first stop. After the file was studied in subcommittee, and if the members deemed it worthy, it would be considered by the full committee. If the Transportation Committee voted in favor of it, SF2085 would be sent to the Senate floor for debate and a vote. Twenty-six senators would need to vote for the bill for it to be sent to the House for a vote. If passed by the House without amendment, the bill would finally reach the governor's office for consideration. Finally, a "yes" vote would be required from the Governor in the form of his signature to become law.

The primary obstacle to SF2085 becoming law was the anti-helmet lobby. ABATE (A Brotherhood Aimed Toward Education) is a non-profit organization of motorcycle enthusiasts with the aim of, among other things, advocating favorable legislation for motorcycle riders. ABATE has been a longtime defender of a motorcycle rider's choice whether or not to wear a helmet on Iowa roads.

ABATE's full-time lobbyist at the statehouse presented at the same subcommittee meeting with the girls. While ABATE applauded the girls' efforts, they restated their longstanding position—although they don't advocate for riders not to wear helmets, they think educating riders to make the proper choice to wear a helmet is preferable to a law requiring it. They respected that the proposed legislation was only applied to minors but still saw the law as an avenue to a helmet law irrespective of age.

Three of the five subcommittee members sided with ABATE. SF 2085 wasn't recommended to the Transportation Committee and died on the subcommittee floor. Senators Bolkom and Dvorsky met with the girls after the subcommittee decision and told the trio not to lose heart. The senators reminded them a typical bill requires between two to three years to get enough traction to become a law.

Another obstacle for the bill was timing. It was an election year, and nothing kills a politician's chances for re-election faster than backing a controversial piece of legislation like SF2085. Finally, the senators suggested it would help if they worked to get their message outside the borders of Iowa City.

As if on cue, Nathan McNurlen, a graduate film student at the University of Iowa, noticed the girls on the news one night and became interested. He and a couple of his classmates created an eighteen-minute YouTube documentary titled: *Hope/Hearts/Helmets* featuring Olivia, Leah, and Caroline on their efforts to get the helmet law passed.

The girls' efforts attracted the attention of the *Huffington Post* which featured them in their series "Greatest Person of the Day." Locally, Olivia, Leah, and Caroline were asked to speak at several events around Iowa City. They were also presented with the "New Advocates Award" from Brain Injury Alliance of Iowa.

The entire process of taking on an issue like a helmet law in Iowa was a huge confidence boost for the three teenagers. They stood toe-to-toe against ABATE and senators opposed to helmet laws and gained firsthand knowledge of the inner workings of the legislative process. In a local news article, Olivia was gracious, "It's been an amazing experience—something no government class can teach you."

Although a rewarding experience, confidence and experience wasn't their objective. The three admitted they faced an uphill battle. They have since gone off to colleges in different states but remain resolute in their conviction to one day get the law passed. "Whatever it takes, we're in it for the long haul," Leah said.

When Ernie came home from his family Vegas trip in January, he decided it was time to get back to work. Both he and the department thought it best if he ease back into surgery with a lightened workload. His colleagues were thrilled to have him back at work.

Soon after he returned to work, on the evening of January 14, Charlotte Neilson happily closed her deli early. Although maybe a bit unheard of for a restaurant owner to close early, this was the farthest thing from her mind when she agreed to host a surprise sixtieth birthday party for Ernie. Some things are more important than money, and to her, this was one.

At 7 PM, one hundred of Ernie's closest friends and family gathered at Charlotte's. Food and drink was complimentary, but it didn't stop party goers from setting out an impromptu donation bowl and giving hundreds of dollars to offset the owner's lost revenue.

From Charlotte's perspective, hosting was the least she could do for the family who not only had been good friends but played such an instrumental part in her success. "All three of them worked for me. Ellyn was here every Wednesday, Catharine worked here over the summers, and Caroline worked here regularly. Line was here the morning of the eleventh," Charlotte said, her voice quivering.

Family and friends had already exchanged favorite Found stories and reflections for about an hour before Marilyn Found drove Ernie into Charlotte's lot. An unsuspecting Ernie thought his sister had made a wrong turn. She told him they were going to Larry and Linda Marsh's house for a night of darts.

Ernie was surprised to see Charlotte's lot full so late in the evening. "My first impression was, 'Man, Charlotte has a pretty good business going on here,'" he quipped. "All the surrounding business' lights were out so I thought maybe it was a private party. Then we pulled up, and I saw Larry and Paul inside and thought, 'Oh my god.'"

Ernie walked in and was greeted with a resounding, "Surprise!" The theme of the party was to make the night strictly about Ernie. Party organizers wanted to honor the man who had spent the last six months honoring Ellyn and Caroline. A party goer recited a poem she wrote about him:

"His talents and interests abound
this surgeon slash magician named Found.
We are old and decrepit
but we can accept it
when there're old guys like Found around."

The evening was wonderful. Filled with lively stories, many told by Ernie. He spoke of his relationship with Larry at medical school, residency, and moving to Iowa. He talked about his trip to New Hampshire with Paul and their zip lining exploits. Every time Larry, Paul, or any other speaker tried to put the spotlight squarely on Ernie, he just as quickly turned the honor and admiration towards his family.

In February, PrepVolleyball.com named Coach Bresnahan National

Volleyball Coach of the Year for the 2011 season. PrepVolleyball.com is the preeminent national high school volleyball publication, so each year there are several deserving coaches nominated for the prestigious award. Many years the decision is so difficult they select co-coach of the year, but the reporter explained the 2011 selection was easy. "Coach Brez stands alone."

The reporter interviewed several volleyball coaches from Iowa who were quoted as saying what an amazing job Brez did during the exceptional season. The first quote was from Tom Keating. "Kathy will tell you that so many people helped her and the team work through this incredibly challenging time, but the reality is that Kathy was the rock."

The PrepVolleyball article caught the eye of *ESPN Magazine*, and they decided the story would be perfect for their spring high school issue. They assigned Walter Villa to cover the story.

Ernie's cell phone rang one day, and he was reluctant to answer because he didn't recognize the number. He answered anyway, and Villa explained who he was and why he was calling. After a nice conversation, the reporter told Ernie he would send him a copy of the spring issue featuring an article about Caroline and the volleyball team. Ernie called Gregg to see if he had anything to do with the article. Gregg assured his father he was just as surprised when Villa contacted him before the spring edition was released.

Despite an increased work schedule, Ernie maintained his symbiotic relationship with the volleyball girls for the remainder of the school year. They were each other's connection to Caroline.

For the girls, Ernie's adventurous spirit and hospitality was how they were able to stay connected to her. Be it a swimming pool party, a hayride, or just inviting them to bring some friends over and hang out in the barn for the day. "He loves to be like a little kid and does all this crazy stuff. He's definitely where Caroline got her personality," Kelley said.

The volleyball seniors served as surrogate daughters to Ernie by including him in their senior activities. The girls allowed Ernie to experience everything Caroline missed the entire year. In early May, after they posed with their dates for senior prom pictures at their own homes, the girls dragged their dates to the farm to repeat the process for Ernie. Later that month, he was invited to and attended each of the senior volleyball player's graduation parties.

On the evening of May 24, Ernie parked his car, adjusted his coat and tie, with mixed emotions trekked towards Carver Hawkeye Arena for the Iowa City West High Commencement.

As a guest speaker, Ernie patted his coat pocket to ensure he still had the speech he had crafted. While he was honored and happily accepted the invitation from Jerry Arganbright to speak to the senior class, he was morose about the reason. Instead of Caroline probably charging across the stage and jumping into the principal's arms to receive her high school diploma, Arganbright would present Caroline's honorary degree to him.

After the last valedictorian was recognized by the principal, Arganbright announced the honorary diploma recipient and called Ernie forward to accept it. The graduates sprung to their feet with wild applause. The spectators in the stands followed the graduates' lead.

The ovation bathed Ernie in emotion; he choked back tears as he shook Jerry's hand and thanked him. After the two embraced, Ernie took a position behind the podium to say a few words, and the applause intensified. Ernie couldn't hold back his emotions as he waited for the extended standing ovation to subside. These were the people who had been there for him every step of the way. Together they had grieved and memorialized Caroline and Ellyn the past nine months.

Once the applause died down and everyone took their seats, Ernie took a breath and smiled at the Class of 2012. "Well, here we are. We made it. Commencement day. We all know what 'commencement' means; it means to begin something, start anew. When this ordeal is done, we are going to go out and begin our lives doing something entirely new and something quite a bit unknown: a job, more schooling, or a new relationship. You know, these new things will be exciting, but it comes with many unknowns. How are we going to tackle some of these unknowns? Let me provide for you a few anecdotal and action axioms to live by," he began.

Ernie spoke of his own trials and tribulations after high school. He was a big shot scholarship winner for achieving the highest marks in mathematics during his four years at Batavia High. Along with his sports accolades, he left for college supremely confident.

His confidence shriveled up on the first day of calculus class where he was completely lost and got an "F" on the first quiz. He called his parents requesting to come home. They told him to ask for help and keep trying, which is exactly what he told the graduates to do.

Next, Ernie asked the entire graduating class to stand and partake in an exercise. While they stood in place he asked them to smile, kick themselves in the butt, pat themselves on the back, and finally to pat their neighbor on the back. He then asked them to sit back down.

He finished with some words of wisdom: "So here are my few brief axioms: No. 1, ask for help when you need it. No. 2, when it is up to you alone, just get it done. No. 3, feel the fear and then do it. No. 4, smile, it saves a lot of energy. No. 5, don't kick yourself in the can too hard. No. 6, don't pat yourself on the back too often. No. 7, acknowledge others with a pat on the back. Finally, and this will be axioms 8 through 100, 'Live Like Line'. You all know what that means; it's what I do. Congratulations to you all, and thank you very much for sharing your hearts,"

Ernie said. These axioms were what he and Ellyn had been raised on, had raised their children on, and now he had passed them along to Line's friends and classmates, some of whom would pass them on to their children someday.

For more than a few members of the Class of 2012, when Caroline died, a part of their youth died too. Through the loss of someone so close, they had experienced the vulnerabilities of humanity in a way most invincible teenagers hadn't. As they had done all year, the West High Class of 2012 took a negative and turned it into a positive.

Caroline's tragedy made them re-prioritize what was important in their lives. "Life is hard, but you should value every aspect of your life and make every single second that you have with people count. Value the people you have, the support systems you have, and the support you can provide," Hannah Infelt declared.

The graduates would view every day they were given on the earth as a gift and live each to the fullest. They would establish giving hearts and help those less fortunate. In short, they would Live Like Line.

Chapter 27
Summer 2012: A New Friend and a Hollywood Invasion

There's not a word yet, for old friends who've just met.
—Jim Henson, "I'm Going to Go Back There"

It's very unusual in Hollywood. Few people are
trustworthy—a handshake means nothing to them.
—James Cameron

Ernie took a trip to San Antonio to see Catharine graduate from Trinity University. She was one of three students selected by the college to receive a community service award. The presenter listed the reasons for her nomination—her role with the ambassadors, co-chairing the class of 2012 gift committee, her position as captain of the volleyball team, and her involvement with her sorority. The presenter then zeroed in on what he valued about Catharine the person, citing her range of relationships with other students on campus. "She is as comfortable with fellow students in Urban Studies as she is with athletes on the volleyball team and her sorority sisters. She's one of the cool kids without barriers or ego, a harmonizer in all that she does."

After graduation, Catharine moved back to the farm in June. It was comforting to Ernie that, after months alone, he would finally have family back in the house again, even if it was only temporary. Catharine planned to follow in her mother's footsteps by moving to Boston at the end of the summer with her best friend from college, Hannah Schweitzer. Further, Catharine planned to start running and waitress at Hoolihan's.

Ernie and Catharine spent the summer attending West High softball games, going out to eat together, and reorganizing the house. They also prepared for the upcoming memorial trip to New Hampshire in August.

There were still events going on over the summer to honor Caroline, Ellyn, and the volleyball team. One event Ernie and Catharine attended was in downtown Iowa City on the pedestrian mall. The city added park benches and hired artists to paint them. A bench at the east end of the pedestrian mall, beside the public library, was painted to resemble the LIVE LIKE LINE t-shirts. The artist invited the volleyball team to get in the act by painting the front of the bench a cobalt blue base. The artist then painted the familiar "LIVE LIKE LINE" over the top with an addition to the bench in smaller letters, "Love Like Ellyn."

While it was wonderful having Catharine at home, her presence didn't diminish Ernie's pain. There were still things too raw for him to face, like the crash site. He still hasn't been past the accident location on Mormon Trek Boulevard despite the logistical inconvenience this creates to much of the Iowa City/Coralville area. "It's a little embarrassing when I ride with people to ask them to go all the way around," Ernie said.

On July 18, 2012, triple-digit heat and Lisa Bennett, one of the producers for HBO's *Real Sports with Bryant Gumbel* arrived at the Found farm. Lisa explained that an impassioned plea from Hall of Fame sports writer Frank Deford was enough for them to send her to Iowa and find out if the story was worthy of a segment on the show. Coach Brez had sent Deford a letter explaining the events of 2011, not to get on television but with the hope he might be inspired enough to write a book about them.

Deford had penned eighteen books, one of which entitled *Alex: The Life of a Child* (Viking, 1983). The book is a memoir narrating the life of his daughter, Alex, who was diagnosed with Cystic Fibrosis in 1972 and, at the age of eight, died from the disease. Later, the book became a movie starring Craig T. Nelson as Deford.

Lisa was quickly drawn to Ernie's easy ways and natural story-telling ability. For the next few hours, Lisa was regaled with stories about his family while enjoying an ice-cold Arnold Palmer and a magic trick or two. A scheduled flight was the only thing keeping her from staying to hear more.

Lisa reluctantly said goodbye and made her way into the sweltering July evening. By the time she reached her rental parked in Ernie's drive, she had her cell phone in hand and was speaking to Bryant. Lisa not only recommended the story to the show's host, she also said they should fast-track it with a goal of airing it in an October episode.

Part of the rush was that the seniors on the volleyball team were preparing to attend college and their departure dates were spread over the month of August. Bennett would need to split the piece into two visits. She would bring a crew in early August and interview the volleyball players and coaches before the first player was slated to leave for school. They would come back to town later in the summer and interview individuals more anchored to the community.

Initially, Ernie was thrilled when Lisa called and told him Frank Deford was coming to the farm to interview him. As a kid, Ernie was one of countless sports fans entertained and informed by Deford's articles. When young Ernie received his weekly issue of *Sports Illustrated*, he would check the contents to see if Frank had written an article. If he had, Ernie would rifle past everything else to read it first.

He was elated at the prospect of having one of his favorite sports writers at his house. However, as the September interview date closed in, Ernie became concerned the individual he so revered as a child might not match up with the real life person. What if Frank Deford turned out to be a fame hungry, pretentious jerk?

When Frank and the HBO crew arrived in September, Ernie decided to play it cool—taking a play out of his neighbor John Maier's book. He would force Frank to initiate their first social encounter so he could gauge Deford the person. Ernie wasn't disappointed. "Frank likes to talk, but he also likes to listen. He genuinely likes to hear what people have to say. I thought he'd come out here, 'Alright, I'm in the middle of Iowa, when are we going to get this done? Are we about ready to go?' He was not that way at all. We spent an hour outside in the barn talking."

It was late afternoon by the time they had wrapped up all the questions Frank had for Ernie. Deford and the HBO folks were going to call it a night and head back to their hotel when Ernie asked if they would like to hang out for a while and enjoy some genuine Iowa hospitality. Not wanting to face another night of takeout food, they heartily agreed to Ernie's offer of a barbeque dinner.

The guests and their host ate, drank, and made merry. The rest of the crew gave Ernie and Frank some space. The golden hour and the cicadas' song mesmerized the two men as they watched the western corn field slowly consume the amber sun.

Once the light show ended and released its grip on them, the conversation turned to sports, more specifically, baseball. Ernie told Frank how much his eighty-five-year-old father loved Cardinals baseball. He confessed that for his father's eighty-fifth birthday, he tried to recite *Casey at the Bat* while playing original music he commissioned from a local concert pianist. He admitted he got the poem and the music down, but putting them together wasn't as easy as he thought. "It is damn hard to play the piano and talk at the same time," Ernie confessed, "To play and sing is okay because you are singing right along with playing, but when you talk, it throws off your timing and eventually you find yourself talking in time with the music." Two weeks prior to his father's birthday, it became clear he couldn't make it happen. He had recruited Gregg to recite the poem while he played the piece in the background.

Frank said how much he admired the poem too. Ernie decided to test Frank's knowledge of the famous verse and launched into the first line without warning, "The outlook wasn't brilliant for the Mudville nine that day..."

To which Frank replied without skipping a beat, "...The score stood four to two with but one inning left to play."

Back and forth they went, line by line, until they finished the legendary poem. The camera crew kicked themselves for putting their equipment away and not documenting the impromptu recitation. When they finished, Ernie said, "You really do know that poem."

To which Frank simply replied, "Yeah, I'm familiar with it."

With the footage in the can, it was time for Frank and the crew to leave. As an afterthought, the crew wanted to get a few shots of the UIHC building before they left town. Ernie led them around so they could scout for a suitable location. They found a spot and, as the crew set up, Ernie took the opportunity to ask Frank one final question.

"Has there ever been a day that you didn't think about Alex?" Ernie asked.

Frank paused and measured his words. "Yeah, that day came. I remember it was about two years afterwards. I got up one morning and realized I hadn't thought about her the day before. I was shocked and almost mad at myself. It takes time. Time will help and will soften, but time won't heal it."

When the camera crew was packed up, Frank told Ernie they had to go. The two men, who shared the love of baseball and the heartache of losing a child, embraced, and then the sports reporter climbed into the back seat of their rented SUV. Walking back to his car, Ernie turned when he heard his name. Frank leaned out of the open window and yelled, "I'm going to send you something. Be looking for it."

Ernie waved in the direction of the SUV as it accelerated down the street.

Deford left Iowa City as enamored with Ernie as Ernie was with him. Deford found Ernie to be an honorable man, fiercely committed to his family. He was amazed at Ernie's strength and grace in the face of sorrow so deep that even he, a parent who outlived a child, couldn't take its full measure.

About a week later, Ernie opened a package that came in the mail. He pulled out two items: a hand-written letter from Frank and a copy of *Casey on the Loose: What Really Might Have Happened* by Frank Deford, released in 1989. Deford wrote the book using Ernest Thayer's well-known poem to create a fictional account of the trials and tribulations for Casey after his infamous strikeout.

Frank could have easily been indignant when Ernie questioned his knowledge of the poem. He could have spoken down his nose about his published books and his fifty-plus years in the business, but he didn't. That told Ernie all he needed to know about the man he had placed on a pedestal. Ernie was relieved that Deford not only lived up to but surpassed his own legend. Ernie thought Frank may have even passed muster with ol' John Maier.

On October 23, 2012, the story about Caroline and the West High volleyball team titled: "Live Like Line" aired on *Real Sports with Bryant Gumbel*. Frank, Lisa Bennett, and the HBO crew didn't disappoint. They showed the dramatic and heartbreaking loss of Caroline, then Ellyn, and the amazing mountain of grief the volleyball team had to overcome to win another state title.

Bryant closed the segment with an in-studio sit down with Deford. The reporter saved the best for last and finished by telling Gumbel about Ernie learning a new piano piece and reciting *Casey at the Bat* for his father's birthday. On the surface, it was a charming way to end the story, but it was more than that. It was a personal acknowledgment to Frank's new friend from Iowa and the special evening they had spent together amongst the cicadas watching the sunset.

The story's impact on the nation was immediate and dramatic. The local and state media outlets clamored for reaction interviews from Ernie, Coach Brez, the volleyball team, and nearly anyone associated directly or indirectly with the Founds or the volleyball team. An infusion of new Live Like Line t-shirt orders flooded Hollywood Graphic's website from neighboring states—Minnesota, Missouri, and Nebraska, and as far away as Alabama and Arkansas.

It turns out that Hollywood also watches Bryant Gumbel's show, and it wasn't long after the story aired that movie producer, Ross Greenberg, called Ernie and asked if they could meet. Greenberg, the former head of HBO Sports, told him that he was moved by the story and believed it could be an inspiring movie.

Ernie was shocked. He never considered what had happened, while tragic, sad, and inspiring, to be movie-worthy. He felt overwhelmed at the prospect of dealing with Hollywood hotshots, so he reached out to Frank Deford, who had some experience dealing with Hollywood when they made the movie about his daughter. Frank told him if he was really considering it, the most important thing for him was trust. He had to be able to trust the moviemaker to do the right thing with something as precious as his family's story. Ernie discussed it with Catharine and Gregg, who both expressed some reservation with the idea. Ernie took a few meetings but never felt comfortable enough with any of the writers or producers to move forward.

His biggest trepidation with the process of a movie was the lack of control. Ernie wanted the ability to dictate to the producers and directors what would and wouldn't be in the movie. "I wouldn't want any booze or drugs in the movie. I wouldn't want to see any of the girls pregnant," Ernie said. The Hollywood term for what he was asking for was "final cut," but he was never assured by a producer or writer he would get that.

The phone calls from Hollywood persisted. "I continue to be on the fence about it," Ernie said. "Sometimes I think that we should just go ahead with it for all the good things that might come out of it. Other times I think, 'Let's just let the book be it, we don't need any more.'"

Chapter 28
New Hampshire—The Climb

Climb the mountains and get their good tidings.
—John Muir

The frank blessings of the hill
Fall on thee, as fall they will.
"Tis the law of bush and stone—
Each can only take his own.
Let him heed who can and will,—
Enchantment fixed me here
To stand the hurts of time, until
In mightier chant I disappear.
—Ralph Waldo Emerson, *Monadnoc*

[Author Note: Because of what I witnessed on August 10 and 11, 2012, I felt compelled to write these last two chapters in the first person. My fitness level, trepidation of funerals, and bad weather nearly caused me to miss the events, which not only would have been tragic from a personal standpoint, but the story would have suffered.]

In June of 2012, Ernie asked me to attend the August memorial service for Ellyn and Caroline in New Hampshire. He said the plan was for roughly fifty family and friends to climb Mount Monadnock on Friday morning. Pastor Matt Paul would oversee the memorial service and interment of both Caroline and Ellyn's ashes on Saturday at Cathedral of the Pines. I was honored when he asked me, but I had two reservations.

Reservation No. 1: I was carrying way too much around the midsection on two knees without cartilage. The last thing I wanted was to ruin what was sure to be a seminal and emotional weekend for the Found and Slocum families by being airlifted off of a mountain with a heart attack. When I repeatedly expressed my worry to Ernie, he assured me that climbing Monadnock was a misnomer. It was more of a hike than a climb. After hearing about Paul and the zipline, I should have known better than to take his words at face value, but he was very convincing.

My second reservation I kept from Ernie. Before the New Hampshire weekend I had only viewed Ellyn and Caroline's deaths in two dimensions—via second hand accounts or video. I hadn't attended either of their funeral services because I don't handle death well, especially that of a teenager. When I watched Caroline's visitation and funeral service on DVD it truly depressed me. I didn't know I was depressed, but my wife did. I denied it at first but after some self-reflection realized she was right. I stepped away from the Found's story for about a month to regroup.

I talked the trip over with my wife, whose opinion I value more than anyone else on the planet. She thought I should go to New Hampshire. I decided, as hard as it would be, I owed it to Ernie and his family, the volleyball team, the community, and mostly to Ellyn and Caroline to tell the story properly. It would help for me to see and feel these two events first hand. I booked a flight into the Manchester-Boston Regional Airport for Thursday, August 9. The memorial took on an even greater importance when I realized it would be the perfect way to end this book.

An hour before I left for the airport, I checked my email to make sure there wasn't anything that couldn't wait until I returned. There was an alert from the airline, my flight had been delayed a few hours because Atlanta was socked in with weather. This delay put me outside of the window to catch my connecting flight to Manchester, so I immediately called the airline to see what alternatives were available.

Despite my rising tone of frustration, the unsympathetic customer service representative repeatedly told me I had no options. I would just have to fly out Friday morning. Desperate, I gave her a summary of the story and the importance of my being in New Hampshire on Friday morning to "hike" the mountain. After a long pause, presumably to let her heart finish thawing, she choked on the words, "I can get you into Boston at midnight."

At 12:30 AM, I climbed in a rental car, set the GPS for Rindge, New Hampshire, cranked the radio, and steered onto the Interstate 93 North on-ramp for the two-hour drive.

Halfway through my road trip, while passing through yet another blacked out New England town, I received a text message. I normally would ignore a text while at the wheel, but at 1:30 AM I needed an excuse to stretch, so I pulled over to the shoulder and read it. It was from Gregg: "Look, I've had a couple of beers and am really tired, but I'm going to stay awake and guide you in. This place is really hard to find, especially at night." I was extremely touched he thought of me and called to tell him so. The gesture may not have meant nearly as much if I was family, or his close friend, but Gregg and I had only met one other time as interviewer and interviewee. I told him how touched I was of his concern for my well-being, but I had another hour of driving so he should get some sleep and I would see him in the morning.

Friday morning I dressed in cargo shorts and the LIVE LIKE LINE t-shirt Ernie had left for me at the front desk when I picked up my a room key. I had a nice breakfast and met many family members and friends.

Several of Ernie's guests like Mike and Barb Recker, Paul Etre, and Pastor Matt and his wife had arrived earlier in the week and had gone up the mountain the day before. Each had some excellent advice for me, but none of them described getting to the top as a hike. "You'll be huffing and puffing on the way up, but coming down isn't aerobic; it would only be tough for people with bad joints," Mike Recker exclaimed. My left knee throbbed as if it had ears.

After breakfast, I rode with Ernie to the mountain. He led the procession of cars on the ten-minute drive. He turned from the highway onto a narrow lane leading to a small park ranger shack. Ernie stopped, lowered the driver's side window, and extended a five-dollar bill to the ranger.

"We're back again. I guess we just can't get enough," Ernie joked.

"I see that. Welcome back," the park ranger replied with a smile.

"Have an updated weather report?"

"The National Weather Service says there's supposed to be thunderstorms after 3 PM, but I never trust the National Weather Service. It could come a lot sooner."

"Or maybe it won't come at all."

Ernie feathered the gas and drove ahead to the long and narrow parking lot. Other cars in the group trickled in and occupied spots around Ernie's rental car. He unfolded his tall frame from the car with a groan. It was the second time in as many days the sixty-year-old with a worn hip, had climbed the mountain, and his body was rebelling. He secretly hoped that he wouldn't have to go all the way to the top this time and that at least one of his two, Iowa City wild-card climbers,

Jennifer Whitmore and Annette Winkler, would bow out early. Ernie would be their knight in shining armor to escort them to the bottom.

Ernie donned his favorite St. Louis Cardinals cap, which completely clashed with his purple "Team Found" t-shirt. This day wasn't about fashion, not that Ernie ever worried much about such frivolities. I jammed the pockets of my cargo shorts with bottled water.

The parking lot soon turned into a blend of reunited family members being introduced to the Founds' friends from Iowa. Ernie normally would have made every introduction himself, but he looked skyward at the heavy, gray clouds rolling in and decided self-introductions on the way up would have to suffice. Ernie made a few remarks and thanked the collective for sharing the weekend with his family. In his best camp counselor voice, Ernie yelled instructions for all thirty-five in the group to hear, "OK, anyone needing to use the bathrooms, they are in the building to the right. We'll probably get spread out going up, so just follow the White Dot Trail up to the peak and the White Cross Trail back down."

White Dot Trail, so named for the white dots painted on trees and rocks up the mountain, was a 1.9 mile direct route to the summit. The trail, which took most people between three and four hours to complete, started and finished on a flat dirt path splitting the Ranger Station and visitor center.

Once pit stops were completed, we moved as a loosely formed group onto the trail, which started tamely enough. Small rocks embedded into the gradually inclining path were hazards, but nothing too concerning. The majority of the group marched along the trail with a third of the younger and more physically fit climbers pulling away. It wasn't long before the lead pack disappeared out of sight.

People in the slower group eventually spread out and formed smaller clusters. Some groups chatted excitedly on a wide range of topics from sports to food that was packed for the top. Others chose instead to take in the beauty of the woods bracketing the trail in silence.

The path became rockier and less flat. Soon, the path disappeared and was replaced with boulders of all shapes and sizes we had to traverse. I huffed, puffed, and sweated. Things got riskier for us beginners from Iowa when the boulders switched on and off with fifty-foot-long slippery rock faces. To get across, I had to cling to the slick granite with both hands and feet to maintain balance and grip while I crawled on all fours. I powered through this section of the mountain and ignored my burning quadriceps, hamstring, calves, and quaking arm muscles.

I required many breaks along the way. On one such stop between gasps for breath, I took the opportunity to remind Ernie he said we were going on a hike, not a full blown mountaineering excursion. Ernie's half-grin said it all. Oh how he loved a good practical joke.

Eventually, I settled into the rhythms of the climb and hit my stride. Spotting the lead group farther up the mountain, I picked up my pace in an effort to close the gap. Thinking I was at the last steep section and the top was near, I used my last bit of energy to charge up the granite face.

As I got to the crest and peered over, I was only two-thirds finished with some of the steepest climbing yet to come. I was just in time to see the lead group pull themselves on top of the summit. Since I had no shot at catching the leaders, I took a nice long break and finished the last of my water before pressing onward.

By the time I got to the last few steep sections, my clothes were soaked with sweat. I arrived at a large gap between boulders, and decided to jump towards the upper rock. I sprung toward my target, and as I bent my front leg to land on the rock, my wet and sagging shorts caught on my knee, stretching them tight and ripping the entire crotch out of them. The rest of the time on the mountain, some referred to the hole in my shorts as my ventilation system.

When I reached the top, I was greeted by rousing applause from the spry ones. Catharine was in the group and already snacking on sandwiches and other bagged goodies. She handed me a bottle of water and took me to a brass geological survey marker placed where most assume the top of the mountain is and explained, "We kiss this every year when we get to the top." Not one to break tradition, I gave the brass marker a peck.

A local, halfway through his daily climb, explained the official survey point at the summit was not the brass disk. He pointed to a triangle carved into another rock. "This was the official marked top, and neither is on the highest rock," he said, pointing to a peak clearly higher.

Ernie and Gregg escorted the tail end of our group up to the summit about forty-five minutes later. When Jennifer and Annette reached the top, our cheers echoed off the peaks. Ernie walked directly to the brass marker dropped to his knees and bent down to kiss the marker once again.

But kissing that brass circle would forever be incomplete. The realization this single action, which had brought him such joy over the last twenty-five years, was now irreversibly altered came crashing down around him. He collapsed, face down on the disk, and sobbed. Seeing the larger-than-life man reduced to lying on a cold rock and weeping like a child was heart wrenching.

I cried too.

Seeing Ernie experience such sorrow was a powerful image. I felt like a voyeur peeking in his window. I forced myself to push the uneasy feelings aside though. After all, I had been invited to New Hampshire to help me portray the family's story. So, although I felt uneasy, I raised my camera and snapped a picture of Ernie during his moment of deep heartbreak. This was one of the most uncomfortable things I've ever done. I still feel bad for taking the picture, but it was the right thing to do. Capturing the image truly helped me better understand the whole story.

Time slipped by quickly as we sat atop Monadnock eating, laughing, and recounting climbing exploits. In spite of the temperature dropping and rather ominous-looking clouds moving in, no one was much interested in starting our descent. A wind picked up and chilled us, so the group took refuge in a depression behind one of the peaks. Safe from the wind, a portable CD player was pulled from a backpack.

The popular contemporary Christian band Casting Crowns' song "Who Am I" was cued up, and someone hit play. We held hands and sat in silence as the acoustic guitar, piano, and drums wrapped seamlessly around Mark Hall's stirring lyrics:

"I am a flower quickly fading
Here today and gone tomorrow
A wave tossed in the ocean
A vapor in the wind
Still You hear me when I'm calling
Lord You catch me when I'm falling
And You told me who I am
I am Yours, I am Yours."

Other climbers at the top not associated with our group, either out of respect or uncomfortable with the personal and emotional gathering, relocated to the opposite side of the summit creating a buffer between them and us.

No one spoke after the song faded. A time for silent reflection seemed appropriate. Ernie put his arms around Catharine and Gregg, embracing them. He looked up at the fast moving clouds, now low enough we could nearly reach up and touch them, and reminded everyone of the impending weather, "We should really get moving down the mountain soon folks."

As we started down, I witnessed a very special moment between Ernie and another man and his young son. The fellow hiker had caught up to Ernie and asked, "I've been seeing these LIVE LIKE LINE t-shirts on people all over the mountain. What does that mean?"

Ernie smiled and replied, "Have you got a couple of weeks? That's how long it would take me to tell you that story." He recounted an extremely pared down version, and the man was awash with emotion when Ernie finished. So was I.

Five minutes into our descent, the skies opened up on us, and heavy rain fell the remainder of our trip down the mountain. The showers were so heavy the foot paths and crevasses between boulders became streams.

The rain-soaked granite surfaces made our footing unpredictable and at times treacherous. Some of the boulders were covered in moss and slippery as sheets of ice. The only way to traverse the fifty-foot sheets of slick granite was to slide down on your backside and take it on faith you would stop before slamming into a boulder.

At about the halfway point of our descent, K.C.'s husband, Barry, was right in front of me on a set of rocks when his feet shot out from under him and he landed flat on his back. I rushed to help because Barry is an older man. I reached down to give him some assistance. Barry refused my hand and barked, "I'm fine." He righted himself and charged right back down the path without as much as a groan from what was surely a painful fall onto unforgiving rocks. Clearly I didn't need to worry about Barry any longer.

The last person made it down the mountain about three hours after we left the summit. Everyone was muddy and waterlogged. Our physical condition couldn't dampen our enthusiasm after climbing the mountain and getting down safely. Many of us had started the climb as strangers, but we finished as friends.

We successful mountain climbers went back to the Woodbound Inn, cleaned up, and relaxed with a drink or two. Ernie asked us to gather later that evening in the events building behind the Inn. Family and friends gathered, socialized, shared, and remembered as we feasted on a catered seafood dinner. It was yet another chance for friends from the Midwest, as well as family and friends from the East, to solidify our bonds before the memorial the following day.

I moved from table to table listening to beautiful stories about Caroline and Ellyn—they ranged from silly and funny to heartwarming. Ernie worked the room too, spending time at each table. He listened intently with a smile as others shared their favorite memories about his wife and daughter.

I suddenly missed my own family, so I stepped outside in the rain to try to get a signal on my cell phone. Reception was spotty in the woods of New Hampshire, but I was able to secure one bar, which was enough to call. I became extremely emotional speaking with my wife and children. Tears racing raindrops down my cheeks, I thought, "If I can't handle this without falling to pieces, tomorrow, I may be in real trouble."

We said our goodnights, and I headed to my room. I put my head down on the pillow and fell into a deep sleep at 9 PM. At 11 PM, I woke in excruciating pain. Both groin muscles on the inside of my upper thighs had seized into knotted cramps. I was an athlete in high school and college and had experienced countless cramps in nearly every major muscle group, and I could generally alleviate them in short order with stretching and self-massage. However, these cramps were so severe I couldn't move. Each time I tried to stand up, it felt like my groin muscles were being tightened in a vice. I sat in agony for ten minutes, sweating buckets, before the cramps subsided enough for me to charge to the bathroom where I exceeded the maximum recommended dose of Advil.

It seems that Ernie's practical joke had legs, and severely cramped ones at that.

Chapter 29
The Memorial

For everything there is a season, and a time for every matter
under heaven: a time to be born, and a time to die; a time to plant,
and a time to pluck up what is planted; a time to kill, and a time
to heal; a time to break down, and a time to build up; a time to
weep, and a time to laugh; a time to mourn, and a time to dance;
a time to cast away stones, and a time to gather stones together;
a time to embrace, and a time to refrain from embracing.
—Ecclesiastes 3:1-22

I wanted a perfect ending. Now I've learned, the hard way,
that some poems don't rhyme, and some stories don't have a
clear beginning, middle, and end. Life is about not knowing,
having to change, taking the moment and making the best
of it, without knowing what's going to happen next.
—Gilda Radner

I stepped gingerly into the bathroom at 8 AM and took an extra hot
shower to loosen my sore muscles too numerous to list. I dressed and
went downstairs for breakfast at the restaurant. Our group was scattered about the space. Some were eating while others stuck around for
one more cup of coffee and some conversation. The mood was hushed
and somewhat somber, which was understandable because "memorial"
was just another word for funeral.

Ernie was leaving for the Cathedral of the Pines early in case any last minute preparations were needed. Before he left, he gave me the route he and Ellyn took in the carriage after their wedding. "Make sure you stop at Annett Wayside Park. We stopped there after the wedding and had a bottle of champagne."

Woodbound Inn was only three miles from the blacktop lane leading to the Cathedral of the Pines. I turned down the lane, which split two perfectly manicured lawns. On the left, a quarter-mile away was an idyllic two-story white farmhouse bracketed by trees on either side. Beside the house was a weathered wooden barn with red doors and a partially rusted metal roof. The scene could have been seamlessly woven into the *American Gothic* hanging on Ernie's wall.

The lane banked right through a stand of pines. Once I cleared the last of the pines, I saw a fifty-foot bell tower constructed with local stones. Suspended on pillars, the bell tower was dedicated in 1967 to memorialize all women who had served the US during times of war.

I parked the rental car and joined up with some others just arriving. Gravel walkways crunched under our shoes as we searched the pristine grounds for the St. Francis of Assisi outdoor chapel. Ernie chose it because the prayer associated with the saint was always one of Ellyn's favorites:

...O DIVINE MASTER.
GRANT THAT I MAY NOT SO MUCH SEEK TO
BE CONSOLED – AS TO CONSOLE
TO BE UNDERSTOOD – AS TO UNDERSTAND
TO BE LOVED – AS TO LOVE
FOR IT IS IN GIVING – THAT WE RECEIVE
IT IS IN PARDONING – THAT WE ARE PARDONED
IT IS IN DYING – THAT WE ARE BORN TO ETERNAL LIFE.

I found an empty space on the brown wooden benches. Pastor Matt Paul took his spot in front of the congregation. He stood patiently and waited for the last of us to find a seat. Behind him, on a stone cathedral, rested two drawstring bags, each holding a small wooden box with a cross on the lid. Inside the boxes were the ash remains of Caroline and Ellyn.

On that sunny August morning, Pastor Matt looked around at his immediate surroundings. He took in the natural walls of flowers and vegetation framing the boundaries of the St. Francis chapel. He closed his eyes, breathed in the fresh morning air, and smiled.

The pastor opened his eyes and spoke of the majesty all around us. This place wasn't just majestic for its natural beauty or history, he opined, but also for what the place meant to the Founds. "Ernie, for you and Ellyn to be married here, to come back and renew your vows every year, to baptize Gregg, Catharine, and Caroline in this place, and of course as we gather today to inter Ellyn's and Caroline's ashes as their baptisms have been completed in their death."

The Pastor paused while Catharine read the lyrics to "Smile"—
"Smile though your heart is aching
smile even though it's breaking.
When there are clouds in the sky, you'll get by if
you smile through your fear and sorrow.
Smile and maybe tomorrow, you'll see
the sun comes shining through for you."

As tears streamed down my face, I realized how fitting the words were for the occasion. Both Caroline and Ellyn gave very similar advice to people who were hurting, and through Catharine they were giving us the same advice that day.

Gregg stood and read the words to "Evergreen." Ernie had played it for Ellyn countless times over the years. The words weighed heavy on my heart, and more tears fell from my eyes, faster than I could wipe them away, and I wasn't the only one.

Pastor Matt spoke of climbing the mountain. He reflected on how many levels of experienced climbers were in his group—people who had climbed several times and shot up the mountain quickly and first timers like him. Despite being one of the last to reach the summit, he was moved when the experienced climbers on the peak cheered and encouraged the slower climbers up the last small section. They all made it, and they did it with each other's support.

The pastor wondered how we had all made it through the past twelve months. And, though there was more healing to do, we had all made the journey this far. He spoke of lessons to be taken from the mountain and cathedral. While tragedy had led us here, he prayed for renewal to lead us forward.

At the very place where Ernie and Ellyn renewed their vows every year, he invited each of us to make our own vows to live, love, and laugh. "I'd like you to consider them in their fullness. So when you make a vow to live, it's not just going through the motions. Instead, embody God's love and be present fully to the people we encounter. We can say the words, 'to love', but if we are to love fully as Christ loves us, we must give ourselves to one another. I want you to laugh, not just chuckle; not just grin, but a deep laugh from the belly. That laugh is a sign of the love and joy that we have in Christ, it is an expression of hope," Matt declared.

We recited the prayer of St. Francis, and then Marilyn led us in singing "Gloria Patri." Gregg and Catharine walked to the altar, and each grabbed one of the bags holding the small caskets. Matt concluded the service by inviting us to walk to the cemetery for the interment of the ashes. Gregg, Catharine, and Ernie lead the processional to the cemetery.

The group stepped down off of the path on to the grassy area serving as the cemetery. We gathered around two prepared rectangular holes in the ground. I purposely hung back from the crowd, not because anyone asked me to—everyone went out of their way to make me feel like part of the family. I hung back because it was my intention to be an objective observer so as not to miss anything crucial. I felt I needed to separate myself and not get caught up in the emotions. In my mind, I was invited to document the event.

At least that's what I told myself at the time. More likely, the reason was my unease at funerals. A few years before Caroline's death, I had forced myself to go to the service of a teenager who took her own life. Five minutes into it, I was sobbing uncontrollably. I left the sanctuary and couldn't gather myself enough to return. This was the reason I couldn't bring myself to attend Caroline or Ellyn's services. I simply am too embarrassed about falling to pieces.

Pastor Matt opened the interment proceedings with various readings from scripture: "We know that if the earthly structure we live in is destroyed, we have a building from God. A house not made with hands, eternal in the heavens.... You show me the path of life. In your presence there is fullness and joy. In your right hand there are pleasures forever more."

He asked that when we come back to visit this place, we should resist the temptation to think of it as a place for the dead. We should remember instead the pact that we made to live, love, and laugh. He closed with: "It is in the sure and certain hope of the resurrection to eternal life through our Lord, Jesus Christ, we commend to almighty God our sisters, Ellyn and Caroline, and we commit their ashes to their final resting place."

His final nine words turned me from an objective observer and recorder of the event to a blubbering mess.

Everyone was full of emotion. Daughters put their heads on their mother's shoulders, others held hands as the hard truth sunk in—the last year had not been a dream, but all too real.

Gregg opened one of the bags and pulled out the first of the matching small wooden caskets which held Caroline's ashes. He handed it to Catharine, who kissed the box and handed it to her father. Ernie laid his tear-stained cheek on the side of the casket, kissed it, and handed it to Gregg. Gregg kissed the box and gently lowered it into the first hole.

Gregg then pulled the second casket from the remaining cloth bag. He embraced and kissed the box and then handed it to Catharine who did the same. She passed it to Ernie, who now was openly weeping. He closed his eyes, pulled it in close, and whispered a final message to his departed wife. He achingly kissed the box, knelt, and placed it gently into the ground. Gregg and Catharine finished their goodbyes then moved to their father to comfort him. Ernie, understandably, needed more time.

Once Ernie, Gregg, and Catharine were finished, small groups took turns saying their goodbyes. While this was happening, I was standing off to the side failing in my attempt to control my flowing nose and eyes. My instinct was to turn and walk away, but I couldn't. I forced myself to watch each group of people, be they family members or friends, as they knelt on the ground at the base of the side-by-side rectangular holes in the ground. They were people I had bonded with over the weekend, and it was quite difficult to watch my new friends pour out a year's worth of sorrow.

Some left mementos and trinkets by or in the graves—there was a $20 bill, a running shoe, Dunkin' Donuts coffee, Lucky Charms, and Lifesavers candy. It's fascinating, the importance the bereaved place on items that would normally hold little if any significance at all. I took note of who left which item and, for the purposes of the story, hoped I would get to hear the backstory of each.

The last group paid their respects and joined the others on the path leading back to the entrance. As people milled about, I decided I owed it to these amazing people to pay my respects as well. As I approached the graves, I had second thoughts. I felt I wasn't worthy of this—I was just the storyteller. I knelt down by their graves though and, between sniffles, I said the only thing that came to mind, "I'll do the best that I can. I hope that it's good enough."

The service was now complete, but the grieving wasn't. We shared hugs and some more tears with Ernie, Gregg, and Catharine. Although it was painful, getting Caroline and Ellyn's remains to their final resting place had a finality the funerals in Iowa City hadn't. This day gave mourners the closure that had eluded them the past year.

The group moved in waves across the grounds to a garage where refreshments and cookies were served. It was there I had the honor of speaking to Ernie's father and mother.

His mother was a gifted storyteller and had clearly passed the skill along to Ernie. She told me stories of Ernie as a child and young man. Even though I knew many of them, I enjoyed hearing them a second time because she was so entertaining. I waited to speak with Ernie's father until after he finished eating.

Ernie Sr. was sick with Parkinson's and confined to a wheelchair. The aggressive central nervous system disorder may have taken many of his physical abilities, but not his mind and spirit. His eyes lit up when we discussed our common backgrounds of serving in the Navy and working in law enforcement.

He had a wry and ironic smile. It made me feel like he knew an amusing secret about me and, instead of sharing it, decided to hang on to it for a while. Unfortunately, our chat was cut short because he became tired very quickly and needed some rest. I hoped I would have more time with him later, but his disease and scheduling didn't allow it.

Gregg banged a stick on a bottle and opened the floor to anyone who had a story they would like to share about Caroline, Ellyn, or both. Caroline's Aunt Susan spoke of a wild ride on the back of a jet ski with Line as the driver. Uncle Dick relayed the time he stopped in to see his nephew Ernie and his family and was immediately commissioned to be fifteen-month-old Gregg's first babysitter.

Ted Wernimont told a touching story about Caroline. He umpired high school softball and remembered Line as the most enthusiastic substitute player during her junior year. Between innings, the subs would play catch with the outfielders to keep their arms loose.

Ted always carried a pocketful of Lifesavers when he umpired. If the game was a blowout and boring, sucking on candy was a good way to pass the time. When he umpired a West High game, and saw Caroline between innings, he got in the habit of holding up a Lifesaver which she would pluck out of his hand as she ran by.

The last West High game he worked was in August 2011. The bottom half of the last inning was about to start, and here came Caroline back to the dugout. He held up the last Lifesaver in his pocket, and she grabbed it out of his fingers. She took a few steps, looked over her shoulder at Ted, winked, and said, "Thanks, Sugar." This was the last time he saw her alive.

Ellyn's older sister Mary stood up. She talked about sharing everything with Ellyn, including clothing. She was four years older, and their parents allowed her to go out with friends and do fun things that Ellyn wasn't allowed to do. Mary burned through her money while the frugal Ellyn always seemed to have plenty. Mary had devised a plan to get some of Ellyn's money by convincing her it was a good idea if they split the cost of their clothing, that way it would only cost them half as much. That sounded reasonable to Ellyn. The only problem was that Mary never had any money, so Ellyn had to "lend" her older sister the money she owed for the clothing they bought.

When it was Ellyn's turn to wear a particular article of clothing they purchased, Mary would tell her that she was planning to wear it, too. She would let Ellyn wear it as long as Ellyn would knock $5 off of what she owed. "So you see, I never really paid her back," Mary said.

Mary told the group she had no intention of putting anything in the grave. As she stood at her sister's final resting place, however, the memory came rushing back, so she placed a $20 bill in the hole with Ellyn's casket. "People over the years have said that they were amazed that she fell for that because she was so smart. The truth is that she was the wisest person I knew, and I always sought her advice on any issue," Mary said, choking back tears.

Later that afternoon, I had one more interview scheduled, sitting down with all of Ellyn's sisters. Before the meeting, I told their brother Mark what I was about to do, and he said, "On purpose? They'll eat you alive." I found them funny, charming, and though not the life of the party, they were a roving party whenever they get together. When eating in a restaurant, theirs would be the table you'd want to sit next to because you'd have dinner and a show. Some of the best stories about Ellyn came from this interview.

By early evening I was emotionally spent. I looked for Ernie, Gregg, and Catharine to tell them goodbye and thank them for the honor of attending the memorial. During my search, I ran into a few people and said my farewells to them, but never could find the Founds. I called my family one last time, talked to the kids, and gave my wife flight information. I retired to my room around dinner time, too tired to eat.

I left the Woodbound Inn around 3:30 AM for the two-hour drive to the Manchester Airport to catch a 6:30 AM flight back to Iowa.

With the exception of the Founds, most of the Iowans were on the same flight.

When I got home, I drove by the crash site on Mormon Trek. While the Founds were having their memorial in New Hampshire, a one-year anniversary memorial had taken place at the accident location as well. The tree was decorated with dozens of mementos and just as many items on the ground.

Caroline and Ellyn are gone but not forgotten. Their memories live on in those who were lucky enough to have known them. Although we were profoundly affected by their deaths, we were more deeply impacted by their lives. They are all around us. We see it with the No. 9 painted on the park bench on the downtown pedestrian mall. During the annual Ponseti Races, they place a 9 on to the race shirts each year. To this day, if you watch the West High volleyball team play, the number nine jersey is noticeably absent from the roster of players.

And what became of LIVE LIKE LINE? There are any number of the familiar t-shirts that people of all ages still wear around town. The expression can be seen all over West High—painted on the scoreboard in the gym and on a memorial stone outside the softball diamond. Each time "Sweet Caroline" is played at a West High sporting event, fans sing out the words with gusto in honor of the beautiful girl with the same name who was everyone's best friend.

Line will be remembered for generations to come through the retelling of her fun-loving, giving, and caring ways. Each year during West High's freshman orientation, Principal Arganbright holds Caroline up as an example for the newest students to model. Each year a spirit award in Caroline's name is given to a student who Lives Like Line.

Family, friends, teachers, coaches, and teammates spread the stories about the seventeen-year-old who believed in Santa and gave memorable hugs. They speak of her generosity and strong desire to share her good fortune with those less fortunate. Lauren Hansen, Caroline's Rockets volleyball coach, had a baby girl in 2012 and named her Caroline. Baby Caroline was often seen in a Live Like Line onesie.

As for Ellyn, her employer, Steindler Orthopedic Clinic, named the hand clinic after her. The University of Iowa Hospitals and Clinics dedicated its cancer wing visitors' waiting room in her name too. The waiting room is complete with a piano and beautiful stained glass ornaments. On the other side of the LIVE LIKE LINE memorial at the West High softball field, LOVE LIKE ELLYN is engraved.

Ernie came home from New Hampshire and reluctantly eased into a life without his wife and youngest child. He still does plenty in their memory. He was recently invited to participate as a local celebrity at the Dancing with the Stars benefit for the American Cancer Society. Paired with a professional dancer, Ernie stole the show and was the clear winner of the local charity event. When he is in town, you can usually find him at a West High event.

He has also done some things strictly for himself, like going to a week-long music camp one summer. He likes to travel with friends to St. Louis Cardinals games in the summer. He was given an old sousaphone and commissioned my oldest daughter, Morgan, a tuba player in the West High marching band, to teach him how to play. He played piano in a musical lineup of physicians at another charity event. Ernie the farmer began growing hops for friends who brew their own beer.

While he is carving out his new path, his heart is still rooted in New Hampshire, and by his own admission, probably always will be. Ernie, Gregg, and Catharine still make their annual trip there. Additionally, he makes visits back to the Cathedral of the Pines and Monadnock each year. Ernie also purchased a summer home in New Hampshire.

The house is backed up to a lake and has a boat house and dock on the water and a magnificent view of Mount Monadnock from the front yard. Will he make it his permanent residence? Perhaps someday he will. For the time being, he plans on keeping the farm in Iowa City, at least until Gregg and Catharine have homes and families of their own.

His ideal future includes summers at his New Hampshire lake house, packed with his kids and grandkids. Together, they will swim, fish, and go boating. They will gather around the piano, and he will play for them. He may even break out a deck of cards and do some magic. He will take them to visit the Cathedral to pay respects to Caroline and Ellyn, and then everyone will climb the mountain, together.

Afterword

I will always remember reading about Caroline and Ellyn in the local media during the late summer of 2011. My heart ached for the husband and father, Ernie Found. I vaguely knew of the Found family from church, but I certainly wasn't close to them. Reading and hearing about their tragedies, I couldn't help but thank God for blessing me with a healthy family and wonder how I would cope with such monumental losses. Life continued on for me. My initial sadness eventually passed.

Then, in December, 2011, about a month after the Iowa City West High volleyball team defended their state title without Caroline Found, I inexplicably introduced myself to Ernie at church. I explained who I was and the reason for the introduction—I wanted to write the story of Ellyn and Caroline. During our first twenty-minute conversation, Ernie gave me what would become the theme of this book when he said, "I can't believe how many good things have come from something so bad." We concluded our conversation with him agreeing to meet me. He had no firm idea who I was, and I, an unpublished writer, had no experience writing biographies.

Our initial face-to-face meeting was in early January, 2012, at Ernie's house. For two hours, I listened while he told heartwarming stories about Ellyn and Caroline. We also discussed our own expectations about how the story should be told. At the end of this discussion, he said he wanted me to write his family's story. I remember driving home that night wondering how I planned to do that.

I decided to start by doing something I do relatively well, talking to people. Ernie gave me the names of a few people to talk to. I reached out to them, and they told me more and more about Caroline and Ellyn. They, in turn, gave me names of others I should speak with, and so it went.

As the story developed there were plenty of holes I needed filled in. However, it seemed each time I needed missing information I would intersect with just the right person a few days later. It should be noted that because this is a true story, some of the names have been changed.

When Ernie invited me to New Hampshire for the one-year memorial of Ellyn and Caroline's deaths, I decided this event would be the perfect stopping point for my book.

There were way too many obstacles along the way to call the whole process of this book happenstance. I believe that, in the face of the Founds' misfortune and heartbreak, God wanted me to relay their story as a beacon to those who have or may in the future lose a friend or loved-one.

I also believe God wanted me to be there for Ernie. Through hours of retelling his family's legacy to me, I played a role to ease his pain and help him heal. As well, the Lord put Ernie in my life as a model of how to be the best husband and father I can be. I continue striving to be both.

While parts of the process have been difficult, it has truly been my honor and pleasure to create this book. I hope the journey fills your heart with sadness, joy, laughter, and inspiration. I pray that God is always with us, whether we know it or not.

Live Like Line/Love Like Ellyn.

2010 West High
Volleyball Team

Anna Pashkova
Caroline Hartman
Caroline Van Vorhis
Hannah Infelt
Cassie Jenn
Lexi Potter
Olivia Mekies
Caroline Found
Briannie Kraft
Shelly Stumpff
Katie Kelley
Alli O'Deen
Paige Yoder
Cat Rebelskey
Paola Jaramillo
Olivia Fairfield
Kelley Fliehler
Cara Jansen

2011 West High
Volleyball Team

Anna Pashkova
Caroline Hartman
Mollie Mason
Hannah Fairfield
Hannah Infelt
Hannah Harless
Olivia Mekies
Erin Weathers
Shelly Stumpff
Laynie Whitehead
Emily Merdinger
Lynn Jehle
Emily Carpenter
Olivia Fairfield
Kelley Fliehler

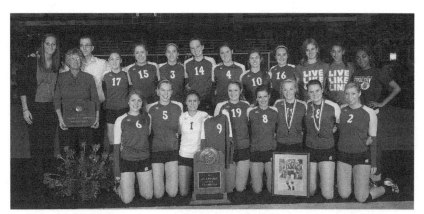

2011 State Champions with Line's Jersey and photo held up.

Special Thanks To:

Ernie Found: Thank you for the trust to tell your family's story, treating me like a family member, and most importantly, your friendship. Your strength, love, commitment, and faith have been a shining example and make me strive to be a better man, husband, and father.

Catharine Found: Your unending support and friendship has been a blessing throughout the process of writing this book. Your grace and wisdom far exceed your years.

Gregg Found: Your contemplative outside the box thinking has been especially helpful during the latter stages of putting this book together. Your ideas challenged me to consider new directions, and reconsider existing aspects of the story that I probably wouldn't have without your guidance.

Mia Hoeft: I could write a book thanking you for being my wife of 27 years, giving me three beautiful children, and for being the love of my life, but for the purposes of this book, thank you for your straight forward advice on every part of the story, and your unwavering support, especially through the difficult parts. I love you with all my heart.

Morgan, Rachel, and Will Hoeft: You three have inspired me from start to finish. You have been enthusiastic supporters, given me countless ideas, and provided me with title and marketing ideas. Most importantly, it makes me happy that you are proud of me.

Steven Semken: What can I say about a guy who guided me through the process of publishing my first book? You have been more than a publisher; you have been a mentor, cheerleader, advisor, therapist, and friend. I am eternally grateful for your direction through the maze of writing and releasing this book.

Jeff Charis-Carlson: Your gentle touch throughout the editing process was greatly appreciated. You polished and shaped the rough edges of my writing style and improved my abilities significantly and I'm extremely appreciative.

Mike and Barb Recker: For providing pictures, text messages, and a unique perspective on Caroline and her friends.

Larry and Linda Marsh: Linda, you provided so many photos and special moments about the family. If I needed something, you had it, or knew where I could find it. Thank you Larry for giving such honest and loving views, as only Ernie's best friend could.

Lisa Murray: You too were there with information, clarification, or photos whenever I needed them. Thanks for opening your home and inviting me to speak with your whole family.

K.C. Wright: I spoke with you several times early on, and you gave me directions to turn regarding family and friends.

Marilyn Found: Thanks for the early stories regarding Danny and growing up with Ernie, and also editing help.

Matt Paul: Thanks for sharing so many ideas along the way to make the story better. Thanks for your special words at the year memorial in New Hampshire, and countless sermons on Sunday, which provided me the strength, peace, love, humility, and courage to press on these past four years.

Additional thanks to those who helped me along the way by providing stories about the Found family, the volleyball team and their season, friendship, moral support, endorsements, guidance on who to speak with, and editing: Dan Gable, Ally Disterhoft, Fran and Margaret Mc-

Caffery, Frank Deford, Geoffrey Lauer, Kyle Otterbein, Kathy Bresnahan, Iowa City Police Officer Todd Cheney, Blair Puetsch, Shannon Harris, Stephanie Onder, Charlie Rogers, Anthony Brown, Richard Bryant, Caroline Van Voorhis, Olivia Laufgren, Erin Muir, Vicky Burketta, Dr. Jerry Arganbright, Paul Breitbach, Scott Sanders, Tom Keating, Lauren Hansen, Earnest Found Sr., Eleanor Found, Grace Found, Marilyn Found, Ted Wernimont, Anna Pashkova, Olivia Mekies, Hannah Infelt, Shelly Stumpff, Olivia Fairfield, Kelley Fliehler, Adrienne Jensen, Annette Winkler, Mark Winkler, Scott Jespersen, Boyd Murray, Lisa Murray, Grace Murray, Anna Murray, Leah Murray, Claire Murray, Julie Jenkins (Trinity University volleyball coach), Mark Vernon, Maddie Vernon, Paul Etre, Larry Marsh, Linda Marsh, Mark Slocum, Bob Slocum, Mary Slocum-Rittle, K.C. Wright, Barry Wright, Aileen Mussleman, Mike Recker, Barb Recker, Jennifer Moy, Dell Richard, Mary Richard, Dave Nicholson, Amy Nicholson, Kyle Nicholson, Emily Nicholson, Claibourne Dungy, and Madgetta Dungy.

To anyone else who contributed that I forgot to include, please forgive me. You have my deepest thanks as well.

Bill Hoeft (left) with Ernie Found. Bill grew up in Des Moines where he attended Lincoln High School until the end of his junior year when he and his mother moved to Monroe, Iowa. It was in Monroe that he met Mia Clevenger, his wife of twenty-seven years (and counting).

After high school he attended Buena Vista College and Mia went to the opposite end of the state to attend the University of Iowa. Two years later he joined the US Navy in 1988. After bootcamp he married, packed up, and moved to San Diego with Mia.

Honorably discharged in 1991, the couple moved to the Iowa City/ Coralville area when Mia was accepted to medical school at the University of Iowa. Most of Bill's adult life has been spent in the service of people. He has served as a police officer, an educator, a correctional officer, as well as in the Navy. His volunteer activities have included coaching numerous sports for children ranging in age from preschool to high school. He has served as an elder at his church, is the father of three children—Morgan, Rachel, and Will—and currently serving his second term on the Coralville City Council.

The Ice Cube Press began publishing in 1993 to focus on how to live with the natural world. We've since become devoted to using the literary arts to better understand how people can best live together in the communities they share, inhabit, and experience here in the Heartland of the USA. We have been recognized by a number of well-known writers including: Gary Snyder, Gene Logsdon, Wes Jackson, Patricia Hampl, Greg Brown, Jim Harrison, Annie Dillard, Ken Burns, Roz Chast, Jane Hamilton, Daniel Menaker, Kathleen Norris, Janisse Ray, Craig Lesley, Alison Deming, Frank Deford, Paul Hawken, Harriet Lerner, Richard Rhodes, Michael Pollan, David Abram, David Orr, Boria Sax, and Barry Lopez. We've published a number of well-known authors including: Governor Robert Ray, Congressman James Leach, Mary Swander, Jim Heynen, Mary Pipher, Bill Holm, Connie Mutel, John T. Price, Carol Bly, Marvin Bell, Debra Marquart, Ted Kooser, Stephanie Mills, Bill McKibben, Craig Lesley, Elizabeth McCracken, Dean Bakopoulos, Dan Gable, and Paul Gruchow. Check out Ice Cube Press books on our web site, join our facebook group, follow us on twitter, visit booksellers, museum shops, or any place you can find good books and discover why we continue striving to, "hear the other side."

Ice Cube Press, LLC (Est. 1993)
North Liberty, Iowa 52317-9302
steve@icecubepress.com
twitter @icecubepress
www.icecubepress.com

to Fenna Marie
a wonderful
loving
line